Bid Protests

A GUIDE TO CHALLENGING FEDERAL PROCUREMENTS

Andrew E. Shipley and Daniel E. Chudd
PRINCIPAL AUTHORS AND EDITORS

ABA
AMERICAN BAR ASSOCIATION
Public Contract Law Section

Cover design by Jill Tedhams/ABA Design

Printed in the United States of America.

25 24 23 22 21   5 4 3 2 1

Library of Congress Cataloging-in-Publication Data

Names: Shipley, Andrew E., author, editor. | Chudd, Daniel E., author, editor.
Title: Bid protests : a guide to challenging federal procurements / Andrew E. Shipley and Daniel E. Chudd, principal authors and editors.
Description: Chicago : ABA, American Bar Association, [2021] | Includes index. | Summary: "A guide to the three primary forums where most federal procurement decisions are contested"—Provided by publisher.
Identifiers: LCCN 2021018180 (print) | LCCN 2021018181 (ebook) | ISBN 9781641058674 (paperback) | ISBN 9781641058681 (ebook)
Subjects: LCSH: Government purchasing—Law and legislation—United States. | Letting of contracts—United States. | Public contracts—United States.
Classification: LCC KF849 .S47 2021 (print) | LCC KF849 (ebook) | DDC 346.7302/3—dc23
LC record available at https://lccn.loc.gov/2021018180
LC ebook record available at https://lccn.loc.gov/2021018181

Discounts are available for books ordered in bulk. Special consideration is given to state bars, CLE programs, and other bar-related organizations. Inquire at Book Publishing, ABA Publishing, American Bar Association, 321 N. Clark Street, Chicago, Illinois 60654-7598.

www.ShopABA.org

Acknowledgments

Principal Authors and Editors

Andrew E. Shipley, Wilmer Cutler Pickering Hale and Dorr LLP
Daniel E. Chudd, Northrop Grumman Corporation

Contributing Authors

Jessica Aldrich, Wilmer Cutler Pickering Hale and Dorr LLP
Chelsea Anelli, Wilmer Cutler Pickering Hale and Dorr LLP
Victoria Dalcourt Angle, Morrison & Foerster LLP
Philip Beshara, Wilmer Cutler Pickering Hale and Dorr LLP
Locke Bell, Morrison & Foerster LLP
Chanda Brown, Wilmer Cutler Pickering Hale and Dorr LLP
Elizabeth D'Aunno, Wilmer Cutler Pickering Hale and Dorr LLP
Ariel Dobkin, Wilmer Cutler Pickering Hale and Dorr LLP
Rachael Plymale, Morrison & Foerster LLP
James Tucker, Morrison & Foerster LLP

Peer Reviewers

Paul Khoury, Wiley Rein LLP
Sharon Larkin, The Larkin Law Group LLP
Cherie Owen, Jones Day
Anne Perry, Sheppard Mullin

The editors also express their sincere appreciation to Emily Theriault, whose dedicated assistance made this publication possible.

The views expressed in this book are solely those of the contributors and editors and do not reflect the views or positions of the organizations with which they are affiliated.

About the Authors

Andrew E. Shipley | Partner, Wilmer Cutler Pickering Hale and Dorr

Andrew has more than 30 years of experience practicing law as both in-house and outside counsel. He is a Chambers and Legal 500 ranked Government Contracts lawyer and was named a Law360 MVP for Government Contracts. He also won the prestigious Burton Award for Distinguished Legal Writing for "Remove Your Case to Federal Court: Lesser Known Options," an article that appeared in the American Bar Association (ABA) *Litigation Journal* and focused on procedural issues unique to government contractors. Andrew served for several years on the ABA's Federal Practice Task Force, working on initiatives designed to improve the practice of law in federal courts across the country, as well as on the board of directors for the DC Chapter of the American Corporate Counsel Association, where he co-founded and served as the initial chair of its Litigation Forum. Andrew supports diverse clients in government contract disputes and litigation, including government enforcement actions, investigations, federal court litigation, board of contract appeals litigation, bid protests, and other contested proceedings. He advises on issues arising in the pursuit or performance of government contracts and has handled an extensive assortment of significant matters for a wide array of companies doing business with the government. He has litigated in state and federal courts across the country and before various government boards of appeal and administrative agencies, including GAO, the Court of Federal Claims, the ASBCA, and ODRA. Andrew also managed an in-house litigation/bid protest group for a FORTUNE 100 multinational government contractor.

Daniel E. Chudd | Northrop Grumman

Daniel E. Chudd is Corporate Counsel with Northrop Grumman Mission Systems, where he counsels on a variety of government contracts matters. Prior to his work with Northrop Grumman, Dan was a partner with Morrison & Foerster in its government contracts group with a focus on government contracts litigation and protest counseling. Dan's interest in government contracts was sparked during his clerkship with Judge Mary Ellen Coster Williams of the U.S. Court of Federal Claims. That experience, combined with his in-depth industry knowledge, makes Dan an effective advocate and counselor on the myriad issues his business partners face.

A Note to the Reader

This book is intended to serve as a guide to bid protests in the three primary forums where most federal procurement decisions are contested: at the procuring agency itself, at the U.S. Government Accountability Office (GAO), and at the U.S. Court of Federal Claims (COFC). It walks the reader through the differences among and the comparative advantages/disadvantages of these three forums, identifies filing prerequisites and deadlines, and discusses various grounds of protest available at the pre-award and post-award stage. Because an encyclopedic treatment of all protest forums is beyond the scope of this volume, certain types of protests (e.g., those brought at the Federal Aviation Administration's Office of Dispute Resolution for Acquisition [ODRA]) are not discussed in these pages.

Table of Contents

Chapter 1
The History of Protest Jurisdiction

A. The Long-Standing Authority of GAO to Hear Bid Protests

A "protest" is a written objection by an interested party to a solicitation, a proposed award, or an actual award of a government contract, and sometimes to the cancellation of a solicitation or a contract. Unsuccessful bidders for government contracts have been protesting the procurement decisions of government agencies for nearly a century. The General Accounting Office (now the Government Accountability Office, GAO) issued its first bid protest opinion in 1926 when it concluded that the "advertising" requirement in federal contracting law was "designed to give all citizens, etc., an equal right to compete for government business; to procure for the government the benefits which flow from competition; and to raise a bar against collusion and fraud in procuring supplies and letting contracts."[1] Since then, GAO has consistently maintained broad authority to hear bid protests, even though an explicit statutory mandate for such authority did not exist until the mid-1980s.

The Budget and Accounting Act of 1921 created GAO and vested it with the authority to settle claims against the government and to investigate and report on federal expenditures.[2] Though not expressly authorizing bid protests, GAO relied on this broad grant of statutory authority to adjudicate protests from its first published protest decision in 1926 up until the enactment of the Competition in Contracting Act (CICA) in 1984.[3] Because GAO lacked any express statutory authorization to sanction or otherwise direct agency action, GAO made its opinions advisory and nonbinding, though in practice they were almost always followed. Congress finally codified GAO's jurisdiction over bid protests in 1984 through CICA.

1. *Comptroller Gen. McCarl to the Sec'y of the Treasury*, 5 Comp. Gen. 717, 718 (Mar. 10, 1926).

2. *See* Pub. L. No. 67-13, §§ 305, 312(a).

3. *See, e.g.*, To Richard A. Mehler, B-142931, Oct. 21, 1964, 1964 CPD ¶ 30 ("Where a bid acceptance is proposed but not yet consummated by a procuring agency, and our Office considers such acceptance undesirable, we may recommend or direct such action as we believe is required by the public policy expressed in applicable statutory enactments to preserve the integrity of the competitive bidding system."); James W. Nelson, *GAO-COFC Concurrent Bid Protest Jurisdiction: Are Two Fora Too Many?*, 43 Pub. Cont. L.J. 587, 590–91 (2014).

Although CICA vested GAO with the authority to hear bid protests it previously lacked, the statute provided for the issuance of only nonbinding recommendations.[4] Thus, GAO's opinions today remain nonbinding and lack preclusive effect in federal courts.[5] GAO's recommendations, however, are almost always adopted by the procuring agency (any failure to do so is reported to Congress), and GAO remains the primary choice of forum for thousands of protesters every year. If GAO finds that an agency's procurement actions did not comply with federal statute or regulations, it may recommend that the agency take any number of corrective actions, including reissuing the solicitation, recompeting the contract, awarding the contract to another party, or terminating an existing contract.[6]

B. The Expansion and Contraction of Federal Court Protest Jurisdiction

Whereas GAO has consistently served as the primary forum for bid protests, federal court jurisdiction over bid protests has had a more uneven history.[7] In *Perkins v. Lukens Steel Co.*,[8] the U.S. Supreme Court found that the Public Contracts Act "was not enacted for the protection of sellers and confers no enforceable rights upon prospective bidders"; thus, the disappointed bidder could not show an injury to its own right and lacked standing to challenge the agency's procurement action in federal court. The Court reasoned,

> [c]ourts should not, where Congress has not done so, subject purchasing agencies of government to the delays necessarily incident to judicial scrutiny at the instance of potential sellers, which would be contrary to traditional governmental practice and would create a new concept of judicial controversies.[9]

Following this decision, the conventional wisdom was that unsuccessful bidders lacked standing in federal district courts to challenge agencies' procurement actions.[10]

---

4. *See* 31 U.S.C. § 3554(b)–(c).

5. *See* Cubic Applications, Inc. v. United States, 37 Fed. Cl. 345, 353 (1997). Under CICA, GAO's bid protest jurisdiction is concurrent with that of the federal courts and protests brought at GAO can subsequently be brought at the Court of Federal Claims (COFC), where the GAO decision and agency record "shall be considered to be part of the agency record subject to review." 31 U.S.C. §§ 3554(b)(3), 3556.

6. 4 C.F.R. § 21.8.

7. *See* Impresa Construzioni Geom. Domenico Garufi v. United States, 238 F.3d 1324, 1331 (Fed. Cir. 2001) ("The history of the judicial review of government contracting procurement decisions is both long and complicated.").

8. 310 U.S. 113, 125–26 (1940).

9. *Id.* at 130.

10. 238 F.3d at 1331.

1. Protest Jurisdiction at Court of Federal Claims

In 1956, however, the Court of Claims asserted jurisdiction over pre-award bid protests, premising such jurisdiction on the Tucker Act (28 U.S.C. § 1491(a)), which gave the court jurisdiction "to render judgment upon any claim against the United States founded . . . upon any . . . implied contract with the United States."[11] In *Heyer Products Co. v. United States,*[12] the lowest-priced bidder challenged the government's selection of the highest-priced bid of the seven offers received. The low bidder argued that the government's actions were arbitrary and capricious and in bad faith. The court held that "it was an implied condition of the request for offers that each of them would be honestly considered," and "when [the government] invited plaintiff to incur [the expense of preparing a bid], it must necessarily be implied that it promised to give fair and impartial consideration to its bid."[13] Since the bidder alleged that the government's actions sounded in fraud and did not reflect an impartial consideration of the offers received, the court found that it had standing to sue for damages.[14] Following *Heyer Products*, the Court of Claims (and subsequently the Court of Federal Claims [COFC]) continued to exercise jurisdiction over pre-award bid protest matters.

The Federal Courts Improvement Act of 1982 (FCIA) created the modern-day COFC and gave it the authority to grant declaratory judgments and injunctive relief. The Tucker Act, as amended by the FCIA,[15] provides:

> To afford complete relief on any contract claim brought before the contract is awarded, the court shall have exclusive jurisdiction to grant declaratory judgments and such equitable and extraordinary relief as it deems proper, including but not limited to injunctive relief.[16]

The following year, however, the Federal Circuit reiterated that COFC's protest jurisdiction extended only to pre-award protests.[17] COFC's jurisdiction remained limited to pre-award protests until the Administrative Dispute Resolution Act (ADRA) amended the Tucker Act in 1996.

---

11. 28 U.S.C. § 1491(a)(1).
12. 135 Ct. Cl. 63, 140 F. Supp. 409 (1956).
13. *Id.* at 412–13.
14. *Id.* at 413.
15. Pub. L. No. 97–164, § 133(a), 96 Stat. 25, 40.
16. Southfork Sys., Inc. v. United States, 141 F.3d 1124, 1132 (Fed. Cir. 1998).
17. United States v. John C. Grimberg Co., 702 F.2d 1362, 1372 (Fed. Cir. 1983) (*en banc*).

2. Prior Protest Jurisdiction in Federal District Court

Although today COFC (an Article I court) is generally recognized as the only judicial forum available for bid protests, beginning in the 1970s protests could also be pursued in Article III U.S. District Courts under the aegis of the Administrative Procedure Act (APA). In *Scanwell Laboratories, Inc. v. Shaffer*,[18] the D.C. Circuit Court of Appeals reversed the dismissal of a post-award bid protest for lack of standing, holding that

> [t]he public interest in preventing the granting of contracts through arbitrary or capricious action can properly be vindicated through a suit brought by one who suffers injury as a result . . . the suit itself is brought in the public interest by one acting essentially as a "private attorney general."

The court explained that disappointed bidders were well-positioned to bring suit against illegal government procurement actions and distinguished the Supreme Court's 1940 decision in *Perkins* by noting that it was "decided during the heyday of the legal right doctrine, and before the passage of the Administrative Procedure Act."[19] Under *Scanwell*, a disappointed offeror that made a "prima facie showing of [an arbitrary or capricious abuse of discretion] on the part of an agency or contracting officer [when considering a bid] ha[d] standing to sue" under the APA.[20] Other circuits followed the D.C. Circuit's lead, confirming district court jurisdiction over bid protests concerning alleged violations of procurement laws or regulations under the APA.[21]

3. ADRA and the Short-Lived Existence of Parallel Jurisdiction

ADRA established jurisdiction in both federal district courts and COFC to hear "the full range of cases previously subject to review in either system," but imposed a sunset provision on district court jurisdiction.[22] ADRA states that

> [b]oth the United States Court of Federal Claims and the district courts of the United States shall have jurisdiction to render judgment on an action by an interested party objecting to a solicitation by a Federal agency for bids or proposals for a proposed contract or to a proposed award or the award of a contract or any alleged violation of statute or regulation *in connection with* a procurement or a proposed

18. 424 F.2d 859, 864 (D.C. Cir. 1970).

19. *Id.* at 866.

20. *Id.* at 868–69.

21. *See, e.g.*, Diebold v. United States, 947 F.2d 787 (6th Cir. 1991); Ulstein Maritime, Ltd. v. United States, 833 F.2d 1052, 1057 (1st Cir. 1987).

22. Emery Worldwide Airlines, Inc. v. United States, 264 F.3d 1071 (Fed. Cir. 2001) (citing 142 Cong. Rec. S11849 (daily ed. Sept. 30, 1996) (statement of Sen. Levin)).

> procurement . . . without regard to whether suit is instituted before or after the contract is awarded.[23]

Thus, the federal district courts and COFC enjoyed co-extensive jurisdiction over bid protests until January 1, 2001, when, by statute, district court jurisdiction lapsed.

The majority view is that COFC is now the sole judicial forum with jurisdiction to hear federal bid protests.[24] The Federal Circuit articulated this view in *Emery Worldwide Airlines, Inc. v. United States*,[25] holding that under ADRA, "it is clear that the Court of Federal Claims is the only judicial forum to bring any governmental contract procurement protest." The Federal Circuit found that Congress's "clear" intent in "enacting the ADRA with the sunset provision [effective Jan. 1, 2001] was to vest a single judicial tribunal with exclusive jurisdiction to review government contract protest actions."[26] Some scholars (and courts) maintain that the federal district courts have retained jurisdiction over certain protests.[27] To date, this has been a minority view.

C. Limits on Task Order Jurisdiction

Orders issued pursuant to an already-awarded indefinite-delivery, indefinite-quantity (IDIQ) contract may *not* be challenged at COFC unless the protest asserts that the order exceeds the scope, period of performance, or maximum dollar value of the underlying contract from which it issued.[28] Rather, the GAO Civilian Task and Delivery Order Protest Authority Act of 2016 and the 2017 National Defense

---

23. 28 U.S.C. § 1491(b)(1) (emphasis added).

24. *See All's Well That Ends Well: Scanwell Jurisdiction in the Twenty-First Century*, 46 Pub. Cont. L.J. 409, 416, 430 (Winter 2017).

25. 264 F.3d 1071, 1080 (Fed. Cir. 2001) (citing Novell, Inc. v. United States, 109 F. Supp. 2d 22, 24–25 (D.D.C. 2000)).

26. *Id.* at 1079; *see also* Rothe Dev., Inc. v. U.S. Dep't of Def., 666 F.3d 336 (5th Cir. 2011) (per curiam); Vero Tech. Support, Inc. v. U.S. Dep't of Def., 437 F. App'x 766, 769 (11th Cir. 2011); Fire-Trol Holdings LLC v. U.S. Forest Serv., 209 F. App'x 625 (9th Cir. 2006).

27. *See, e.g.*, City of Albuquerque v. U.S. Dep't of the Interior, 379 F.3d 901, 911 (10th Cir. 2004) ("[W]e conclude the [ADRA] did not affect the district court's ability to hear cases challenging the government's contract procurement process so long as the case is brought by someone other than an actual or potential bidder."); K-Mar Indus. v. U.S. Dep't of Def., 752 F. Supp. 2d 1201, 1211, 1213–14 (W.D. Okla. 2010) (finding district courts have jurisdiction over protests challenging an agency's decision to insource procurement contracts under the APA).

28. Recently, however, COFC exercised jurisdiction over a protest challenging a simultaneously evaluated and awarded IDIQ contract and associated task order, denying the government's request to dismiss. *See* PAE-Parsons Global Logistics Servs. LLC v. United States, 145 Fed. Cl. 194 (2019). The government argued that the protest challenged only alleged errors with respect to the award of the task order, but the court concluded that because the evaluation and award of the IDIQ contract and its associated task order were inextricably intertwined, declining jurisdiction would deprive the protester of any judicial review of the award of the IDIQ contract itself.

Authorization Act (NDAA) granted GAO *exclusive* and permanent jurisdiction over task order protests for both civilian and Department of Defense (DoD) task orders.[29]

GAO's jurisdiction over task order protests, however, is generally circumscribed by dollar limits. For civilian agencies, a task order may be protested if its value exceeds $10 million. For DoD agencies, NASA, and the Coast Guard, the task order value must exceed $25 million for it to be protestable.[30] In addition, as with COFC, GAO will hear protests asserting an order exceeds the scope, period of performance, or maximum dollar value of its underlying contract, regardless of the dollar value of the order at issue.

For post-award protests, GAO determines whether the jurisdictional dollar threshold is met by looking at the value as stated in the order itself.[31] Thus, if a task order is awarded at an amount below the threshold amount, GAO will not hear a task order protest even if the protester's offer is above the threshold and technically superior. For pre-award protests, GAO will either look to the values of the remaining offers (if the challenge is to an exclusion from the competitive range) or to the government estimate to determine jurisdiction.

Given that different dollar thresholds apply to civilian and defense agency task order protests, one issue of which potential protesters should be aware arises when the order is placed by an agency other than the one that awarded the IDIQ. In such instances, GAO will look to the statutory framework under which the IDIQ contract was awarded to determine which jurisdictional threshold applies. DoD IDIQ contracts are authorized under Title 10 of the U.S. Code; civilian agency IDIQ contracts are awarded under Title 41. Thus, GAO's jurisdiction over a protest challenging a "task order" issued by the DoD against a civilian agency IDIQ contract would be determined by the applicable dollar limits for civilian agency task orders under Title 41.

GAO made its jurisdictional boundaries clear during the three-month period between September and December 2016 when its jurisdiction over non-DoD (i.e., civilian) authorized task orders lapsed.[32] During that period, GAO considered a

---

29. The jurisdiction is permanent in the sense that it no longer has an automatic sunset provision.

30. *See* 10 U.S.C. § 2303; 10 U.S.C. § 2304c (discussing task order protests); Amar Health IT, LLC, B-414384.3, Mar. 13, 2018, 2018 CPD ¶ 111 (dismissing protest for lack of jurisdiction to entertain protests of task orders issued under civilian agency multiple-award IDIQ contracts that are valued at less than $10 million); NCS Technologies, Inc., B-413500.2, Feb. 14, 2017, 2017 CPD ¶ 123, at 2 n.3 (referencing the $25 million threshold applicable to task orders issued under NASA umbrella contracts after 2017 NDAA).

31. *See* Goldbelt Glacier Health Servs., LLC, B-410378, Sept. 25, 2014, 2014 CPD ¶ 281, at 2 (stating that "where an order has in fact been issued by the government, [GAO] view[s] the jurisdictional limit to turn on the value of the disputed order, which is reflected in the terms of the order itself").

32. GAO Civilian Task and Delivery Order Protest Authority Act of 2016, Pub. L. No. 114-779, 130 Stat. 1361 (2016).

handful of protests challenging DoD task orders issued against civilian agency IDIQ contracts. GAO dismissed the protests for lack of jurisdiction, explaining that the fact that a defense agency will place, fund, manage, and benefit from a task order issued by a civilian agency was not relevant to the question of jurisdiction.[33]

Finally, as noted earlier, the dollar thresholds for jurisdiction over task order protests do not apply where the protest alleges that the task order at issue exceeds the IDIQ contract's period of performance, maximum dollar value, or scope of work, or where the protest challenges a Federal Supply Schedule (FSS) order.[34]

D. Protesting Other Transaction Agreements

In recent years, the government, and in particular the DoD, has significantly increased its spending on nonprocurement instruments known as "other transactions" (OTs) or "other transaction agreements" (OTAs). These instruments, which often involve the acquisition of goods or services and can look exactly like traditional procurement contracts, are by definition *not* procurement contracts, and thus they are not subject to the same bid protest rules and jurisdiction.

As a rule, GAO will not consider protests challenging the award of an OTA or objecting to the terms in an OTA solicitation.[35] GAO will review OTA-related bid protests only in the limited case of a timely pre-award protest that "an agency has failed to comply with its statutory OTA authority, and therefore is improperly using an OTA to acquire goods or services in lieu of acquiring the goods or services using a procurement contract."[36]

Historically, in such cases, GAO has used a "direct benefit" test derived from the Federal Grants and Cooperative Agreements Act (FGCAA) to determine whether a procurement contract, rather than an OTA, is required.[37] For example, in *Rocketplane Kistler* and *Exploration Partners, LLC*, GAO explained that if the "principal purpose" of a legal instrument is "to acquire (by purchase, lease, or barter) property or services for the direct benefit or use of the United States Government," then an agency must use a procurement contract.[38] GAO articulated a different test, however, in *MorphoTrust USA, LLC*,[39] in which it required only that the agency's use of an OTA be "knowing and authorized." Although GAO in *MorphoTrust* disavowed reliance on

33. Wyle Labs., Inc., B-413989, Dec. 5, 2016, 2016 CPD ¶ 345; Analytic Strategies, LLC, B-413758.2, Nov. 28, 2016, 2016 CPD ¶ 340.

34. *See* Analytic Strategies LLC; Gemini Indus., Inc., B-413758.2, Nov. 28, 2016, 2016 CPD ¶ 340.

35. *See* 4 C.F.R. § 21.5(m); MD Helicopters, Inc., B-417379, Apr. 4, 2019, 2019 CPD ¶ 120.

36. *Id.* at 2 (citing 4 C.F.R. § 21.5(m)).

37. 31 U.S.C. §§ 6301–6308.

38. *Id.* § 6303; *see* Rocketplane Kistler, B-310741, Jan. 28, 2008, 2008 CPD ¶ 22, at 4; Exploration Partners, LLC, B-298804, Dec. 19, 2006, 2006 CPD ¶ 201, at 5.

39. B-412711, May 16, 2016, 2016 CPD ¶ 133, at 9.

the FGCAA, it did not expressly disagree with the Office's prior decisions in *Rocketplane Kistler* and *Exploration Partners*. Furthermore, after the *MorphoTrust* decision, GAO revised its Bid Protest Regulations to provide specifically that GAO will review whether an agency is "improperly using a non-procurement instrument to procure goods and services," an apparent reference to the "direct benefit" requirements of the FGCAA.[40] Thus, it is unclear what standard GAO will use in such cases going forward, although the authors posit that the two rules can be harmonized if GAO recognizes that a use of an OTA in violation of the FGCAA (i.e., to acquire goods or services for the government's direct benefit) is not "authorized" except in those limited instances where Congress has granted a specific superseding authority (e.g., the DoD's authority for prototyping projects in 10 U.S.C. § 2371b).

Whether federal courts have jurisdiction over OTA bid protests is unclear. In *MD Helicopters Inc. v. United States*,[41] the court declined jurisdiction over a challenge to the government's use of an OTA to update its helicopter fleet. Although the court acknowledged that an OTA was not a "procurement" contract subject to the FAR, it determined that the specific OTA before it was still a "contract" and therefore subject to the Tucker Act, depriving the court of jurisdiction. Conventional wisdom holds that COFC, like GAO, would review a protest alleging that an agency is improperly using an OTA where a procurement contract is required.[42] But recent cases have suggested COFC might also exercise jurisdiction over protests challenging the award of an OTA if the award is "in connection with a procurement."[43] Furthermore, even if the OTA is not "in connection with a procurement" and COFC does not have jurisdiction, arguably a federal district court of general jurisdiction could hear the protest as a challenge to an adverse agency action under the APA.[44] Although this area of the law is still in flux, the limited cases to date appear to be coalescing on a standard whereby an OTA award is subject to bid protest in COFC if the OTA, by its own terms, provides for the award of follow-on production work, which would otherwise need to be acquired through a procurement contract.[45]

---

40. 4 C.F.R. § 21.5(m).

41. 435 F. Supp. 3d 1003 (D. Ariz. Jan. 24, 2020).

42. *See* Hymas v. United States, 810 F.3d 1312, 1324 (Fed. Cir. 2016) (reviewing whether an agency properly construed certain agreements as cooperative agreements rather than procurement contracts subject to the court's bid protest jurisdiction under the Tucker Act).

43. *See* Space Exploration Techs. Corp. v. United States, 144 Fed. Cl. 433, 442–45 (2019) ("*SpaceX*").

44. *See id.* at 445–46; *see also* Scanwell Labs., Inc. v. Shaffer, 424 F.2d 859 (D.C. Cir. 1970) (setting out bid protest jurisdiction in federal courts, prior to ADRA transferring such jurisdiction to COFC for all bid protests in connection with a "procurement").

45. The authority to provide for follow-on production work in an OTA is unique to the DoD's authority to award OTAs to carry out prototyping projects and is expressly set forth in 10 U.S.C. § 2371b(f).

Finally, to the extent a protester seeks only to recover its bid and proposal costs related to an agency's award of an OTA, on the theory that the government breached its implied duty of good faith and fair dealing in considering the protester's proposal, such a claim may be brought in any federal district court, including COFC, up to $10,000, while all such claims valued at more than $10,000 must be brought at COFC.[46]

46. *See* 28 U.S.C. § 1346(a)(2) (granting district courts original jurisdiction over claims based on an implied contract with the United States, up to $10,000); 28 U.S.C. § 1491(a)(1) (granting COFC jurisdiction to render judgment on any claim based on an implied contract with the United States).

Chapter 2
Comparing Protest Forums

There are three primary forums in which a disappointed offeror may file a bid protest: the contracting agency (i.e., an "agency-level protest"), GAO, and COFC. The most significant differences among these forums are the time to decision, level of formality, scope of discovery, costs to prosecute, and the ability to obtain a stay of award or performance. In addition, government counsel vary by forum. Agency counsel represent the government in agency-level and GAO protests, whereas Department of Justice (DOJ) attorneys represent the government at COFC (albeit typically with assistance from agency counsel).

Agency-level protests are less formal and less costly to pursue than protests at GAO or COFC. On the other hand, an agency-level protest essentially asks the procuring agency to review its own procurement process and acknowledge it made a mistake. Accordingly, agency-level protests are often more suitable for fairly straightforward procurement errors, whereas GAO and COFC, both of which allow for discovery, are more appropriate for protests involving more complex issues.

Another difference that may inform a protester's choice of forum involves the protester's ability to obtain a stay of contract award or performance. Both agency protests and GAO protests provide protesters with the ability to halt an agency from awarding or performing a contract if a protest is filed within specified periods of time. At COFC, however, there is no automatic stay. DOJ may stipulate to a stay, but if it declines to do so, the protester must move for injunctive relief. Each of these issues, and others, are discussed further later in the chapter.

Although the three forums are available for protests of awards from nearly all federal agencies, there are exceptions. Two executive branch agencies have special forums with exclusive jurisdiction over their protests, and two have no forum in which to file a protest. The Federal Aviation Administration (FAA) Office of Dispute Resolution (ODRA) is an independent tribunal that handles all FAA bid protests, and the U.S. Postal Service handles all bid protests internally within its Postal Service Law Department. By regulation, neither GAO nor COFC will consider protests involving certain Small Business Administration (SBA) issues, including small business size standards (i.e., "size protests") and procurements under section 8(a) of the Small Business Act.[1]

1. *See, e.g.*, 4 C.F.R. § 21.5(b); 13 C.F.R. § 121.1003 (requiring size protests to be filed with agency contracting officers before being adjudicated by the cognizant SBA Area Office).

As discussed in Chapter 6, however, there are certain SBA-related issues that GAO will consider. Finally, both the U.S. Mint and the Presidio Trust are federal agencies that are statutorily exempt from the federal procurement laws and regulations and for which there is no bid protest forum.[2]

A. Agency-Level Protests

Agency protests provide offerors with a relatively simple and straightforward dispute resolution process. The disappointed offeror files its protest directly with the contracting officer or other designated official and may request that the protest be reviewed by someone at a higher level.[3]

The informal nature of agency-level protests is enshrined in FAR section 33.103 (Protests to the Agency), which states that agencies "should provide for inexpensive, informal, procedurally simple, and expeditious resolution of protests."[4] The FAR instructs agencies to make their "best efforts" to resolve protests within 35 days of the protest filing.[5] Little is provided in terms of discovery, with the FAR providing that "the parties may exchange relevant information"; in practice, discovery is essentially nonexistent in agency-level protests.[6]

Agency-level protests must include basic information such as the protester's contact information, the solicitation or contract number, a detailed statement of the legal and factual grounds of protest (including resulting prejudice), facts establishing the protester's standing as an interested party, the timeliness of the protest, and the requested ruling and form of relief.[7] A protest that fails to comply with any of these requirements risks dismissal.[8] The protest, however, need not contain any specific wording or adhere to any specific format. If a communication with the agency

---

2. *See* A-Z Cleaning Solutions, B-415228, Nov. 6, 2017, 2017 CPD ¶ 343 (dismissing protest of U.S. Mint award because, like the Presidio Trust, the Mint is exempt from federal procurement laws and regulations). Other specialized protest forums include the U.S. Senate's Office of the Sergeant at Arms, which has its own set of procurement regulations and procedures and is not subject to GAO or COFC protest jurisdiction. *See, e.g.*, GAO Bid Protest Docket, Sun Group LLC, B-416587.1, July 18, 2018 (dismissed without published opinion). The Library of Congress, on the other hand, has been defined as an agency over which GAO may exercise protest jurisdiction. *See* 41 C.F.R. § 300-3.1; AOC Connect, LLC, B-416658, Nov. 8, 2018, 2018 CPD ¶ 384 (sustaining protest against Library of Congress award).

3. *See* FAR 33.103(d)(3)–(4) (providing for an independent review at a level above the contracting officer as either an alternative to adjudicate the protest or as an appeal from the decision of the contracting officer, depending on agency-specific procedures).

4. FAR 33.103(c).

5. FAR 33.103(g).

6. *Id.*

7. *See* FAR 33.103(d).

8. *Id.*

contains the required information, it may very well be deemed a protest even if that was not the contractor's intent.

An important feature of agency-level protests is the ability for protesters to obtain a stay of award in a pre-award protest or stay of performance in a post-award protest. The FAR prohibits agencies from awarding a contract pending resolution of a protest if it received the protest prior to award.[9] Similarly, the FAR requires that agencies immediately suspend performance of an awarded contract if a protest is received within ten days of the award or within five days after a debriefing date offered to the protester, whichever is later.[10] In both the pre-award and post-award contexts, however, an agency may override a stay where award or performance "is justified, in writing, for urgent and compelling reasons or is determined, in writing, to be in the best interest of the Government" and approved by an official "above the contracting officer."[11] Such "override" decisions may be challenged by seeking injunctive relief from COFC to halt the award or performance.

A broad spectrum of relief, as well as attorneys' fees, may be available in agency-level protests.[12] If a protester is unsuccessful at the agency level, it may still generally file a protest at GAO or COFC. GAO's Bid Protest Regulations, however, require that a protest challenging the same issue as the one filed with an agency be brought "within 10 days of actual or constructive knowledge of initial adverse agency action."[13] This seemingly clear deadline is actually far less straightforward than it appears, and a body of GAO case law presents a cautionary tale of contractors that engaged in what they believed to be informal communications (e.g., e-mails or letters) with an agency, only to learn that GAO viewed them as agency-level protests.

In *Coulson Aviation (USA), Inc.*,[14] GAO found that letters previously sent by the protester to the agency constituted agency-level protests, and that the agency's responses to those letters constituted an "adverse agency action." GAO held that even though the contractor did not intend to file agency-level protests, its letters met the definition of a protest because they "clearly expressed dissatisfaction with the solicitation by disagreeing with the [agency]'s decision to use FAR part 15, rather than FAR part 12," and "specifically requested corrective action by asking that the [agency] revise the RFP to follow the commercial item procurement procedures under FAR

9. *See* FAR 33.103(f)(1).

10. FAR 33.103(f)(3).

11. FAR 33.103(f)(1), (3).

12. *See* FAR 33.102(b) ("If, in connection with a protest, the head of an agency determines that a solicitation, proposed award, or award does not comply with the requirements of law or regulation, the head of the agency may—(1) Take any action that could have been recommended by [GAO]; (2) Pay appropriate costs as stated in 33.104(h).").

13. 4 C.F.R. § 21.2(a)(3).

14. B-411525, Aug. 14, 2015, 2015 CPD ¶ 272.

part 12."[15] As GAO explained, "to be regarded as a protest, a written statement need only convey the intent to protest by an expression of dissatisfaction and a request for corrective action."[16] The protester filed its GAO protest before proposals were due, but months after the agency declined to revise the RFP. GAO found that the protester's ten-day clock to file at GAO started to run when the agency refused to amend the solicitation. Thus, GAO dismissed the protest as untimely.[17]

Accordingly, when considering whether to communicate with an agency regarding concerns about a procurement, contractors and protest counsel should carefully consider whether they want to posture their communication as an agency-level protest, and if not, how to frame the communication to avoid having it treated as such.

Overall, as a forum for protesting, agencies offer a cheaper, faster, and more direct route to decision than either GAO or COFC. Speed of resolution, however, goes hand in hand with a lack of discovery and the attendant challenge to developing a fulsome understanding of the rationale for the agency's procurement decision. Moreover, as noted earlier, in an agency-level protest, it is the agency itself that resolves the protest, whereas protests at GAO and COFC are adjudicated by an independent arbiter. The protester's ability to request review above the contracting officer level may serve to mitigate (at least partially) concerns about having the contracting officer revisit his or her own decision, but that does not address the other perceived advantages with proceeding at GAO or COFC. Thus, as noted at the outset, agency-level protests are best employed to address the most obvious of errors or to put an agency on notice of perceived problems with a solicitation or procurement decision.

B. GAO Protests

With over 2,000 bid protests annually, the GAO is the most widely used bid protest forum.[18] GAO offers protesters adjudicative efficiency and procurement law expertise, along with the ability to obtain a stay of award or performance and engage in protest-specific discovery—all within a 100-day protest-to-decision timeframe.

GAO provides protesters with a more thorough process than is available through an agency-level protest, but a more streamlined process than employed by COFC.

---

15. *Id.* at 6.

16. *Id.*

17. Interestingly, in *Tribologik Corp.*, B-417532, Aug. 2, 2019, 2019 CPD ¶ 248, GAO accepted as timely a protest filed more than ten days after the agency e-mailed the protester the denial of the agency-level protest. The e-mail was sent on Good Friday, a day on which the protester's office was closed. Although Good Friday is not a federal holiday, GAO looked to the protester's business hours, not the government's, to determine the start of the ten-day period from which the protester was charged with knowledge of the adverse decision.

18. *See* B-158766, GAO Bid Protest Annual Report to Congress for Fiscal Year 2019, Nov. 5, 2019 (noting that GAO received 2,198 protest filings during the 2019 fiscal year).

Despite functioning in many ways like an administrative board or judicial tribunal, GAO is neither. GAO is not part of the executive or judicial branches of government; it is an agency of Congress with protest authority granted through CICA.[19] Because GAO cannot, as an arm of the legislative branch, issue binding judgments on procuring agencies in the executive branch, its protest decisions are technically non-binding "recommendations." In practice, however, agencies rarely decline to accept these recommendations, as CICA requires GAO to "promptly" inform Congress if an agency declines to implement GAO's recommendation and advise whether "in order to correct an inequity or to preserve the integrity of the procurement process," Congress should consider private relief legislation, the recession or cancellation of agency funds, an investigation, or other action.[20] By way of example, from Fiscal Year 2016 through Fiscal Year 2019, there was not a single instance in which an agency declined to fully implement a GAO recommendation. In 2015, GAO advised Congress of a single such occurrence involving the State Department.[21]

Protests filed at GAO are governed by the Bid Protest Regulations found at 4 C.F.R. Part 21, with guidance set forth in FAR 33.104.[22] GAO's Bid Protest Regulations prescribe the requirements for bid protest filings and address a myriad of procedural issues such as standing (i.e., interested party status), timeliness, and stays of award or performance. These procedural issues and what they mean for protesters are discussed in depth in Chapters 3 and 4.

GAO's popularity as a forum is driven largely by its perceived advantages over COFC, which include rapid resolution of the dispute, knowledgeable arbiters whose practice focuses exclusively on bid protest issues, and the availability of an automatic stay of award or performance. By regulation, GAO must issue a decision resolving a protest within 100 days after it is filed.[23] Although this is a longer period than the 35-day period applicable to agency protests, it is typically much shorter than the time to decision at COFC (which can take four to six months or longer). Within this 100-day window, protesters, government agencies, as well as any interested-party intervenors (e.g., contract awardees) engage in a mini-litigation complete with targeted

19. 31 U.S.C. § 3553(a) (providing that the Comptroller General of the United States—the formal head of GAO—shall decide bid protests).

20. 31 U.S.C. § 3554(e).

21. *See* B-158766, GAO Bid Protest Annual Report to Congress for Fiscal Year 2015, Dec. 10, 2015, https://www.gao.gov/assets/680/674134.pdf.

22. While FAR Part 33 (Protests, Disputes, and Appeals) addresses agency-level, GAO, and COFC protests, it explains that GAO's Bid Protest Regulations are the governing set of procedures in that forum. *See* FAR 33.104 ("Procedures for protests to GAO are found at 4 CFR Part 21 (GAO Bid Protest Regulations). In the event guidance concerning GAO procedure in this section conflicts with 4 CFR Part 21, 4 CFR Part 21 governs."). With respect to COFC protests, the FAR directs readers to the rules of that court. FAR 33.105.

23. *See* 4 C.F.R. § 21.9(a).

discovery, briefing, and, on occasion, an evidentiary hearing.[24] The protest is presided over by a GAO attorney who, in essence, functions as an administrative judge or similar neutral adjudicator.

A significant characteristic of GAO protests is the automatic stay of performance or award. For post-award protests, the contracting agency must notify contract awardees that a protest has been filed. Most often such notification comes through a Stop Work Order or similar correspondence advising awardees of the protest and the stay of award or performance resulting from the filing. In pre-award protests, agencies are to "notify all bidders or offerors that have a substantial chance of receiving an award."[25]

A GAO protest proceeds in phases marked by distinct filings from the protester, the agency, and the intervenor(s), if any. The principal features of a GAO protest include the initial protest, third-party interventions, requests for dismissal, the five-day letter, the Agency Report, comments, supplemental protests, Supplemental Agency Reports and comments, and GAO's decision. These features are discussed as follows.

1. *Initial Protest*

GAO protests are filed electronically on GAO's Electronic Protest Docketing System (EPDS), through which all filings and correspondence related to the protest are submitted.[26] The initial protest filing, typically styled as a letter to GAO (but containing the substantive content of a legal brief, e.g., background facts and legal argument), initiates the protest proceedings. The requisite components of the protest document are set forth in GAO's Bid Protest Regulations, and the failure to meet any one requirement may result in the protest being dismissed.

Specifically, any protest filed at GAO must (1) include the protester's contact information; (2) be signed; (3) identify the agency and solicitation and/or contract number; (4) set forth a detailed statement of the legal and factual grounds of the protest, including copies of relevant documents; (5) establish that the protester is an

---

24. Evidentiary hearings are relatively rare at GAO. Although GAO averages about 2,500 protests per year, it held hearings in only 42 cases in FY 2014, 31 cases in FY 2015, 27 cases in FY 2016, 17 cases in FY 2017, and five cases in FY 2018. U.S. Gov't Accountability Off., B-158766, GAO Bid Protest Annual Report to Congress for Fiscal Year 2018 at 4 (2018), https://www.gao.gov/assets/700/695707.pdf. More common, although still not routine, are informal conference calls with counsel for the parties in which the GAO attorney seeks additional information relating to one or more specific issues.

25. U.S. Gov't Accountability Off., GAO-18-510SP, Bid Protests at GAO: A Descriptive Guide at 15 (2018), https://www.gao.gov/assets/700/691596.pdf.

26. GAO provides various instructive resources on EPDS at https://www.gao.gov/legal/bid-protests/file-a-bid-protest.

interested party; (6) establish the timeliness of the protest; (7) request a specific ruling from GAO; and (8) state the form of relief being requested.[27] GAO's Bid Protest Regulations also recognize the ability of protesters to request a protective order, specific documents relevant to their protest allegations, and a hearing. As a best practice, protesters should make these requests.

A protective order ensures that the protester's proprietary information and material will be safeguarded from public disclosure; coupled with document requests, it also provides protester's counsel the ability to review relevant proprietary or source-selection sensitive information regarding the awardee or other offerors that would not otherwise be made available. Because generally only outside counsel or consultants and sufficiently walled-off in-house counsel may be admitted under GAO's Protective Order, one challenge faced by protesters who proceed without being represented by counsel is the inability to access this information. This lack of access can doom an unrepresented protester's chances of success.

In the days after a protest is filed, GAO will assign the protest a Comptroller General file number (or "B-number," as it is styled "B-" followed by six numerical digits, e.g., B-123456) and assign a GAO attorney who will serve as the adjudicator of the protest. GAO will also issue an "Acknowledgement of Protest" providing the dates for the filing of the Agency Report (30 days after the protest filing) and GAO's decision (100 days after the protest filing). The document will include a copy of GAO's Protective Order if one is requested. GAO Protective Orders are discussed further in Chapter 5. Counsel for the procuring agency typically enter their notices of appearance within a few days of the protest being filed.

2. *Intervention*

Protests often include intervening parties. GAO's Bid Protest Regulations define "intervenor" as "an awardee if the award has been made or, if no award has been made, all bidders or offerors who appear to have a substantial prospect of receiving an award if the protest is denied."[28] A party wishing to intervene must file a notice of intervention requesting admission to the matter.

---

27. *See* 4 C.F.R. § 21.1(c). The "copies of relevant documents" commonly included with a protest are copies (or excerpts) of the governing solicitation, a notice of award, or other relevant information available to the protester when filing (e.g., evaluation documents or written debriefing materials). Although these materials are often also included in the Agency Report, it is best practice for the protester to file key documents if available with the protest so that GAO will have them in the intervening month before the Agency Report is produced. It is not uncommon, however, for the protest letter to reference such documents without including them as attachments, and GAO rarely, if ever, dismisses a matter for this reason alone.

28. 4 C.F.R. § 21.0(b)(1).

GAO must admit contract awardees that seek to intervene in post-award protests. In pre-award protests, however, GAO applies what in practice has become an "exceptional circumstances" test to determine whether an offeror has a "substantial prospect" of receiving an award. For example, although GAO typically allows the intended awardee of a planned sole-source contract to intervene, it routinely denies pre-award intervention requests where several viable offerors remain eligible for award and the protest challenges either the terms of the solicitation or the protester's exclusion from the competitive range.[29] Under circumstances such as an intended sole-source contract where potential competitors were not afforded a chance to submit proposals, GAO will allow intervention if the protester can otherwise establish standing (e.g., by submitting a timely response to a Notice of Intent). Chapter 3 includes a detailed discussion on interested parties and standing at GAO and COFC.

3. Requests for Dismissal

GAO may dismiss protests that fail to meet any of the requirements set forth in 4 C.F.R. § 21.1(c), either sua sponte or upon request from an agency or intervenor.[30] Common grounds for dismissal include a failure to state a sufficient ground of protest, lack of interested party status, or untimeliness. In addition, GAO's bid protest regulations set forth a number of grounds of protest that GAO will not hear.[31] Protest grounds that GAO will generally not consider include matters of contract administration, issues with SBA programs, affirmative determinations of contractor responsibility, and protests by subcontractors.[32]

One argument often asserted by the agency and/or intervenor in a request for dismissal is that the protest is based on speculation. GAO's bid protest regulations require that a protest include a detailed statement of the legal and factual grounds for the protest, and that the grounds stated be legally sufficient.[33] Under this framework, protesters must provide, at a minimum, either allegations or evidence sufficient, if uncontroverted, to establish the likelihood that it would prevail on its claim of improper agency action.[34]

---

29. *See, e.g.*, U.S. Gov't Accountability Off., GAO-18-510SP, Bid Protests at GAO: A Descriptive Guide at 15 (2018), https://www.gao.gov/assets/700/691596.pdf ("permitting intervention in a preaward protest is generally the exception, not the rule").

30. 4 C.F.R. § 21.1(i).

31. *See id.* § 21.5.

32. *Id.*

33. *Id.* § 21.1(c)(4).

34. *Mark Dunning Indus., Inc.*, B-413321.2, Mar. 2, 2017, 2017 CPD ¶ 84, at 2 (protest dismissed where "protester merely speculates as to the contents of [awardee's proposal], having no actual knowledge as to its contents."); *see also* Mission 1st Grp., Inc., B-413028.4, Nov. 20, 2017, 2017 CPD ¶ 364, at 3 ("bare allegations or speculation are insufficient to" support a protest); CAMRIS Int'l, Inc., B-416561,

Although an agency or intervenor may file a request for dismissal at any time, in practice, such requests are typically made soon after the protest has been filed. Agency requests for dismissal are usually accompanied by a request that the obligation to produce the Agency Report be suspended until GAO rules on the request. When a request for dismissal is filed, GAO usually affords the protester an opportunity to respond in writing before deciding the issue.

4. Five-Day Letter

If the protest includes specific document requests—as most protests do—the agency must respond in writing at least five days before filing the Agency Report (i.e., the legal response to the protest and relevant factual record). GAO's Bid Protest Regulations require the Five-Day Letter (as it is commonly called) to

> identify [i] whether the requested documents exist, [ii] which of the requested documents or portions thereof the agency intends to produce, [iii] which of the requested documents or portions thereof the agency intends to withhold, and [iv] the basis for not producing any of the requested documents or portions thereof.[35]

Protesters have two days following receipt of the Five-Day Letter in which to object to the scope of the agency's proposed document production.[36] It is not uncommon for agencies to argue that relevancy be narrowly defined so as to limit the scope of production, and for protesters to argue the opposite. GAO typically resolves disputes over the scope of document production within one to two days in order to ensure the protester may timely file its comments.

5. Agency Report

The agency's formal response to the protest is known as the "Agency Report." The Agency Report contains three parts: (1) the agency's memorandum of law prepared by agency counsel, (2) the contracting officer's statement of facts, and (3) the contemporaneous record of procurement documents related to the grounds of protest and responsive to the protester's document requests.[37] These documents include relevant portions of the protester's proposal, relevant portions of the awardee's proposal, the solicitation, and relevant evaluation documents. Some agencies have adopted the practice of combining the legal memorandum and the contracting officer's statement

---

Aug. 14, 2018, 2018 CPD ¶ 285 (protest ground relating to evaluation of awardee's price proposal dismissed as based on speculation concerning contents of the proposal).

35. 4 C.F.R. § 21.3(c).

36. *Id.*

37. *See id.* § 21.3(d).

of facts into a single document. The Agency Report is filed within 30 days of the initial protest, unless otherwise directed by GAO.[38]

6. Comments on the Agency Report

Within ten days of the Agency Report, the protester must file "comments" on the Agency Report, which function in many ways as a reply brief in support of the initial protest grounds and as an opposition to the legal memorandum and statement of facts submitted by the agency.[39] Intervenors also have the option to file comments (e.g., in support of a protested award). It is not uncommon for intervenors to coordinate their efforts with agency counsel, and even to provide support to the agency, such as assisting with legal research.[40] GAO will dismiss a protest if a protester fails to timely file its comments and, importantly, will also dismiss any individual protest ground that the protester fails to address in its comments.[41]

7. Supplemental Protests

During the course of proceedings at GAO, a protester may learn of and file additional (i.e., "supplemental") grounds of protest. Any supplemental ground of protest, however, "must independently satisfy GAO's timeliness requirements."[42] Often, a protester will learn of new grounds of protest from information contained in the documents produced with the Agency Report. Thus, under the routine scenario where the agency produces the documents simultaneously with its legal memorandum and statement of facts, the ten-day comment period matches the ten-day window for the filing of a supplemental protest. Accordingly, protesters frequently combine their comments and any supplemental protest grounds in a single filing.

But, the two dates do not always align. For example, agencies sometimes produce documents several days before they file their memorandum of law. If those documents contain information that gives rise to supplemental grounds of protest, then the supplemental protest clock starts to run upon the production of those

38. *Id.* § 21.3(c).

39. *Id.* § 21.3(i)(1).

40. Agency responses to offers of help vary widely among agency counsel. Some agency counsel readily accept assistance, while other agency counsel decline assistance out of concern that today's intervenor may be tomorrow's protester on the very same procurement. Best practice for intervenor counsel is to contact agency counsel as soon as possible after intervention has been allowed to make the offer of help, and to follow up after admission under the protective order has been granted when help may actually be provided.

41. 4 C.F.R. § 21.3(i)(2)–(3).

42. U.S. Gov't Accountability Off., GAO-18-510SP, Bid Protests at GAO: A Descriptive Guide at 12 (2018), https://www.gao.gov/assets/700/691596.pdf.

documents. Alternatively, GAO will sometimes extend the protester's ten-day comment period. Such an extension, however, would not change the ten-day window for filing a supplemental protest based on information obtained from previously produced documents.[43] In sum, protesters must keep a close eye on the date they received information underpinning their supplemental grounds of protest, and file within ten days thereafter.

8. *Supplemental Agency Report and Supplemental Comments*

If a protester files supplemental grounds, GAO will direct the agency to file a "Supplemental Agency Report" (SAR) on which the protester and any intervenors will file comments. The filing of supplemental protest grounds and the subsequent SAR rarely, however, cause GAO to postpone its originally planned decision date, which is 100 days from the filing of the initial protest. Instead, GAO almost always issues a single decision covering both initial and supplemental protest grounds by the original decision date. For this reason, GAO will usually direct the agency to file the SAR on a shorter timeframe than the 30 days it had for the Agency Report, and protesters (and intervenors) may also be given fewer than ten days to comment.[44]

9. *Decision*

A hallmark of GAO as a protest forum is the requirement set by 4 C.F.R. § 21.9(a) that a final decision on the protest be issued within 100 days after it is filed. The decision will either sustain, deny, and/or dismiss each ground of protest. A sustained decision represents a finding for the protester on the merits of all or specific grounds of protest and is accompanied by a recommendation of corrective action to remedy the violation. A denial of any protest ground represents a finding for the agency on the merits (i.e., that the agency acted reasonably and lawfully). A dismissal reflects a non-merits-based resolution of all or certain grounds of protest (e.g., for lack of GAO jurisdiction, or where a protest is rendered academic by virtue of agency's voluntary corrective action). In adjudicating the merits, GAO looks to the protest allegations, the Agency Report (including the agency's response to the allegations and

43. 4 C.F.R. § 21.2(c) provides that GAO may, for good cause shown, consider an untimely protest. Missing the ten-day deadline because of confusion as to the day the clock started to run would almost certainly not meet GAO's definition of good cause.

44. GAO's publicly available website (not to be confused with EPDS) will automatically generate dates for supplemental protests that put the decision 100 days from the date of filing. Those unfamiliar with GAO's practices may be confused by this and operate under the assumption that GAO will issue separate decisions for the initial and supplemental protests in seriatim fashion. This is not the case. Absent extremely unusual circumstances, GAO will issue a decision covering both the initial and supplemental protests by the first 100-day deadline.

record documents), and the comments filed on the Agency Report by the protester and any intervenors. GAO reviews the protested agency action for reasonableness and whether it complies with applicable law.[45]

Where a protest is sustained, the corrective action chosen by GAO may differ from the specific relief sought by the protester, and can take any number of forms including termination of award, the resubmission of proposals, or "other recommendation(s) as GAO determines necessary to promote compliance" with statute or regulation.[46] In the event a protest is sustained, GAO will typically recommend that the agency reimburse the protester its costs incurred in filing and pursuing its protest, "including attorneys' fees and consultant and expert witness fees."[47]

Similarly, when an agency takes voluntary corrective action before GAO issues its decision, GAO may recommend that the agency reimburse the protester for the costs of the protest.[48] When an agency takes corrective action prior to a decision, the protester must file a request that GAO recommend that costs be paid; this request to GAO must be made no later than 15 days after the protester has learned (or should have learned) that GAO closed the protest based on the agency's corrective action. The agency then has 15 days after the request is filed to respond, and the protester is then given ten days to file comments on the agency response. GAO's decision in these circumstances depends on whether it concludes that the protest grounds are "clearly meritorious" and that the agency "unduly delayed taking corrective action in the face of a clearly meritorious protest, thereby causing the protester to expend unnecessary time and resources to make further use of the protest process in order to obtain relief."[49]

In determining whether a protest argument is clearly meritorious, GAO does not look merely at whether an agency decided to take corrective action. Rather, a protest will be considered clearly meritorious "where an agency's reasonable inquiry into the protester's allegations would reveal facts showing the absence of a defensible legal position."[50] Issues that GAO considers to be "close questions" and where the agency has provided a reasonable response are not likely to be considered clearly meritorious.[51] To determine if an agency "unduly delayed" in taking corrective action, GAO

45. *See, e.g.*, Alliance Worldwide Distrib., LLC, B-408491, Sept. 12, 2013, 2013 CPD ¶ 223 (GAO reviews agency action "solely to determine if it was reasonable and consistent with the solicitation's evaluation scheme, procurement statues [sic] and regulations.").

46. 4 C.F.R. § 21.8(a).

47. *Id.* § 21.8(d). It is not uncommon for a protester and agency to disagree on the fees to be paid. While there is a protester-agency claim process laid out in GAO's regulations (*see id.* § 21.8(f)), GAO will entertain separate protests challenging an agency's decision on a protester's cost claim. *See id.* § 21.8(f)(3)–(6).

48. *Id.* § 21.8(e).

49. Remote Diagnostics Technologies, LLC—Costs, B-413375.3, Feb. 6, 2017, 2017 CPD ¶ 52, at 2.

50. *Id.* at 3.

51. *Id.*

will consider whether the agency waited until after it submitted the Agency Report to take corrective action. Where the agency takes corrective action as a result of supplemental protest grounds, GAO regards corrective action taken prior to submission of the supplemental report to be timely and not unduly delayed.[52]

Once GAO recommends *entitlement* to the reimbursement of costs, whether in a final protest decision or as a result of a request following corrective action, the parties should attempt to reach an agreement on the *amount* of costs to be reimbursed. GAO's rules provide that the protester must submit its claim for costs "detailing and certifying the time expended and costs incurred" with the agency within 60 days of GAO's recommendation.[53] Failure to submit a timely claim may result in forfeiture of the protester's rights.[54] The agency must then issue a decision on the cost claim as soon as practicable. GAO anticipates that the parties may try to negotiate the costs, but provides that the protester may file a request that GAO recommend the amount of costs to be paid and must do so within ten days of when the agency states that it will not participate in further discussions.[55] Again, the agency is given 15 days to respond and the protester is given ten days to submit comments on the response before GAO issues a decision.[56]

When GAO recommends that a procuring agency pay a protester's attorneys' fees, fees are capped by CICA at $150 per hour.[57] This limit, however, may be (and often is) adjusted based on an increase in the cost of living from when CICA took effect (1995) or a special factor such as the limited availability of qualified attorneys for the proceedings.[58] In making any adjustment, October 1995 is considered the proper base month and year for the $150 per hour rate.[59] In addition, costs of consultants or expert witnesses are limited to "the highest rate of compensation for expert witnesses paid by the Federal Government."[60] Under CICA, small businesses are not subject to these restrictions.[61]

52. *Id.*

53. 4 C.F.R. § 21.8(f)(1).

54. *Id.*

55. *Id.* § 21.8(f)(3).

56. *Id.* § 21.8(f)(4).

57. 31 U.S.C. § 3554(c)(2)(B).

58. *Id.*; *see also* Dep't of the Army; ITT Fed. Servs. Int'l Corp. - Costs, B-296783.5, Apr. 26, 2006, 2006 CPD ¶ 72 (allowing attorneys' fees at a rate of $192.12/hour based on the Dep't of Labor's Consumer Price Index); Dep't of State - Costs, B-295352.5, Aug. 18, 2005, 2005 CPD ¶ 145 (approving attorneys' fees between $196.89 and $197.77 based on the Consumer Price Index for the San-Francisco-Oakland-San-Jose, California, area).

59. *See* Sodexho Management Inc. - Costs, B-289605.3, Aug. 6, 2003, 2003 CPD ¶ 136, at 35 (finding that the proper baseline for computing CPI increases for hourly rates is October 1995—the month when FASA's original $150 ceiling took effect).

60. 31 U.S.C. § 3554(c)(2)(A).

61. *Id.* § 3554(c)(2).

Another challenge that a protester may face in seeking costs arises if GAO sustains some but not all of the grounds of protest. GAO may rule that the protester is only permitted to recover costs for the meritorious protest grounds. It is often not easy to segregate the costs of drafting each protest ground, especially where timekeeping must necessarily be somewhat broadly stated in attorneys' invoices to avoid protective order violations. Under these circumstances, GAO has found that "an estimate based on the number of pages in the protester's submissions to our Office that were devoted to a particular issue – is a reasonable means of determining" the amount that is incurred in pursuit of the successful protest issues.[62] When calculating the percentage of pages associated with the meritorious protest grounds, however, protesters may want to exclude the pages associated solely with administrative matters or the general description of the solicitation, which would be required for any protest arguments, not merely those that are meritorious.

C. COFC Protests

COFC provides a formal, structured bid protest process that more closely resembles standard litigation than agency-level or GAO protests.[63] COFC reviews bid protests under the "arbitrary and capricious" standard of the APA.[64] The APA standard of review is highly deferential to the contracting agencies. In applying the APA, the court may set aside an award if "(1) the procurement official's decision lacked a rational basis; or (2) the procurement procedure involved a violation of regulation or procedure."[65] With respect to the first basis for setting aside an award, the court determines "whether the contracting agency provided a coherent and reasonable explanation of its exercise of discretion"; under the second basis, the protester "must show a clear and prejudicial violation of applicable statutes or regulations."[66]

COFC offers several advantages as a forum that make it an appealing option for prospective protesters. Chief among them is the protester's ability to obtain a more comprehensive procurement record than is available in other forums. The "Administrative Record" filed by DOJ at COFC includes the agency's complete procurement file and is therefore almost always more fulsome than the Agency Report at GAO. As previously noted, discovery is essentially nonexistent in agency-level protests.

62. BAE Tech. Servs., B-296699.3, Aug. 11, 2006, 2006 CPD ¶ 122, at 3.

63. Congress established COFC under Article I of the Constitution and by statute provided that the court shall consist of 16 presidentially appointed and Senate-confirmed judges that serve 15-year terms with the option to continue hearing cases as a senior judge thereafter. *See* 28 U.S.C. § 171 *et seq.*

64. 5 U.S.C. §§ 701–706; *see* DataMill, Inc. v. United States, 91 Fed. Cl. 722, 728 (2010).

65. Axiom Res. Mgmt., Inc. v. United States, 564 F.3d 1374, 1381 (Fed. Cir. 2009) (quoting Impresa Construzioni Geom. Domenico Garufi v. United States, 238 F.3d 1324, 1332 (Fed. Cir. 2001)).

66. *Id.* (quoting *Impresa*, 238 F.3d at 1333).

In addition, COFC does not impose specific bid protest timeliness rules; instead, protests are technically subject to the Tucker Act's general six-year statute of limitations.[67] Thus, COFC may be the only option available to prospective protesters that miss the very short filing deadlines at GAO. Despite the lack of protest-specific timeliness rules, protesters at COFC should still file promptly upon learning of the basis for their protest. Doing so avoids any risk of a laches argument and minimizes the risk that performance will have proceeded so far along that meaningful relief will be unavailable.

One advantage that agency-level and GAO protests have over COFC protests is the CICA-mandated automatic stay on performance or award. To obtain a stay at COFC, the protester must either obtain injunctive relief from the court, or agreement from the government to voluntarily stay award or performance for a stipulated period of time. Although not required, in practice, DOJ (which, as noted earlier, represents the contracting agency) often agrees to a stay where the protester intends to seek a temporary restraining order and/or preliminary injunctive relief.

Another potential disadvantage of pursuing a protest at COFC is the cost, which typically exceeds the costs of pursuing agency-level or GAO protests. For example, recent DoD bid protest statistics reflect an average protest resolution time of 133 days at the court compared to just 41 days at GAO—and although GAO protests must be resolved within a 100-day window, there is no comparable limit at COFC and protests may extend well beyond that timeframe.[68]

Protesters sometimes use COFC for a "second-bite" protest. This refers to the situation where the protest is initially filed and litigated at GAO, but in the wake of an unfavorable decision, the protester files a similar protest at COFC. Although GAO decisions are not binding, the court may look to a GAO opinion for guidance or as persuasive authority.[69]

Protests at COFC proceed in phases with filings from the protester, the government, and the intervenor(s), if any. The principal components of COFC protests include the pre-filing notice, the complaint and accompanying filings, requests for injunctive relief, the initial status conference, the Administrative Record, motions for judgment on the record, oral argument, and the court's written decision. These and

67. *See* 28 U.S.C. § 2501 ("Every claim of which the United States Court of Federal Claims has jurisdiction shall be barred unless the petition thereon is filed within six years after such claim first accrues.").

68. *See* Mark V. Arena, et al., *Assessing Bid Protests of U.S. Department of Defense Procurements*, RAND Corp. (2018), https://www.rand.org/content/dam/rand/pubs/research_reports/RR2300/RR2356/RAND_RR2356.pdf.

69. Idea Int'l, Inc. v. United States, 74 Fed. Cl. 129, 136 n.11 (2006) ("Although GAO decisions are not binding on this Court, the Court 'recognizes GAO's longstanding expertise in the bid protest area and accords its decisions due regard.'") (quoting PHT Supply Corp. v. United States, 71 Fed. Cl. 1, 9 n.6 (2006)).

other elements of protest practice at COFC are governed by the Rules of the Court of Federal Claims (COFC Rules, or RCFC), including Appendix C thereto (which sets forth the "Procedure in Procurement Protest Cases").[70] These common COFC protest components are discussed next.

1. Pre-Filing Notice

COFC Rules require that protesters submit a pre-filing notice at least 24 hours prior to filing a bid protest at the court and encourage them to provide notice even earlier if possible "as a courtesy to the court and to government counsel."[71] The notice must be sent to the following recipients: the DOJ, Commercial Litigation Branch, Civil Division; the COFC Clerk of Court; the procuring agency's contracting officer; and the apparently successful offeror where there has been an award and plaintiff received notice of the awardee's identity.[72] The notice may be sent by e-mail, and a Sample Bid Protest Pre-Filing Notice is provided on COFC's website along with the methods of contact for the Clerk and DOJ to whom the notice must be sent.[73]

The notice must provide standard corporate disclosure information, information regarding the procuring agency, whether the protester anticipates seeking injunctive relief and has discussed the need for such relief with the DOJ, information regarding any preceding GAO protest, and whether a protective order is contemplated.[74] Although the notice is required to be filed at least 24 hours before a protest, a protest need not be filed on the day specified in the notice (or at all).

2. Complaint and Initial Filings

To commence a bid protest at COFC, a protester[75] must file a complaint and associated documents.[76] Depending on the nature of the matter as noted later, the initial bid protest filing at COFC typically includes:

---

70. COFC's Rules and accompanying appendices and forms are publicly available on its website at https://www.uscfc.uscourts.gov/rcfc.

71. *See* RCFC, Appx. C, § II, ¶ 2.

72. *Id.*

73. *See* U.S. Fed. Cl., Bid Protest Information, https://www.uscfc.uscourts.gov/bid-protest-info.

74. *See* RCFC, Appx. C, § II, ¶ 3.

75. At COFC, the protester is referred to as the "plaintiff"; the government is the "defendant"; and any admitted intervenor is designated either a "defendant-intervenor" (if defending against the protest) or, though less common, a "plaintiff-intervenor" (if supporting the protest).

76. *See* RCFC 3.

- **Complaint.** The complaint must include short and plain statements regarding both the court's jurisdiction and the protester's entitlement to relief, and a demand for the relief sought (which may include relief in the alternative or of different types).[77]
- **Civil cover sheet.** If a complaint is filed in paper form, it must include a cover sheet (shown in Form 2 of the RCFC Appendix of Forms). A cover sheet is not required, though is often included, with electronic filings.[78]
- **Disclosure statement.** A disclosure statement identifying any parent corporation or publicly held corporation owning 10 percent or more pursuant to RCFC 7.1.
- **Motion to file under seal.** If the protester believes its complaint or material filed therewith contains confidential or proprietary information, a motion to have the pleadings sealed must be concurrently filed.[79] The complaint and any material filed with it must be marked or highlighted to indicate confidential or proprietary information.[80]
- **Redacted complaint.** If the protester seeks to file the complaint under seal, a proposed redacted version must be filed along with the sealed version that omits any confidential or proprietary information so that it may be released to the public. Failure to file a proposed redacted version may result in denial of the motion for leave to file under seal.[81]
- **Motion for protective order.** A protester seeking to have a protective order issued must file a motion for a protective order (typically filed along with the complaint and motion for leave to file under seal).[82] The RCFC Appendix of Forms includes a model protective order for bid protests (Form 8) that may be included with the requesting motion as the proposed order. COFC Protective Orders are discussed in detail in Chapter 5.B.
- **Request for preliminary injunctive relief.** If the protester seeks a temporary restraining order (TRO) or preliminary injunction, the complaint must be accompanied by an application for such relief as well as any "affidavits,

77. *See* RCFC 8(a).

78. *See* RCFC, Appx. E (Electronic Case Filing Procedure); RCFC, Appx. of Forms, Form 2 (Cover Sheet).

79. *See* RCFC, Appx. C, § III *et seq.* ("the complaint or related material will be treated as though filed under seal while the motion is pending").

80. *See* RCFC, Appx. C, § III, ¶ 6(a).

81. *See* RCFC, Appx. C, § III, ¶ 6(b).

82. *See* RCFC, Appx. C, § VI, ¶ 17(a).

supporting memoranda [of law], and any other documents upon which the [protester] intends to rely."[83]

- **Filing fee.** A fee (currently $400) must be submitted along with the complaint.[84]

In addition to the materials just described, protesters at COFC must be represented by an attorney of record admitted to practice at the Court of Federal Claims.[85]

3. Intervention

COFC Rules provide for intervention by a third party on a timely motion to intervene either as a matter of right or permissively.[86]

Although the process for intervening at GAO is simpler and faster (requiring only a letter to GAO), COFC generally provides greater latitude to intervention requests. For example, in a pre-award protest at GAO, "intervenor" is defined as a bidder or offeror with a substantial prospect of winning the award if the protest is denied.[87] COFC's Rules, however, are more permissive in terms of intervening parties and do not prohibit intervention by nonbidders who would not, for example, be interested parties with standing to file a protest.[88]

4. Initial Status Conference and Scheduling Order

Promptly upon receipt of the complaint, the court will convene an initial status conference among the parties. Often conducted telephonically, the status conference will address matters such as intervenor admissions, any request for temporary

83. RCFC, Appx. C § V, ¶ 10.

84. U.S. Court of Federal Claims Schedule of Fees, https://www.uscfc.uscourts.gov/sites/default/files/19.10.01%20UPDATED%20Fee%20Schedule.pdf (last visited July 8, 2020).

85. *See* RCFC 83.1(c)(1); *but see* RCFC 83.1(a)(3) ("An individual who is not an attorney may represent oneself or a member of one's immediate family, but may not represent a corporation, an entity, or any other person in any proceeding before this court."); RCFC, Appx. C, § VIII, ¶ 25 (allowing protests to be filed by nonadmitted attorneys when conditioned upon pursuit of admission within 30 days from filing).

86. *See* RCFC 24(a)(2) ("the court must permit anyone to intervene who . . . claims an interest relating to the property or transaction that is the subject of the action, and is so situated that disposing of the action may as a practical matter impair or impede the movant's ability to protect its interest, unless existing parties adequately represent that interest"); RCFC 24(b)(1) ("the court may permit anyone to intervene who: (A) is given a conditional right to intervene by a federal statute; or (B) has a claim or defense that shares with the main action a common question of law or fact").

87. 4 C.F.R. § 21.0(b)(1).

88. *See, e.g.*, CHE Consulting, Inc. v. United States, 71 Fed. Cl. 634 (2006) (finding original equipment manufacturer subcontractor entitled to intervention as of right in pre-award challenge to solicitation where successful protest would impact subcontractor's direct economic interest); Northrop Grumman Info. Tech., Inc. v. United States, 74 Fed. Cl. 407 (2006) (permitting contractor to intervene that assisted agency with A-76 procurement for purpose of protecting proprietary information).

or preliminary injunctive relief (or, alternatively, agreed-upon stays of award or performance), protective order issues, the content of and time for filing the Administrative Record, supplementation of the Administrative Record, and the schedule for the proceedings.[89] Shortly thereafter, the court will typically enter a Scheduling Order setting forth the date by which the agency must file the Administrative Record, a briefing schedule for motions and cross-motions on the Administrative Record, and a date for any oral argument on the merits. If a protester seeks preliminary injunctive relief, the Scheduling Order will also likely include dates for briefing arguing the motion for a preliminary injunction.

5. Temporary Restraining Order/Preliminary Injunctive Relief

As noted, unlike GAO or agency-level protests, bid protests filed at COFC do not obtain an automatic stay of performance or award. Accordingly, a COFC protester seeking a stay must either reach agreement with the government on the terms of a voluntary stay or move for injunctive relief.[90] The basis for obtaining injunctive relief is discussed in Chapter 4.B.

6. Administrative Record

Section VII of Appendix C to the RCFC addresses the content and filing of the Administrative Record. RCFC, Appendix C, section VII, paragraph 22(a)–(u) identifies 21 categories of "core documents relevant to a protest" that include many more documents than are typically included in the Agency Report at GAO. For example, COFC Rules identify as "core documents" the agency's source selection plan—a document that agencies routinely seek to avoid producing at GAO protests.[91] Also included in the COFC definition of "core documents" are "records of any discussions . . . between the agency and the protester, awardee, or other interested parties . . ."; the "awardee's, or other interested parties' offers, proposals, or other responses to the solicitation"; and "the agency's evaluations of the protester's, awardee's, or other interested parties' offers, proposals, or other responses to the solicitation, including supporting documentation."[92] At GAO, agencies will seek to withhold these documents in whole or in part if they are not relevant to a specific ground of protest.

In short, the Administrative Record at COFC is almost always more fulsome than the Agency Report at GAO. COFC has interpreted its rules to mean that the

89. *See* RCFC, Appx. C, § IV (Initial Status Conference).
90. *See* RCFC, Appx. C, § V (Injunctive Relief).
91. RCFC, Appx. C, § VII, ¶ 22(b).
92. RCFC, Appx. C, § VII, ¶ 22(j), (l), (n).

Administrative Record should essentially be the agency's record of the procurement.[93] Thus, for example, although the Agency Report at GAO may not include cost evaluation materials in a protest challenging only a technical evaluation, at COFC the Administrative Record would likely contain such documents. If the COFC protest is a "second-bite" protest (i.e., filed after the disappointed offeror protested and lost at GAO), the Administrative Record will include the GAO Agency Report, all filings made at GAO, and GAO's decision.

The protester may seek to supplement the Administrative Record at COFC, but supplementation is not easy to obtain, and the need for it must be demonstrated. "As a general rule, in determining whether an agency's actions are arbitrary or irrational, the 'focal point for judicial review . . . should be the administrative record already in existence, not some new record made initially with the reviewing court.'"[94] Although the court recognizes that "the administrative record is a fiction,"[95] and eschews the use of "an iron-clad rule automatically limiting its review to the administrative record,"[96] supplementation remains the exception rather than the rule.[97]

The court will, however, distinguish between a motion to supplement the record and a motion to complete the record, readily granting the latter if the agency failed to include information relevant to its procurement decision. As explained by COFC, "insofar as [a] plaintiff's request focuses on documents created during the evaluation process, the matter appears to the Court to involve more a question of completing the administrative record, rather than supplementing it," and under the APA "the relevant doctrine entails 'limiting review *to the record actually before the agency*' . . . not to the record the agency chooses to present."[98]

---

93. *See, e.g.*, Bannum, Inc. v. United States, 89 Fed. Cl. 184, 189 (2009) ("The 'primary focus of the court's review should be the materials that were before the agency when it made its final decision.'") (quoting Cubic Applications, Inc. v. United States, 37 Fed. Cl. 345, 349–50 (1997)).

94. DataMill, Inc. v. United States, 91 Fed. Cl. 722, 728 (2010) (quoting Knowledge Connections, Inc. v. United States, 79 Fed. Cl. 750, 759 (2007)).

95. Al Ghanim Combined Group Co. Gen. Trad. & Cont. W.L.L. v. United States, 56 Fed. Cl. 502, 508 (2003).

96. GraphicData, LLC v. United States, 37 Fed. Cl. 771, 779 (1997).

97. *See* Axiom Res. Mgmt., Inc. v. United States, 564 F.3d 1374, 1379–81 (Fed. Cir. 2009) ("While we recognize the need for an adequate record during judicial review, the parties' ability to supplement the administrative record is limited" and should be allowed only "if the existing record is insufficient to permit meaningful review consistent with the APA.").

98. Tauri Grp., LLC v. United States, 99 Fed. Cl. 475, 480 (2011) (quoting Axiom Res. Mgmt., Inc. v. United States, 564 F.3d 1374, 1380 (Fed. Cir. 2009)) (emphasis added by quoting opinion); *see also* Murakami v. United States, 46 Fed. Cl. 731, 740 n.4 (2000) ("allowing the record to be supplemented by evidence that the agency considered but did not include in the record might be viewed as not supplementation at all, but merely requiring that the administrative record be complete").

7. Motions for Judgment on the Administrative Record

After the Administrative Record is filed, the protester, government, and any intervenor(s) will file motions and cross-motions for judgment pursuant to RCFC 52.1.[99] Because the relief sought by a protester in its bid protest complaint involves a request for injunctive relief, the parties may also file declarations to establish (or disprove) the prongs for injunctive relief, for example, the existence of irreparable harm.[100]

The court will advise the parties during the Scheduling Conference whether the protester or the government (and intervenor(s), if any) will submit the first set of briefs. In practice, however, the court typically directs the protester to submit the first round of briefing.

The following reflects a typical (but not mandated) timeline of events:

- Within 30 to 45 days of the filing of the complaint, the agency files the Administrative Record.
- Within 14 to 21 days after the Administrative Record is filed, the protester files its Motion for Judgment on the Administrative Record (MJAR). The MJAR must not exceed 40 pages, double-spaced.[101]
- Within 14 to 21 days after the protester files its MJAR, the government and intervenor file their respective responses to the protester's MJAR, as well as their respective cross-MJARs and any motions to dismiss (e.g., based on procedural grounds separate from the merits of the allegations). A combined MJAR response and cross-MJAR must not exceed 50 pages, double-spaced.[102]
- Within 10 to 14 days after the government and intervenor file their MJAR responses and cross-MJARs, the protester files its reply in support of its MJAR and cross-MJAR responses. A combined MJAR-reply and cross-MJAR response must not exceed 30 pages, double-spaced.[103]

---

99. *See* Bannum, Inc. v. United States, 404 F.3d 1346, 1356 (Fed. Cir. 2005) ("[T]he judgment on an administrative record is properly understood as intending to provide for an expedited trial on the record.").

100. *See* Holloway & Co., PLLC v. United States, 87 Fed. Cl. 381, 391 n.12 (2009) ("In a protest before the court, factual matters respecting relief rest on a separate and distinct footing" subject to resolution by the Court rather than decision by the procuring agency in the administrative record.); *see also* Ashbritt, Inc. v. United States, 87 Fed. Cl. 344, 366–67 (2009) ("[I]t is appropriate to add evidence pertaining to prejudice and the factors governing injunctive relief to the record in a bid protest—not as a supplement to the AR, but as part of this Court's record."), *clarified*, 87 Fed. Cl. 654 (2009).

101. *See* RCFC 5.4(b)(1).

102. *Id.*

103. *Id.* 5.4(b)(2).

- Within 10 to 14 days after the protester files its cross-MJAR responses, the government and intervenor file their replies in support of their cross-MJARs. An MJAR-reply must not exceed 20 pages, double-spaced.[104]

8. Decision and Appeal Options

After briefing has been completed, the court will usually hold a hearing in which the parties present oral argument. The Tucker Act provides COFC with the authority to provide "any relief that the court considers proper, including declaratory and injunctive relief except that any monetary relief shall be limited to bid preparation and proposal costs."[105] If the court sustains the protest, it will often issue declaratory judgment and/or a permanent injunction—both of which are binding on federal agencies.[106]

COFC decisions may be appealed to the Court of Appeals for the Federal Circuit in accordance with the Federal Rules of Appellate Procedure.[107] Because the United States is a party to the protest, an appeal may be filed by any party within 60 days after COFC enters its judgment.[108] Review of Federal Circuit decisions may be sought at the Supreme Court of the United States.

---

104. *Id.*

105. 28 U.S.C. § 1491(b)(2). The Equal Access to Justice Act (EAJA), 28 U.S.C. § 2412, allows prevailing protesters at COFC to recover attorney's fees and other expenses under certain limited circumstances. The EAJA limits award to protesters with a net worth of $7,000,000 or less and that have 500 or fewer employees. § 2412(2)(B). As a result, the EAJA does not provide for recovery for all protesters. To obtain costs, the court must not find that the government's position was "substantially justified or that special circumstances make an award unjust." § 2412(d)(1)(A). The prevailing protester must submit an application for fees and other expenses within 30 days after final judgment in the action, and the application must include an itemized statement supporting the amount sought. § 2412(d)(1)(B). Recovery of attorney's fees is capped at $125 per hour unless the court determines that an increase in the cost of living or other factors justify a higher fee. § 2412(2)(A).

106. *But cf.* McAfee, Inc. v. United States, 111 Fed. Cl. 696, 714 (2013) (finding protester demonstrated likelihood of success on the merits but declining to grant injunctive relief because "the national security interests at stake here are overpowering . . . this is a situation in which McAfee has demonstrated a violation by the Air Force of statutes and the FAR, but no viable remedy is at hand").

107. *See* RCFC Rule 58.1.

108. *See* F.R. App. P. 4(a)(1)(B).

Chapter 3

Who May Protest, and When and Whether to Do So

A. Who May Protest

1. Interested Parties and Standing Generally

In protests, as in other litigation matters, one of the threshold questions for GAO or COFC will be whether the protester has standing to file a protest, that is, whether the protester is an "interested party." GAO rules define "interested party" as "an actual or prospective bidder or offeror whose direct economic interest would be affected by the award of a contract or by the failure to award a contract."[1] Likewise, the Federal Circuit has defined this term to mean it "(1) is an actual or prospective bidder; and (2) possess[es] the requisite direct economic interest."[2] An actual or prospective offeror has a direct economic interest if it suffered a competitive injury or prejudice as a result of an alleged error in the procurement process.[3] For practical purposes, this means the protester must be a potential offeror or bidder to file a pre-award protest and an actual offeror or bidder that did not receive a contract award in the post-award context.

Notably, this definition also excludes a number of entities that might be substantially affected by procurement decisions from protesting. Subcontractors, even substantial subcontractors, or other team members may *not* file a protest, even if their direct economic interests may be affected by the award of the contract.[4]

1. 4 C.F.R. § 21.0(a)(1).

2. Sys. Application & Techs., Inc., 691 F.3d 1374, 1382 (Fed. Cir. 2012) (citing Weeks Marine, Inc. v. United States, 575 F.3d 1352, 1359 (Fed. Cir. 2009)); *see also* Orion Tech., Inc. v. United States, 704 F.3d 1344, 1348 (Fed. Cir. 2013).

3. Myers Investigative and Security Servs. v. United States, 275 F.3d 1366, 1370 (2002) (holding that "prejudice (or injury) is a necessary element of standing").

4. *See* Dash Eng'g, Inc.; Engineered Fabrics Corp.—Reconsideration, B-246304, May 4, 1993, 93-1 CPD ¶ 363 ("A prospective subcontractor does not have the requisite interest to be an interested party because it is not a prospective or actual offeror.").

For the same reason, individual joint venture partners and substantial investors do not have standing to protest. Only the actual bidder or offeror may do so.[5] Thus, where a joint venture loses a contract award, the joint venture entity itself must file the protest. It is important, therefore, to have clear provisions in any joint venture agreements—especially special joint venture agreements for purposes of pursuing a single contract—concerning which party controls the decision to protest and who will pay for any such protest.

2. *Sole-Source Award Protests*

Sole-source contract awards come up in a number of settings. Most often challenges to such awards arise when an agency has stated that its needs are so urgent and compelling as to require it to avoid the time for competition, where the agency concludes that only one offeror has the capability to meet the agency's requirements, or where an agency makes a change to the scope of an already existing contract. While this section discusses the confines of standing, the particulars of protests challenging the use of sole-source or other noncompetitive procedures are discussed in Chapter 6.

Generally, GAO and COFC rely on their definitions of an "interested party" in the context of a protest challenging a sole-source procurement (i.e., a protester must be an actual or prospective supplier whose direct economic interest would be affected by the award of a contract or the failure to award a contract).[6] For sole-source procurements, this means that the protester must demonstrate that it could have competed for the contract "but for" the agency's decision to award on a sole-source basis.[7]

This means, however, that a contractor that is unable to meet the agency's technical requirements at the time it submitted its bid cannot be an interested party.[8] An exception to this rule may exist where a protester asserts that it would be an interested party but for the agency's sole-source action.[9]

---

5. Matter of Yona-Brixtel, LLC, B-416649, Sept. 12, 2018, 2018 CPD ¶ 317 (stating that a joint venture, not an individual venture partner, is the appropriate "interested party" to protest).

6. *See* 4 C.F.R. § 21.0(a).

7. *See* Int'l Training, Inc., B-272699, Oct. 2, 1996, 96-2 CPD ¶ 132 ("Since the protesters would have been eligible to compete for award but for the protested delivery terms, they were interested parties."); *see also* Cubic Def. Sys., Inc. v. United States, 45 Fed. Cl. 239, 247, *dismissed*, 230 F.3d 1375 (Fed. Cir. 1999) (noting that protester's "but for" argument "plainly reveals that Cubic's claim points to the Government's actions as the cause of its inability to compete and as the root cause of the alleged CICA violation").

8. *See* Merlin Int'l, Inc., B-310611, Jan. 2, 2008, 2008 CPD ¶ 66 (finding that protester was "not an interested party to challenge the Army's determination to proceed on a sole-source basis" where it could not meet all of the requirements).

9. *See Cubic Def. Sys., Inc.*, 45 Fed. Cl. at 247.

Finally, where the procuring agency publicized its intent to award on a sole-source basis and invited expressions of interest, GAO has held that a potential source may protest only if it timely responded to the agency's notice of intent (NOI).[10] At GAO, the protester's response to the NOI must have been more than a fleeting expression of interest or mere suggestion that it could meet the requirements. The protester must have provided sufficient information to allow the agency to assess whether or not there was only one source capable of meeting the requirement.[11]

COFC tends to be more lenient in this regard. For example, the court found that a telephone call by a contractor to the agency expressing interest in a procurement is sufficient to confer standing.[12]

3. Competitive Range Decision Protests

Competitive range protests arise after an agency decides to enter into discussions with some, but not all, offerors and narrows the field through a competitive range determination pursuant to FAR 15.306(c). An offeror removed from the competitive range may have the ability to protest the agency's determination. To do so, however, the excluded offeror should, within three days of receipt of the notice that it has been removed from the competitive range, request a *pre-award* debriefing under FAR 15.505. As discussed in more detail in the timeliness discussion in section B of this chapter, although FAR 15.505(a)(2) states that an offeror may elect to delay its debriefing to be a post-award debriefing, and although the post-award debriefing may provide more information, doing so could result in a GAO protest filed after the debriefing being deemed untimely.

4. Multiple Award IDIQ Contracts

One area in which GAO and COFC have diverged is whether an awardee under a multiple award IDIQ contract can protest the award of additional contracts. At

10. Tech. Advancement Grp., Inc., B-417609, Aug. 8, 2019, 2019 CPD ¶ 290, at 5–6; Forensic Quality Servs. Int'l, B-299723, May 23, 2007, 2007 CPD ¶ 97 ("as a prerequisite to filing a protest against a sole-source procurement, a protester must have submitted a timely expression of interest in response to the published notice and the agency must have rejected its proposal and proceeded with the noncompetitive procurement").

11. Simula Gov't Prods., Inc., B-274730, 96–2 CPD ¶ 219, at 2 (finding insufficient a submission of only an "undocumented, unexplained, assertion that it could meet the requirement") (citing Litton Computer Servs., B-256225.4, July 21, 1992, 94–2 CPD ¶ 36).

12. *See Cubic Def. Sys.*, 45 Fed. Cl. 239 at 251 (noting that the court has previously declined to "reach the broader question of whether a timely-submitted proposal is, in every instance, a prerequisite for challenging an award decision") (quoting FN Mfg., Inc. v. United States, 41 Fed. Cl. 186, 188 (1998)); *see also* KSD, Inc. v. United States, 72 Fed. Cl. 236, 249 (2006) (finding unconfirmed allegations of contact with agency sufficient).

GAO, once a contractor receives an award, it does not have standing to challenge additional awards to other offerors. In *National Air Cargo Group v. United States*,[13] GAO explained that such an awardee is no longer "an interested party to challenge the agency's decision to award another contract." Subsequent to this decision, the contractor in *National Air Cargo Group* filed a protest at COFC, which reached a different conclusion than GAO and concluded that an awardee under a multiple award IDIQ contract can challenge an agency's decision to award further contracts.[14]

In *PAE-Parsons Global Logistics Services, LLC v. United States*,[15] COFC cited to *National Air Cargo* in denying a motion to dismiss brought by the government against a protest filed by PAE-Parsons, an IDIQ contract awardee, explaining that "[e]ssentially, an awardee still has an 'economic interest' in 'stopping the government from stepping outside stated procurement terms in making further awards.'" Although COFC's decisions in *National Air Cargo Group* and *PAE-Parsons* are not binding precedent, and the Federal Circuit has not yet weighed in, these cases provide support for standing at COFC should one IDIQ contract awardee wish to challenge another contractor's award.

B. When to Protest

1. Pre-Award Protest Filing Deadlines

The deadline for filing a pre-award protest depends on the basis for the protest and the forum in which it is brought. Agency-level protests are governed by FAR 33.103, which provides that "[p]rotests based on alleged apparent improprieties

13. Nat'l Air Cargo Grp., Inc., B-411830.2, Mar. 9, 2016, 2016 CPD ¶ 85.

14. Nat'l Air Cargo Grp., Inc. v. United States, 126 Fed. Cl. 281, 297 (2016).

15. PAE-Parsons Global Logistics Servs. LLC v. United States, 145 Fed. Cl. 194 (2019) (internal citations omitted). The *PAE-Parsons* case is notable for another reason. The government also argued that the plaintiff was merely complaining about task orders it did not receive rather than the fact that another offeror also won an IDIQ contract. The court noted that the case presented "a fact pattern" it had never seen before in which the IDIQ contract and task order awards were merged into a single evaluation process. The court denied the government's motion to dismiss for lack of jurisdiction, explaining that the Army's procurement scheme presented a unique circumstance in which the task orders could not be separated from the IDIQ contracts under which they issued, and that absent jurisdiction, contractors would be deprived of any judicial review of the award of the IDIQ contract itself. As the court subsequently explained in another protest challenging the same procurement, "[t]o hold that this Court lacks jurisdiction over this massive IDIQ procurement would effectively gut a significant part of federal procurement law by using the Federal Acquisition Streamlining Act of 1994 (FASA), 10 U.S.C. § 2304c(e) (2018), to nullify a broad area of contract scrutiny. This misuse of FASA would not streamline the procurement and protest process, but, rather, would eliminate a significant part of it, directly contradicting the legislative intent behind both FASA and the Competition in Contracting Act." Fluor Intercontinental, Inc. v. United States, 147 Fed. Cl. 309, 316 (2020).

in a solicitation shall be filed before bid opening or the closing date for receipt of proposals."[16] "In all other cases, protests shall be filed no later than 10 days after the basis of protest is known or should have been known, whichever is earlier."[17] If a protester is dissatisfied with the outcome, it has the option to file a subsequent protest at GAO or COFC. As discussed in Chapter 2, however, a special timeliness rule applies to GAO protests initially filed with an agency: the protester must file its GAO protest "within 10 days of actual or constructive knowledge of initial adverse agency action."[18]

For the most part, the timeliness rules at GAO and COFC align in that a protest challenging a solicitation impropriety may be filed any time prior to the date for submission of proposals. GAO's Bid Protest Regulations specify that "[p]rotests based upon alleged improprieties in a solicitation which are apparent prior to bid opening or the time set for receipt of initial proposals shall be filed prior to bid opening or the time set for receipt of initial proposals."[19] Thus, protests related to the language in the solicitation (e.g., of overly restrictive requirements, improper evaluation methods, or patent ambiguities) must be filed prior to the date for submission of proposals. In addition, where alleged improprieties do not exist in the initial solicitation but are subsequently incorporated by amendment, such improprieties must be protested no later than the next closing time for receipt of proposals.[20]

The filing deadlines for the most common pre-award protest grounds are discussed later. The substantive discussion of these and other pre-award grounds of protest are found in Chapter 6.A.

a. Challenges to the Terms of a Solicitation

Under GAO's Bid Protest Regulations, challenges to the terms of a solicitation (e.g., an assertion that an RFP is unduly restrictive because it includes a brand-name requirement not needed to meet the agency's minimum needs) must be brought prior to the time proposals are due.[21] GAO strictly adheres to this requirement, explaining that "late is late."[22]

Although COFC does not have specific protest timeliness rules, the Federal Circuit has similarly held that pre-award protests challenging patent (i.e., obvious) errors

16. FAR 33.103(e).
17. *Id.*
18. 4 C.F.R. § 21.2(a)(3).
19. *Id.* § 21.2(a)(1).
20. *Id.*
21. 4 C.F.R. § 21.2(a)(1).
22. *See, e.g.*, Baldt Inc., B-402596.3, June 10, 2010, 2010 CPD ¶ 139, at 1 (dismissing untimely challenge to solicitation) ("Underlying our timeliness rules regarding solicitation improprieties is the principle that challenges which go to the heart of the underlying ground rules by which a competition is conducted, should be resolved as early as practicable during the solicitation process, but certainly in advance of an award decision if possible, not afterwards.").

in a solicitation must be filed prior to the submission of proposals.[23] In *Blue & Gold Fleet, L.P. v. United States*, the Federal Circuit concluded that "a party who has the opportunity to object to the terms of a government solicitation containing a patent error and fails to do so prior to the close of the bidding process waives its ability to raise the same objection subsequently in a bid protest action in the Court of Federal Claims."[24] The Federal Circuit's rationale for this rule was a "desire to prevent contractors 'from taking advantage of the government and other bidders' and to 'avoid[ ] costly after-the-fact litigation.'"[25] Thus, potential protesters "cannot sit on their rights to challenge what they believe is an unfair solicitation, roll the dice and see if they receive [the] award."[26]

b. Agency Decision to Proceed with Sole-Source Award

At GAO, protests of an agency's decision to issue a sole-source award through non-competitive procedures must be filed within ten days of when the basis of protest is known or should have been known. Thus, where an offeror's expression of interest in a sole-source procurement is rejected, a protester must protest within ten days of this rejection.[27]

An issue that often confronts protesters is determining whether the agency has, in fact, decided to proceed with a sole-source award. For example, an NOI indicating that the agency plans to award a sole-source contract that also invites potential competitors to submit expressions of interest typically does not constitute a "final" decision against which a protest may be lodged. In this regard, GAO stated,

---

23. *See* Blue & Gold Fleet, L.P. v. United States, 492 F.3d 1308, 1313 (Fed. Cir. 2007). Recently the decision in *Blue & Gold Fleet, L.P. v. United States* has come under criticism that its bar to bringing claims for patent errors after award is contrary to Congress's intent in enacting a six-year statute of limitations. Inserso Corp. v. United States, 961 F.3d 1343, 1354–55 (Fed. Cir. 2020) (Reyna, J., dissenting) ("Congress has spoken to the timeliness of challenges to patent errors in the solicitation. Congress provided that '***[e]very claim*** of which the United States Court of Federal Claims has jurisdiction,' which includes challenges to patent errors in the solicitation, 'shall be barred unless the petition thereon is filed within six years after such claim first accrues.' . . . Given this clear congressional directive, we cannot curtail the six-year limitations period for challenges to patently defective solicitations." (quoting 28 U.S.C. § 2501)) (emphasis in original) (citing SCA Hygiene Prod. Aktiebolag v. First Quality Baby Prod., LLC, 137 S. Ct. 954, 197 L. Ed. 2d 292 (2017)).

24. 492 F.3d 1308.

25. CRAssociates, Inc. v. United States, 102 Fed. Cl. 698, 712 (2011), *aff'd*, 475 F. App'x 341 (Fed. Cir. 2012) (quoting *Blue & Gold Fleet*, 492 F.3d at 1314).

26. *Blue & Gold Fleet*, 492 F.3d at 1314.

27. It is important to note that the ten-day rule applies even to alleged solicitation improprieties if they arise when "no closing time has been established, or if no further submissions are anticipated." 4 C.F.R. § 21.2(a)(1).

a protest of a sole-source procurement where the agency has provided an opportunity for interested firms to submit an expression of interest is premature, and [ ] the protester can protest the sole-source and related issues within 10 days of when it knows or should have known that its response was rejected and that the sole-source procurement is proceeding.[28]

Thus, to protest a planned sole-source procurement in the wake of an NOI, "a protester must have submitted a timely expression of interest in response to the published notice and the agency must have rejected its proposal and proceeded with the noncompetitive procurement."[29]

There are occasions, however, when the NOI contains language strongly indicating that a "final" decision has been made and that the invitation to potential offerors to submit expressions of interest is a mere formality. Under such circumstances, it is not uncommon for would-be offerors to file "protective" protests that may be subsequently withdrawn if the agency acknowledges that no final decision has been made.

c. Exclusion from Competitive Range—the "Competitive Range Trap"

An offeror excluded from the competitive range may protest its exclusion. But many contractors have been caught in the "competitive range trap." At GAO, a protest is timely if it is filed within ten calendar days after "the basis of protest is known or should have been known (whichever is earlier)" or within ten calendar days of the protester receiving a *requested and required debriefing.*[30] A debriefing is the agency's written or oral explanation of its procurement decision.

Under CICA, where an offeror is eliminated from a competitive range, the agency is required to provide a pre-award debriefing if requested by the offeror within three days of receiving notice of its exclusion. But the FAR allows the offeror to request that the debriefing be delayed until after award.[31] At first blush, deferring the debriefing may seem more advantageous to the offeror: after all, the agency is required to provide more information in a post-award debriefing than it is in a pre-award debriefing.[32]

However, the FAR warns, rather understatedly, that "[d]ebriefings delayed pursuant to [the contractor's request] could affect the timeliness of any protest filed

28. Forensic Quality Servs.-Int'l, B-299723, May 23, 2007, 2007 CPD ¶ 97 (citing Bombardier, Inc., B-244328, June 17, 1991, 91-1 CPD ¶ 575, at 2; Keco Indus., Inc., B-238301, May 21, 1990, 90-1 CPD ¶ 490, at 3).

29. *Forensic Quality Servs.-Int'l, B-299723*, at 1.

30. 4 C.F.R. § 21.2(a)(2).

31. FAR 15.505(a)(2).

32. *Compare* FAR 15.506(d) (post-award debriefing requirements including information about the awardee) *with* FAR 15.505(f) (pre-award debriefing requirements).

subsequent to the debriefing."[33] GAO, in fact, has consistently held that an offeror that learns of its exclusion from the competitive range but chooses to delay the debriefing until after award gives up its opportunity to protest.[34] Thus, it is important for offerors to be aware of this trap and to request a pre-award debriefing whenever they think they may want to protest their exclusion from the competitive range. If the agency then determines it would rather delay the debriefing until after award, there will be no effect on the timeliness of the potential protest.

2. Post-Award Protest Filing Deadlines

a. GAO Filing Deadlines

The timeliness rules for post-award protests differ dramatically between GAO and COFC. At GAO, post-award timeliness depends not only on when a protest ground was or should have been known but also on whether a debriefing was required and requested, and when the debriefing closed. In addition, protesters at GAO face another question as to whether they want to seek a CICA stay (most do), which requires compliance with an even more stringent timeliness standard.

i. GAO's Standard Ten-Day Rule

The timeliness of a post-award protest at GAO often depends on whether a debriefing was required and requested within three days of notice of award. In a procurement where a debriefing is not required, the protest must be filed within ten days of when the protest ground was known or should have been known.[35] In almost all cases, this will be from the date of the offeror's notice of award (or from when the award is otherwise publicly announced).

Agencies often provide debriefings even if not required. Debriefings not required by the FAR do not toll the ten-day clock, and this can be an unpleasant surprise for the unwary contractor. The most common type of procurement for which debriefings are required, if requested, are those under FAR Part 15 (Contracting by Negotiation). Award decisions for which the agency need not provide debriefs include those made under FAR Part 8 (Federal Supply Schedule), FAR Part 12 (Commercial Item), and FAR Part 13 (Simplified Acquisitions). Whether a debrief is required for a task

33. FAR 15.506(a)(4)(ii).

34. *See* Loc Performance Prod., Inc., B-417431, Apr. 22, 2019, 2019 CPD ¶ 149 ("In this respect, we have specifically concluded that where, as here, a protester elects to delay a required pre-award debriefing, the protester has failed to diligently pursue any protest grounds which the protester would have discovered in that pre-award debriefing.") (citing United Int'l Investigative Servs., Inc., B-286327, Oct. 25, 2000, 2000 CPD ¶ 173, at 3); *see also* VMD Sys. Integrators, Inc., B-412729, Mar. 14, 2016, 2016 CPD ¶ 88 (applying very strict interpretation of timeliness rules).

35. 4 C.F.R. § 21.2(a)(2).

or delivery order award made under FAR Part 16 depends on whether the award is for more than $5.5 million.[36] No debriefing is required for task/delivery order awards below the $5.5 million threshold.[37] For such orders, a protest must be filed within ten days of when the protest ground was known or should have been known.[38]

ii. GAO's Debriefing Exception

In a procurement where a debriefing is requested and required, "the initial protest shall not be filed before the debriefing date offered to the protester, but shall be filed not later than 10 days after the date on which the debriefing is held."[39] It is imperative, however, that a contractor submit a request for debriefing in writing within three days of the notice of award for the timeliness rules related to required debriefings to apply (otherwise the debriefing is voluntary, and the debriefing exception will not apply).

It is also important for the contractor to understand when the debriefing is closed. For example, if an agency agrees to respond to questions at a time following an oral debriefing and confirms that the debriefing will be held open until such questions are answered, the clock will begin to run only when the agency has responded. If, on the other hand, the agency refuses to answer questions or is unclear as to whether it will hold the debriefing open until it has responded to unanswered questions, then the safest interpretation is that the agency closed the debriefing on the date of the oral debriefing.

In 2018, the DoD amended its rules for debriefings pursuant to the 2018 NDAA section 818.[40] According to these new rules, DoD agencies must provide disappointed offerors with an opportunity to ask follow-up questions "within two business days after receiving the [post award] debriefing."[41] The procuring DoD agency has five business days to provide written responses to those questions. Thus, so long as the contractor elects to ask follow-up questions, the closing of its debriefing, and the deadline to submit a protest, is automatically delayed. If a contractor does not timely submit follow-up questions, however, the debriefing will be considered closed on the day in which it was held.

---

36. FAR 16.505(b)(6).

37. *Id.*

38. As orders below $5.5 million would not meet GAO's jurisdictional threshold amount, any such protest would have to assert that the order exceeded the scope, period of performance, or maximum value of the umbrella contract under which it issued.

39. 4 C.F.R. § 21.2(a)(2).

40. *See* Dep't of Def., Class Deviation 2018-O0011, Enhanced Post Award Debrief Rights (2018), https://www.acq.osd.mil/dpap/policy/policyvault/USA000563-18-DPAP.pdf.

41. *Id.*

Once the agency has closed a required debriefing, a contractor wishing to file a protest has ten days to submit its protest to GAO. This is true even if the agency continues to respond to questions after the debriefing is closed. In *State Women Corp.*, the unsuccessful offeror submitted follow-up questions on May 28, and the Army provided written responses on June 1, along with a statement that the debriefing was closed.[42] The offeror continued to submit questions, which the Army continued to answer until June 20. The offeror filed its protest on June 24, and the Army requested summary dismissal on timeliness grounds. Because the debriefing closed on June 1, GAO held that the June 24 protest was untimely.[43] GAO also made clear, however, that the new, enhanced debriefing rules applicable to DoD enhanced debriefing do not alter the timeliness rules for filing a protest or obtaining a stay of performance. As discussed more fully in Chapter 4, to ensure a stay of contract performance, the agency must receive notice of a protest by GAO within five days of the close of the requested and required debriefing.[44]

b. COFC Filing Deadline

COFC does not have a specific deadline for filing post-award protests other than the standard six-year statute of limitations generally applicable to claims. Thus, a contractor disappointed with the outcome of a GAO protest is not time barred at COFC even if the protest is filed months after the award decision. As a practical matter, however, it behooves the would-be protester to file at COFC as soon as practicable to avoid or minimize the risk either that its claim would be dismissed on the equitable ground of laches or that performance of the contract would have proceeded so far as to preclude meaningful relief.[45]

In addition, the court will consider how quickly a protester acts in its review of a request for a temporary restraining order or a motion for preliminary injunction to stay contract performance during the pendency of the protest. If a protester waits a lengthy period of time to protest, the delay may suggest that the protester does not anticipate immediate and irreparable harm associated with performance of the contract, which will weaken any injunctive arguments.

---

42. B-416510, July 12, 2018, 2018 CPD ¶ 240, at 2–3.

43. GAO distinguished *Harris IT Servs. Corp.*, B-406067, Jan. 27, 2012, 2012 CPD ¶ 57. In *Harris*, the agency's provision of additional responses to a protester's questions following a written debriefing and silence as to the status of the conclusion of the debriefing created an ambiguity as to whether the debrief had concluded.

44. 31 U.S.C. § 3553(d).

45. *See* Nat'l Telecommuting Inst., Inc. v. United States, 123 Fed. Cl. 595, 602 (2015) (holding that laches barred a protest filed six months after award where the delay was avoidable and caused the government and the awardee economic prejudice).

C. Whether to Protest

1. *Gathering Information*

In assessing whether to protest, a contractor should collect and analyze all the information it can about the procurement action(s) that would be challenged, and whether the protest would likely lead to business. In the post-award context, the first step upon receipt of the disappointing notice of award to another offeror would be to request a debrief. As noted earlier, if the procurement is one in which a debriefing is required, the request must be made in writing within three calendar days of notice of the award. In fact, both awardees and disappointed offerors should request debriefings, as awardees can profit by learning how the agency assessed their proposals. In-person or telephonic debriefings are preferable to written debriefs, as the opportunity to engage with the agency and ask questions in real time often leads to more informative debriefings.

Contractors should request redacted copies of the evaluation documents and source selection decision. In the past, agencies were not always willing to provide these documents, but recently more agencies have been willing to provide more fulsome debriefings as a way to avoid "fishing expedition" protests that may occur when a contractor leaves a debriefing without having any meaningful sense of why it did not receive the award.

In addition, contractors should make sure to get any questions they have about the evaluation and award decision answered during the debriefing. Contractors must be mindful, however, that an agency's refusal to answer questions does not support a ground of protest. Put simply, GAO does not entertain protests related to debriefing inadequacies—and the timeline for filing a protest will not be tolled.

As previously noted, even when a debriefing is not required, or where a debriefing is not requested in a timely manner, offerors can still request a voluntary debriefing in an attempt to gain more information. Contractors should keep in mind that the deadline to file a protest is not tolled under such circumstances and thus would be due within ten days of when the protester knew or should have known the grounds for protest.

2. *Assessing Prospects*

The would-be protester should consider the strength of the grounds it would advance as well as the likely remedies that would result if the protest succeeds. Where the most likely outcome is a re-evaluation that leads to the same disappointing result, winning the protest may provide little more than a moral victory, and at a considerable cost. Although contractors have at times protested to make a point to an agency with which they do repeat business, that is not a path that necessarily leads to favorable long-term outcomes.

To consider its prospects, a disappointed offeror should ask itself the following:

- Did the debriefing or other information reveal errors in the evaluation of the offeror that materially impacted the evaluation?
- Did the agency appear to ignore certain aspects of the offeror's proposal?
- Were discussions conducted and, if so, did the discussions concern all significant weaknesses or deficiencies associated with the proposal?
- Was the agency's award decision rational and did it adhere to the solicitation's evaluation scheme?

Disappointed offerors should keep in mind that any potential protest ground that it knows about (or should know about) at the time of the initial protest must be included in the initial protest. Protesters cannot merely argue that the evaluation included a large number of errors, then identify two or three as "examples" with a plan to describe the rest during comments on the agency record. Instead, each error should be described in as detailed a manner as possible to ensure that its future arguments are not deemed untimely. This may also assist an offeror in alleging the necessary prejudice.

Disappointed offerors should also try to identify any arguments they may be able to make about the awardee. Although this may be difficult in an initial protest, GAO's rules on the agency record require only that the agency provide documents concerning the protest grounds alleged. Thus, if an offeror cannot include any arguments about the awardee, it is unlikely to receive any of the awardee's proposal or evaluation information in the protected agency record. That is not to say that an offeror should speculate entirely about the awardee's proposal and the agency's evaluation. But to the extent an offeror has publicly available information about an awardee's offerings, prior contract performance, or what it has offered in the current procurement, the offeror may be able to use that information to build an argument that the awardee's proposal was not evaluated properly.

In analyzing the strengths of the protest grounds, the disappointed offeror should consider the amount of information it has and does not have. Very often protests are sustained not on the basis of an initial protest but on what is found in the agency record and potential supplemental protest grounds. If an agency has been forthcoming in its debriefing, however, and has already provided the offeror with the full evaluation record with respect to the offeror's evaluation, there may not be much more that the offeror will expect to receive in the agency record.

In addition to considering the strength of available protest grounds, the disappointed offeror should assess the potential remedies available to it. As discussed previously, a winning protest could result in having the agency re-evaluate offers in accordance with the solicitation or conduct discussions and request revised proposals. Under the first scenario, a disappointed offeror may not feel confident that it will ultimately win the contract. Depending on the nature of the errors and their significance, the agency may very well re-evaluate the offers, better document its evaluations, and come to the same award decision it had previously made—but this time with a potentially stronger record to withstand any protest. This process, referred to as an agency's "papering the record," is not unusual.

The arguments that are most likely to lead to the submission of revised proposals and a new award decision are those that affected the way in which offerors proposed under the solicitation. These may include latent ambiguity claims, the agency's use of unstated evaluation criteria, and errors during discussions that may have resulted in an offeror amending its proposal. Although the resubmission of proposals could still result in the same award decision, it opens the door of opportunity wider for an offeror to revise its proposal and rectify any weaknesses the agency had previously found.

Finally, disappointed offerors may want to consider the potential business impact of protesting or not protesting beyond the outcome of the protest itself. For example:

- Will the contract serve as a foothold for a much larger set of procurements so that an offeror may want to take a chance on what may seem like weak protest grounds in the hopes of finding something better in the record?
- Will the contracting agency be upset by a protest? A protest, by definition, involves litigating against the customer. Although most procurement officials view protests as a fact of life and a sign of a healthy procurement system, less experienced officials may not share that view. That said, protests that are well-grounded and are not overly speculative or inflammatory are far less likely to upset a customer than those that the customer may view as spurious.
- For incumbent contractors, does the automatic stay provide enough of a business case for protesting, so long as there are reasonable grounds of protest?
- Are there less obtrusive ways to express disappointment with the agency's procurement decision? Where a disappointed offeror does not think it has a strong protest but still has concerns about the evaluation or the outcome, there may be other ways to express this concern to the agency, including setting up a meeting with the contracting officer or those higher up (especially after the deadline for protests has expired), going to the agency ombudsmen, or drafting a letter (as opposed to a protest) to the agency to raise these concerns and ask how the offeror can improve its position in future procurements.

3. Choosing a Forum

Once an offeror decides to file a protest, it must also decide where to file the protest. As previously noted, GAO and COFC are the most popular, so this discussion focuses on those forums. There are instances, however, when an agency-level protest may be appropriate. A pre-award agency-level protest may provide an effective means of flagging a concern with the agency without putting the agency into a defensive position before a third-party tribunal. Protests based more on "business" arguments rather than legal arguments may also have a better chance at the agency level. For example, a protester that made a mistake in its proposed costs, but thinks the agency should have recognized the mistake, might argue that the agency would have been better off clarifying the mistake. This type of argument is not likely to receive a sympathetic ear at GAO but may persuade an agency to revisit its decision. Finally, protests based on obvious errors that would likely result in quick voluntary corrective action if protested at GAO may also succeed as agency-level protests.

Most disappointed offerors, however, will assert protest grounds that go beyond obvious errors or the desire merely to flag a concern with an agency's action. How, then, should a protester decide between GAO and COFC? There are a number of factors to consider:

Will the Forum Hear the Case: One of the first questions may be simply whether the court or GAO has jurisdiction to hear the protest. As discussed earlier, the court does not have jurisdiction to hear protests associated with task and delivery orders, except to the extent the order exceeds the scope of the contract or is an order under an FSS contract. Thus, any protests of a task order award, assuming the award exceeds the statutory threshold, must be filed at GAO. Similarly, protests by an awardee of an IDIQ contract that another offeror should not have been awarded the contract will not be heard at GAO, but some judges at COFC have exercised jurisdiction over such protests. Finally, of course, if a protester misses the deadline to file a post-award protest at GAO, it likely could still file a protest at COFC, assuming the court would otherwise have jurisdiction.

Legal Consistency and Agency Discretion: For the most part, both COFC and GAO give the agency a great deal of discretion in its evaluation and conclusions. That said, some judges at the court appear to probe more deeply into agency decisions, or may require more detailed, contemporaneous documentation than GAO. On the other hand, earlier COFC cases may be instructive but are not binding on later decisions, so, absent Federal Circuit precedent, judges have the leeway to disagree with prior decisions. At GAO, the Comptroller General is the formal issuing authority. As a result, GAO attorneys strive to maintain consistency among their opinions. GAO also hears many more protests than COFC in any given year, so there are likely to be far more GAO decisions addressing the particular issues at hand, giving protesters a larger body of precedent on which to base their protest and to assess the likely outcome.

Document Production: GAO limits the Agency Record to documents associated with the particular protest grounds. Thus, if a protest challenges only the agency's evaluation of costs, a protester may not receive any additional information about how the agency evaluated technical proposals. Or, if a protest challenges the evaluation only of the protester's proposal, the agency may not provide any information about the evaluation of the awardee. These restrictions may foreclose any possible supplemental protest grounds related to other areas of the evaluation about which the protester was not given information in the debriefing.

As previously discussed, at COFC, protesters usually receive a more fulsome record. Because it is performing an APA-style review of the agency's award decision, the court will generally require that the DOJ (and, therefore, the agency) provide the record of the procurement, that is, the documents and information before the decision maker at the time the award decision was made. This means that the protester is often granted access to documents and information not explicitly tied to its specific grounds of protest.

Timing, Stays, and Cost: GAO protests tend to move very quickly, not only because of the early deadlines to submit the protest but also because GAO, by statute, has only 100 days within which to issue its decision. Although the court does not have any such deadline, protests at COFC move fairly quickly as the judges understand the importance of an early resolution. In practice, COFC protests typically take longer to resolve than those at GAO (four to six months instead of 100 days). But if the protester requests and is required to litigate a TRO or Preliminary Injunction (PI), the protest may be resolved more quickly than it would at GAO, as the "likelihood of success on the merits" prong for such relief is often treated as outcome determinative by the parties.

A primary reason most protesters choose to go to GAO is that doing so within the deadlines specified by CICA will likely result in an automatic stay of award or performance. At COFC, there is no such automatic statutory stay. As previously discussed, DOJ may voluntarily stay contract award or contract performance for a period of time sufficient to allow COFC to decide the matter. Because there is no guaranteed stay, however, many protesters still feel safer going to GAO.

Although the costs of filing a protest will vary dramatically in either forum, generally the costs of protesting at GAO are likely to be lower than protesting at COFC for the following reasons:

- COFC requires more formal briefing and more initial papers to be filed in addition to the complaint including the possible need for a motion for TRO or PI.
- COFC often holds hearings, both telephonically and in-person, including oral argument on motions for injunctive relief, motions to supplement or complete the administrative record, and motions for judgment on the administrative record. In contrast, hearings at GAO are rare. Although hearing officers will at times convene conference calls to work through certain issues, these are

often less formal and do not very often involve "oral argument" on the substantive issues.

- The potentially larger record anticipated in a COFC protest also may result in higher costs.

Finally, the court requires that parties, other than individuals, be represented by counsel admitted to practice before COFC. GAO, in contrast, will allow parties to represent themselves pro se. Although this is a potential cost savings for protesters at GAO, we do not recommend protesters represent themselves at GAO because they will not be allowed to access protected material, which often provides the basis for successful protests.

Chapter 4
Stays, Overrides, and Injunctions

A. Stays

One of the prime benefits of filing a protest at GAO, as opposed to COFC, is the possibility of receiving an automatic stay under CICA.[1] CICA provides for two kinds of protest stays: pre-award stays, or a stay of contract *award*, and post-award stays, or a stay of contract *performance*. On rare occasions, agencies may seek to override the stay.

1. Stay of Contract Award

Pre-award protests usually involve challenges to the terms of a solicitation or to the exclusion of an offeror from the competitive range. Generally, in GAO and agency-level protests, challenges to the solicitation must be filed before the date set for submission of proposals (or, for improprieties introduced by an amendment, by the date and time set for the next revisions to proposals).

When a protest is filed with GAO or directly with an agency before contract award, the contracting officer is generally prohibited from proceeding to award the contract until the protest is resolved.[2] Notably, although this stay prevents contract award, it does not prevent the agency from proceeding with the other pre-award stages of the procurement, including receiving proposals, conducting discussions, and evaluating offers.

2. Stay of Contract Performance

For protests filed with an agency or GAO after contract award, there is a stay of contract performance, provided the protester meets special timeliness standards. Congress intended the stay to preserve the status quo during the pendency of a GAO

1. 31 U.S.C. § 3553(c)(1), (d)(3). Notably, the CICA stay applies only to GAO protests. FAR 33.103(f)(1) provides similar assurance to protesters at the agency level that the agency will not award the contract while the protest is pending, "unless contract award is justified, in writing, for urgent and compelling reasons or is determined, in writing, to be in the best interest of the Government."

2. FAR 33.103(f)(1); FAR 33.104(b)(1).

bid protest. Without the stay (as was often the case before the stay was instituted), the challenged awardee might begin and perhaps complete a substantial portion of the work by the time the protest is adjudicated. If the protest was meritorious, the absence of the performance stay often would result in the victorious protester being left with a less meaningful remedy, or no meaningful remedy at all. That remains true today in protests where the stay is not triggered or is overridden.

Generally, to receive the automatic stay under CICA, the protester must file the protest at GAO within ten calendar (not business) days after contract award or within five calendar days after a required debriefing. Take note: these deadlines for triggering a stay of performance run on different rules from the deadline for filing a timely GAO protest. Usually (but not always), the deadline for the CICA stay is prior to the deadline for filing a timely GAO protest.

As discussed in Chapter 3, for DoD procurements, Class Deviation No. 2018-O0011, titled "Enhanced Postaward Debriefing Rights," holds open debriefings to allow disappointed offerors an opportunity to ask the agency questions.[3] The Class Deviation requires contracting officers to provide unsuccessful offerors "an opportunity to submit additional questions related to the debriefing within two business days after receiving the debriefing."[4] Agencies must respond in writing within five business days after the receipt of timely questions and must hold the debriefing open until it "delivers its written responses to the unsuccessful offeror."[5] The Class Deviation states: "The agency shall not consider the postaward debriefing to be concluded until the agency delivers its written responses to the unsuccessful offeror."[6] Most importantly, the new rules provide that the "five-day period" associated with the timeline for a CICA stay does not commence until the day the government delivers to a disappointed offeror the written responses to any questions submitted. In sum, the Class Deviation requires agencies to "comply with the requirements of FAR 33.104(c) regarding the suspension of contract performance . . . upon receipt of a protest filed by an unsuccessful offeror" at GAO within:

- Ten calendar days "after the date of contract award";
- Five calendar days "after a debriefing date offered to the protester under a timely debriefing request and no additional questions related to the debriefing are submitted"; or

---

3. The 2018 NDAA § 818 required the Secretary of Defense to issue new regulations aimed at improving the usefulness of the post-award debriefing process under FAR 15.506(d) in connection with defense procurements. On March 22, 2018, the DoD issued Class Deviation No. 2018-O0011, titled "Enhanced Postaward Debriefing Rights," to implement this mandate.

4. Dep't of Def., Class Deviation 2018-O0011, Enhanced Post Award Debrief Rights (2018), https://www.acq.osd.mil/dpap/policy/policyvault/USA000563-18-DPAP.pdf.

5. *Id.*

6. *Id.*

- Five calendar days "after the Government delivers its written response to additional questions submitted by the unsuccessful offerors, whichever is later."[7]

If a protest is filed within this period, the contracting officer must direct the awardee to stop performance of the contract until the protest is resolved.[8] Notably, pursuing an agency-level protest first does not toll the clock for obtaining a stay of a later-filed GAO protest. If a disappointed offeror's post-award agency-level protest is denied after the ten-day/five-day clock has run out, it can still go to GAO for a second try, but it will not get a stay of performance.[9]

Note that to trigger the stay in a GAO protest, the agency must receive notice of the protest from GAO within ten days after award or within five days after a required debriefing.[10] Prior to institution of GAO's electronic filing system, this meant that a protester could not wait until the close of business on the last day to file its protest. Today, however, GAO's electronic filing system automatically notifies the agency of the protest as soon as it is filed.

3. *Stay Overrides*

Although it is a fairly rare occurrence, an agency may override a stay of award or performance.

For pre-award agency-level protests, "a contract may not be awarded, pending agency resolution of the protest, unless contract award is justified, in writing, for urgent and compelling reasons or is determined, in writing, to be in the best interest of the Government."[11] For post-award agency-level protests, "the contracting officer shall immediately suspend performance, pending resolution of the protest within the agency, . . . unless continued performance is justified, in writing, for urgent and compelling reasons or is determined, in writing, to be in the best interest of the Government."[12] In both pre- and post-award protests, the agency's justification or determination must be "approved at a level above the contracting officer, or by another official pursuant to agency procedures."[13]

---

7. *Id.*

8. FAR 33.103(f)(3); FAR 33.104(c)(1).

9. The procuring agency may voluntarily agree to continue the stay pending the resolution of the protest at GAO but is not required to do so.

10. If the agency receives notice directly from the protester on the last day but does not hear from GAO until the following day, the agency is not required to stay performance. If a protester is not using the electronic filing system for some reason (e.g., the system is down), to be sure to obtain the stay, it is a good practice to aim for a filing no later than noon on the day the protest would be due for purposes of the stay.

11. FAR 33.103(f)(1).

12. FAR 33.103(f)(3).

13. FAR 33.103(f).

For pre-award protests before GAO, an agency may override a stay of award if the head of the contracting activity, on a nondelegable basis, makes a written finding that "(i) Urgent and compelling circumstances [that] significantly affect the interest of the United States will not permit awaiting the decision of the GAO; and (ii) award is likely to occur within 30 days of the written finding."[14] For post-award protests before GAO, an agency may override a stay of performance if the head of the contracting activity, on a nondelegable basis, authorizes performance upon a written finding that "(i) performance will be in the best interests of the United States; or (ii) urgent and compelling circumstances that significantly affect the interests of the United States will not permit waiting for the GAO's decision."[15]

Although CICA provides for automatic stays at GAO, it does not give GAO jurisdiction to hear override challenges. In the event of a stay override, a protester may challenge the override by filing a new suit in COFC. This suit does not need to bring the entire protest to COFC, though that is an option. Rather, the challenge to the stay override can be distinct from the underlying protest and focus specifically on the override decision, arguing that it was arbitrary and capricious, or an abuse of discretion. COFC assesses the reasonableness of the override decision by looking to the agency's rationale as stated in its justification and approval. Some judges have applied a four-part test to determine whether an override was rational. This test, known as the "*State Farm* test," considers

> if the agency has relied on factors which Congress has not intended it to consider, entirely failed to consider an important aspect of the problem, offered an explanation for its decision that runs counter to the evidence before the agency, or is so implausible that it could not be ascribed to a difference in view or the product of agency expertise.[16]

Although some COFC judges use this test, others do not.[17] The Federal Circuit has yet to weigh in on the issue.

B. Injunctive Relief

No automatic stay applies to protests filed at COFC. To get a "stay" of contract award or performance at the court, the protester must move for a preliminary injunction. The court considers injunctions to be extraordinary equitable relief, although the DOJ, working with the procuring agency, will on occasion agree to a stay, thus

14. FAR 33.104(b)(1).
15. FAR 33.104(c)(2).
16. PMTECH, Inc. v. United States, 95 Fed. Cl. 330, 343 (2010) (quoting Motor Vehicle Mfrs. Ass'n v. State Farm Mut. Auto. Ins. Co., 463 U.S. 29, 43 (1983)).
17. *Id.*

avoiding the need to seek injunctive relief. The uncertain ability to obtain injunctive relief is one of the reasons that GAO is a far more popular forum for filing protests.

If the protester moves for injunctive relief, the court will decide the issue based on the same four factors employed by the U.S. District Courts: (1) the movant's likelihood of success on the merits, (2) whether the movant will suffer irreparable injury in the absence of injunctive relief, (3) the balance of hardship on all parties, and (4) whether injunctive relief will serve the public interest.[18]

The "[d]enial of the opportunity to compete [fairly] for a contract can constitute irreparable harm."[19] To establish the factual bases for irreparable harm, best practice often involves attaching with the motion a declaration from a knowledgeable person attesting to the nature and extent of irreparable harm that the protester will experience absent such relief.

In arguing that the balance of harms tips their way, protesters often assert that the government will suffer minimal harm in being forced to engage in a fair, rational procurement compared to the harm occasioned by locking the protester out of a fair opportunity to compete. Delay in conducting the procurement, in and of itself, is not sufficient to demonstrate that the balance of hardships favors the government.[20]

The "public interest" prong often takes on added importance as compared to non–bid protest cases given the involvement of the public fisc and the greater chance that national security interests will be implicated when the United States is a party:

> It is axiomatic that the public has an interest in honest, open, and fair competition in the procurement process. Whenever a plaintiff is improperly excluded from that process, that interest is compromised. Conversely, a procuring agency should be able to conduct procurements expeditiously and with minimal judicial encroachment upon an agency's discretion. Public interest, however, militates against awarding injunctive relief when national defense and national security interests are concerned.[21]

To counteract the national security interests cited by the government, protesters often rely on the principle that "the public has an interest in honest, open, and fair competition in the procurement process."[22]

---

18. *See* Cont'l Servs. Grp., Inc. v. United States, 130 Fed. Cl. 798, 800 (2017); *aff'd in relevant part,* 722 F. App'x 986 (2018).

19. DZSP 21, LLC v. United States, 139 Fed. Cl. 110, 121 (2018) (internal citations omitted); *see also* AshBritt, Inc. v. United States, 87 Fed. Cl. 344, 378–79 (2009) (internal citations omitted) ("loss of profits stemming from a lost opportunity to compete on a level playing field has been found sufficient to constitute irreparable harm").

20. 2M Research Servs., LLC, 139 Fed. Cl. 471, 480 (2018).

21. Cincom Sys., Inc. v. United States, 37 Fed. Cl. 266, 269 (1997) (internal citations omitted).

22. *2M Research Servs.*, 139 Fed. Cl. at 480.

Chapter 5
Protective Orders

Protests, especially post-award protests, often require the agency and the parties to review the awardee's and the protester's proprietary technical and/or pricing information. To protect against the misuse of such information, both GAO and COFC issue protective orders limiting access only to those persons admitted under the order and their support staff (paralegal, clerical, and administrative personnel) employed or supervised by admitted individuals.

A. GAO Protective Orders

A routine component in nearly all GAO bid protests is the request for the issuance of a protective order as contemplated by GAO's Bid Protest Regulations.[1] From the outset, initial protest filings must advise GAO if they contain proprietary, confidential, or otherwise business-sensitive information requiring the issuance of a protective order. Even before GAO issues its protective order and admits parties thereunder, within one day of filing a protest with GAO the protester is required to submit a redacted version omitting the putative protected information.[2]

As has long been recognized, this protective order process is "essential to the proper functioning of GAO's bid protest process."[3] GAO's standard application for access to material under a protective order requires the attorney to affirmatively state that he or she is not involved with

> competitive decision making as discussed in *U.S. Steel Corp. v. United States*, 730 F.2d 1465 (Fed. Cir. 1984) for or on behalf of the party [he or she] represent[s], any entity that is an interested party to this protest, or any other firm that might gain a competitive advantage from access to the material disclosed under the protective order. . . . This means that [he or she does] not, for example, provide advice concerning or participate in decisions about marketing or advertising strategies, product

1. *See* 4 C.F.R. § 21.1(d)(1). GAO publishes a comprehensive guide to its protective orders, which includes detailed guidance on the topics discussed herein as well as sample form documents. *See* U.S. Gov't Accountability Off., GAO-19-613SP, Guide to GAO Protective Orders (June 2019), https://www.gao.gov/assets/700/699422.pdf.
2. *See* 4 C.F.R. § 21.1(g).
3. Waterfront Techs., Inc., B-401948.16, June 24, 2011, 2011 CPD ¶ 123.

research and development, product design or competitive structuring and composition of bids, offers, or proposals with respect to which the use of protected material could provide a competitive advantage.[4]

The attorney seeking admission under the protective order must identify any attorneys in his or her firm who cannot make the representations set forth above, and any immediate family members who serve as officers or hold management positions with an interested party or with any other firm that might gain a competitive advantage from access to protected material. Although applications from outside counsel generally pass without objection, that is not always the case.[5] GAO will not, however, deny an application based on allegations that outside counsel previously represented the objecting party and should therefore be disqualified to prevent the use of confidential information. Put simply, GAO does not adjudicate allegations relating to attorney rules of professional conduct.[6]

Typically, applicants seeking admission under the protective order are outside counsel for the protester and intervenor. In-house counsel may also be admitted provided they are not involved with competitive decision making and are able to assure GAO that no one in a competitive decision-making role will have access to protected material.[7] As a practical matter, admitted in-house counsel tend to be litigation specialists who work within large law departments that wall off their attorneys from competitive decision making.[8] Smaller companies and smaller law departments often require in-house counsel to wear multiple hats, including some that place them within the ambit of competitive decision making. In-house litigators co-located with competitive decision makers may need to agree that they will access protected material only at their outside counsel's office. In other instances, GAO has qualified the admission of in-house attorneys by limiting the type of protected material they may access.[9]

In-house counsel seeking admission to GAO's protective order must provide the following information on their application:

---

4. U.S. Gov't Accountability Off., GAO-19-613SP, Guide to GAO Protective Orders (June 2019), *available at* https://www.gao.gov/assets/700/699422.pdf.

5. Allied-Signal Aerospace Co., B-250822, Feb. 19, 1993, 93-1 CPD ¶ 201 (outside counsel denied admission under protective order where he had served as corporate officer for various subsidiaries, suggesting a management relationship).

6. *See, e.g.*, Enterprise Servs., LLC, B-417329, May 30, 2019, 2019 CPD ¶ 205, at 3–4.

7. *See* Baldi Bros. v. United States, No. 15-1300, 2016 WL 5462448, at *1 (Fed. Cl. Sept. 27, 2016); Robbins-Gioia, Inc., B-274318, Dec. 4, 1996, 96-2 CPD ¶ 222.

8. *See* US Sprint Commc'ns Co. Ltd. Partnership, B-243767, Aug. 17, 1991, 91-2 CPD ¶ 51 (application approved for attorney in company's litigation section, a separate operation focused exclusively on litigation that walled its attorneys off from competitive decision making).

9. *See, e.g.*, SRI Int'l, Inc., B-250327.4, Apr. 27, 1993, 93-1 CPD ¶ 344, at 4 n.1 (in-house counsel granted access to counsel's company's evaluation documents but not to competitor's information).

- His or her position and responsibilities, including any role in providing procurement-related advice;
- The person(s) to whom he or she reports and their position(s) and responsibilities;
- The number of in-house counsel at the office where the applicant works and their involvement in competitive decision making;
- The applicant's relationship to the nearest person involved in competitive decision making (both in terms of physical proximity and corporate structure); and
- Measures taken to isolate the applicant from competitive decision making and efforts to protect against inadvertent disclosure.

Consultants are experts retained by attorneys to assist in pursuing or defending a protest.[10] Consultants seeking admission must provide:

- A current resume describing their education and experience to date;
- A list of all clients for whom they have worked in the two years prior to the date of the application and a brief description of the work performed;
- A list of all clients for whom their employers have performed work within the two years prior to the application and for whom the use of protected material could provide a competitive advantage, and a brief description of the work performed;
- A statement of the services expected to be performed on the bid protest;
- A description of the financial interests that they, their spouses and/or family has in any interested party in the protest or whose protected information will be reviewed;
- A list of all instances in which they have been admitted or been denied admission to a protective order, had an admission revoked, or were found to have violated a protective order; and
- A list of professional associations to which they belong, including identification numbers.[11]

Consultants seeking access under the protective order must also attest that for two years following the date the application is granted, they will not engage or assist in the preparation of a proposal to be submitted to any agency of the U.S. government relating to the subject of the procurement at issue in the protest where any party to the protest will be a competitor, subcontractor, or team member. Consultants must

10. *See* U.S. Gov't Accountability Off., GAO-19-613SP, Guide to GAO Protective Orders 12 (June 2019), https://www.gao.gov/assets/700/699422.pdf ("GAO's policy is to allow protesters to choose the assistance they deem necessary to pursue their protest.").

11. *Id.* at 44.

also agree that for two years after the application, they will not engage or assist in the preparation of a proposal for submission to the contracting agency for the procurement at issue in the protest.

Objections to an applicant's admission to a protective order should be raised within two days of receipt of the application. Any such objection should identify a legitimate concern that the person's admission "would pose an unacceptable risk of inadvertent disclosure."[12] Such objections typically arise in connection with applications from in-house counsel who provide advice on competitive decision-making issues or outside consultants (e.g., experts) whose resumes reveal that they or their firms could receive a competitive advantage from accessing protected material.[13]

GAO's standard protective order limits each party to four copies of protected documents. The term "party" refers to the entity that is the protester or intervenor, not the number of individuals admitted to a protective order. A "copy" refers to any duplication, electronic or hard copy, and the original document counts as one of the permitted four copies. Thus, if multiple attorneys or law firms represent a party, they must share the four copies. The parties may seek to enlarge the number of permitted copies (e.g., one for each attorney admitted under the protective order), but enlargement is generally available only upon agreement of all parties, and GAO consent is required.

The first page of each protected document must include the following legend:

PROTECTED MATERIAL

TO BE DISCLOSED ONLY IN ACCORDANCE WITH

GOVERNMENT ACCOUNTABILITY OFFICE PROTECTIVE ORDER

Once the protective order issues, documents submitted in connection with the protest that lack the protective legend are treated as protected for two days, thereby giving the submitting party an opportunity to correct any inadvertent failure to mark the material as protected.

Any agency or party filing protected material shall, upon request by another party, provide to the other parties admitted under the protective order an initial proposed redacted version of the document within one day of the request. The party authoring the document shall file a final redacted version of the document that has been agreed to by the parties. Only the final agreed-to version must be filed. GAO

12. Sys. Research & Applications Corp., B-299818, Sept. 6, 2007, 2008 CPD ¶ 28, at 8; McDonnell Douglas Corp., B-259694.2, June 16, 1995, 95-2 CPD ¶ 51, at 4.

13. *See, e.g.*, Harmonia Holdings Grp., LLC, B-417475.3, Sept. 23, 2019, 2019 CPD ¶ 333 (proposed consultant's application for admission to protective order denied because it provided proposal support services, including writing proposals for clients).

will resolve disputes upon request, but strongly prefers and will encourage the parties to make all possible efforts to negotiate an agreed-upon set of redactions.

Material obtained under the protective order is to be used only for the protest in which it was produced absent express prior authorization from GAO. Protected material may, however, be used in a bid protest filed at COFC without GAO's prior authorization, so long as it is filed under seal with COFC, the court is advised of GAO's protective order, and the submitting party requests COFC to issue its own protective order to cover the material. The filing party must also notify GAO that suit has been filed within one business day of filing suit.

Excluding materials filed with COFC and governed by the court's protective order, each party admitted to the protective order must destroy all protected material, including all electronic copies, with the exception of a single copy of a protected decision or letter issued by GAO, within 60 calendar days after the protest concludes. Parties can agree or seek permission from GAO to hold protected materials longer than 60 days after the protest concludes. Once the parties destroy the protected materials, however, they must certify to each other party that the documents have been destroyed; alternatively, the parties may return protected information to the party from which it was obtained. As a practical matter, parties typically destroy and certify rather than return protected material. Individuals outside the protective order who inadvertently receive protected information have a duty to return the information to counsel, and to refrain from reading or disseminating the information.[14]

GAO may sanction the attorney admitted to the protective order, or in certain circumstances take adverse action against a party to the protest, for violations of the protective order. GAO considers the ability to dismiss a protest or impose other sanctions as part of its inherent authority.[15] Sanctions for violating the protective order include dismissal of the protest, referral of the violation to appropriate bar associations or other disciplinary bodies, and restricting the violating attorney's ability to practice before GAO. The issue of whether and what sanctions to impose on individuals who violate the protective order is considered by GAO subsequent to, and apart from, resolution of the protest.

GAO considers dismissal to be a severe sanction, to be employed only in the rarest of cases, as it "weighs against . . . the general public policy favoring a decision on the merits."[16] Among the factors GAO considers

14. *See* PWC Logistics Servs. Co. KSC(c), B-310559, Jan. 11. 2008, 2008 CPD ¶ 25.

15. *See* Latvian Connection LLC, B-413442, Aug. 18, 2016, 2016 CPD ¶ 194, at 4 ("[O]ur Office necessarily reserves an inherent right to dismiss any protest, and to impose sanctions against a protester, where a protester's actions undermine the integrity and effectiveness of our process.").

16. PWC Logistics Servs. Co. KSC(c), B-310559, Jan. 11, 2008, 2008 CPD ¶ 25, at 8.

are the inadequacy of lesser available sanctions, the protester's (as opposed to its counsel's) responsibility for what occurred, the gravity of what occurred and the prejudice to the intervenor and the agency resulting from it, and the salutary deterrent effect of dismissal on others who might be tempted to such conduct in the future.[17]

B. COFC Protective Orders

Although the request for a protective order at GAO is included in the body of the initial protest filing, parties seeking a protective order in protests at COFC file a separate motion requesting its issuance. Protesters are able to include proposed protective orders using COFC's model, known as Form 8 under the COFC Rules.

To this end, Section VI, Rules 16–20, of Appendix C to the RCFC detail the court's procedures for issuing protective orders. Rule 16(a) explains that the protective order is the

> principal vehicle relied upon by the court to ensure protection of sensitive information. . . . The protective order defines the procedures to be followed to identify protected information, to prepare redacted versions of such information, and to dispose of protected information at the conclusion of the case.

Information identified as protected "may be disclosed only to the court and to individuals who have been admitted to the protective order."[18]

Once the court issues a protective order, individuals seeking access to protected information must file an application.[19] Outside and inside counsel must complete Form 9—Application for Access to Information Under Protective Order by Outside or Inside Counsel; and consultants must fill out Form 10—Application for Access to Information Under Protective Order by Expert Consultant or Witness. Both forms are available online[20] and require the applicant to attest that he or she is not involved in competitive decision making as discussed in *U.S. Steel Corp. v. United States.*[21]

---

17. *Id.* (protest dismissed where counsel sent protected material to client's general counsel, who reviewed and further distributed the information within the company); *see also* Dep't of Hous. & Urban Dev.-Reconsideration, B-414459.5, Sept. 26, 2018, 2018 CPD ¶ 341 (citing *PWC Logistics*).

18. RCFC, Appx. C, § VI, ¶ 16(b).

19. *Id.* ¶ 16(c).

20. United States Court of Federal Claims, Appendix of Forms, https://www.uscfc.uscourts.gov/forms.

21. 730 F.2d 1465 (Fed. Cir. 1984). *See, e.g.*, Baldi Bros. v. United States, No. 15-1300, 2016 WL 5462448, at *1 (Fed. Cl. Sept. 27, 2016) ("Protective orders may be granted to deny persons involved in competitive decision-making any access to a competitor's confidential information.") (citing U.S. Steel Corp. v. United States, 730 F.2d 1465 (Fed. Cir. 1984); Ross-Hime Designs, Inc. v. United States, 109 Fed. Cl. 725 (2013); Fairholme Funds, Inc. v. United States, 118 Fed. Cl. 795 (2014); Hitkansut LLC v. United States, 111 Fed. Cl. 228 (2013)).

In-house counsel must provide a narrative describing:

- His or her position and responsibilities, including any role in providing procurement-related advice;
- The person(s) to whom he or she reports and their position(s) and responsibilities;
- The number of in-house counsel at the office where the applicant works and their involvement in competitive decision making;
- The applicant's relationship to the nearest person involved in competitive decision making (both in terms of physical proximity and corporate structure); and
- Measures taken to isolate the applicant from competitive decision making and efforts to protect against inadvertent disclosure.[22]

Expert consultants and witnesses must provide:

- A current resume;
- A list of all clients for whom they have worked in the two years prior to the date of the application and a brief description of the work performed;
- A statement of the services expected to be performed on the bid protest;
- A description of the financial interests that they, their spouses and/or family has in any interested party in the protest or whose protected information will be reviewed;
- A list of all instances in which they have been admitted or been denied admission to a protective order, had an admission revoked, or were found to have violated a protective order; and
- A list of professional associations to which they belong, including identification numbers.[23]

Notably, unlike GAO's standard form, the COFC form does not require consultants to identify the clients for whom their employers have worked within the past two years. Similar to GAO's application form, the COFC form requires consultants and expert witnesses to forbear for a two-year period from engaging or assisting in the preparation of a proposal to be submitted to any agency of the U.S. government relating to the subject of the procurement at issue in the protest where any party to the protest will be a competitor, subcontractor, or team member. They must also agree that for two years after the application, they will not engage or assist in the preparation of a proposal for submission to the contracting agency for the procurement at issue in the protest and will not have any personal involvement in any such activity.

22. RCFC, Appx. of Forms, Form 9.
23. *Id.* Form 10.

If no one objects to a person's application by the close of the second business day after other parties have received it, he or she will be granted access without further action of the court. If any party objects, then the applicant will be admitted only upon order of the court. Persons admitted under the protective order must take the necessary steps to ensure that protected information is handled in accordance with the terms of the order, including oversight of support personnel with access to the information.[24] The court, procuring agency, and DOJ personnel are automatically admitted to protective orders.[25]

COFC issues protective orders at its discretion upon motion of a party.[26] As a practical matter, the court will issue a protective order in any bid protest involving confidential awardee or protester information. COFC provides a sample protective order (Appendix of Forms, Form 8), but cautions that the parties and the judge "may want to amend the sample protective order to meet the needs of a specific case or their individual preferences."[27] Form 8—entitled "Protective Order in Procurement Protest Cases"—defines "protected information" to mean "information that must be protected to safeguard the competitive process, including source selection information, proprietary information, and confidential information. . . ."[28]

The sample form instructs that the subject line of any electronic transmission providing protected information must read: "CONTAINS PROTECTED INFORMATION."[29] If protected information is provided in paper form, it must be sealed in a parcel that bears the following conspicuously marked legend: "PROTECTED INFORMATION ENCLOSED."[30] The first page of each document containing protected information must contain a banner stating, "Protected Information to Be Disclosed Only in Accordance with the U.S. Court of Federal Claims Protective Order."[31] Portions of any document containing protected information must be clearly identified.[32]

A party that files protected information must promptly serve on the other parties a proposed redacted version bearing the legend "Agreed-Upon Redacted Version" in the upper right-hand corner. Any party seeking to include additional redactions must do so within two business days unless the parties agree to a different deadline. The filing party must circulate a second redacted version with the legend "Agreed-Upon

24. RCFC, Appx. C, § VI, ¶ 16(c).
25. *Id.* ¶ 16(d).
26. *Id.* ¶ 17(a).
27. *Id.* ¶ 17(b).
28. RCFC, Appx. of Forms, Form 8.
29. *Id.*
30. *Id.*
31. *Id.*
32. *Id.*

Redacted Version" bearing the additional redactions. After the parties reach agreement on additional redactions, the filing party must file with the court the final redacted version marked "Redacted Version." If the parties are unable to reach agreement, the objecting party may submit the matter to the court. Until the court decides the issue, the disputed information must be treated as protected.

COFC has made clear, however, that the "purpose of redaction . . . is to safeguard the competitive process, not to withhold information that a party frowns on making public."[33] Moreover, if the proposed "redactions would be so extensive as to render the affected document incomprehensible, the court may exercise its discretion and decline to make them."[34]

Within 30 days after the protest is concluded (including any appeals and remands), each party must destroy all protected information received pursuant to the bid protest and certify destruction in writing to each of the other parties. Alternatively, the receiving party may return the protected information to the parties from which it was received.

33. Torres Advanced Enterprise Sols., LLC v. United States, 135 Fed. Cl. 1, 4–5 (2017) (quoting Linc Gov't Servs. LLC v. United States, 96 Fed. Cl. 672, 724 (2010)).

34. *Id.*; *see also* Allied Tech. Grp., Inc. v. United States, 94 Fed. Cl. 16, 51 n.1 (2010).

Chapter 6
Grounds of Protest

Regardless of tribunal, for a protester to prevail, it must demonstrate that it was prejudiced by the agency's procurement error. That is, the protester must show that "but for" the agency's error, the protester would have (or would have had) a substantial chance for award. Notably, this does not mean that a protester must show that it would have received the award; it must only show that there was a "substantial chance it would have received the contract award" but for the agency's error.[1] The following discussion walks through the most common grounds of protest, but it must be remembered that they all share the same requirement that they resulted in prejudice to the protester.

A. Pre-Award Grounds of Protest

Pre-award protests may be brought on a number of grounds, including alleged improprieties with the terms of the solicitation, improper exclusion from the competitive range, a decision to award a sole-source contract, the decision to cancel a solicitation, and, depending on the circumstances, the decision to insource a product or service rather than obtain it through full and open competition in the marketplace.

1. Patent Ambiguities

Solicitations that are patently ambiguous or defective are subject to pre-award protest. Indeed, as discussed later, such protests can be brought only as pre-award challenges and must be brought prior to the time proposals are due.[2] GAO has found that "[a]n ambiguity exists where two or more reasonable interpretations of the terms or specifications of the solicitation are possible. A patent ambiguity exists where the

1. *See, e.g.*, Alfa Laval Separation, Inc. v. United States, 175 F.3d 1365, 1367 (Fed. Cir. 1999).

2. With respect to patent ambiguities not found in the initial solicitation, but which are subsequently incorporated into it, the protest must be filed not later than the next closing time for receipt of proposals following the incorporation. DCR Servs. & Constr., Inc., B-415565.2, Feb. 13, 2018, 2018 CPD ¶ 125 (citing 4 C.F.R. § 21.2(a)(1); Draeger, Inc., B-414938, Sept. 21, 2017, 2017 CPD ¶ 308, at 4).

solicitation contains an obvious, gross, or glaring error, while a latent ambiguity is more subtle."[3] COFC has a similar standard:

> The United States Court of Appeals for the Federal Circuit has explained that a contract provision is only ambiguous if susceptible to more than one reasonable meaning. In addition, this Court has held that, to be patently ambiguous, each meaning must be consistent with the contract language. But the mere fact that the parties disagree with regard to the interpretation of a specific provision does not, standing alone, render that provision ambiguous. To that end, a patent ambiguity exists when there is a facial inconsistency between provisions or terms within the contract, and such an ambiguity should be, to the reasonable contractor, apparent on the face of the contract. And so, a patent ambiguity is one that is obvious, gross, glaring, so that the plaintiff contractor has a duty to inquire about it at the start.[4]

At GAO a protester must protest the existence of a patent ambiguity prior to the due date for receipt of proposals or quotations.[5] Similarly, at COFC a protester must protest a patent ambiguity prior to the close of the bidding process, not after the award decision is made.[6]

The presence or absence of a patent ambiguity or defect is not determined by the protester's actual knowledge at the time of proposal submission, but by what a reasonable bidder would have perceived in studying the solicitation packet.[7] In *System Dynamics International, Inc. v. United States*,[8] the protester, SDI, complained that the Army's evaluation of its proposal was unreasonable because the Army had withheld vital testing information SDI needed to provide the technical wiring recommendations required by the solicitation. COFC found that this allegation stemmed from a patent defect in the solicitation and dismissed for lack of jurisdiction, explaining that the omission of the testing information would have been discovered by "an offeror exercising 'reasonable and customary care.'"[9] Separately, SDI protested that it was unable to propose on an equal footing with the incumbent contractor (and ultimate

---

3. Fei Sys., B-414852.2, Nov. 17, 2017, 2017 CPD ¶ 349, at 3 (citations omitted).

4. Land Shark Shredding, LLC v. United States, No. 18-1154C, 2018 WL 6719720, at *5 (Fed. Cl. Nov. 27, 2018) (internal quotations omitted) (citations omitted) (first quoting Barron Bancshares, Inc. v. United States, 366 F.3d 1360, 1375–76 (Fed. Cir. 2004); and then quoting West Bay Builders, Inc. v. United States, 85 Fed. Cl. 1, 15 (2008)).

5. Anders Constr., Inc., B-414261, Apr. 11, 2017, 2017 CPD ¶ 121, at 5 ("Under our Bid Protest Regulations, a patent ambiguity must be protested prior to the time set for receipt of initial proposals or quotations, when it is most practicable to take effective action against such defects.") (citing 4 C.F.R. § 21.2(a)(1); Cleveland Telecomms. Corp., B-247964.3, July 23, 1992, 92–2 CPD ¶ 47, at 3–5).

6. Blue & Gold Fleet, L.P. v. United States, 492 F.3d 1308, 1315 (Fed. Cir. 2007).

7. Sys. Dynamics Int'l, Inc. v. United States, 130 Fed. Cl. 499, 520 (2017).

8. *Id.*

9. *Id.* at 518.

awardee) because the solicitation identified only the labor categories needed for the work, not the labor mix. COFC held that this omission was obvious from the face of the solicitation and dismissed this claim as well.[10]

2. *Failure to Provide for Full and Open Competition*

CICA establishes a mandate for "full and open competition" in government procurements, which should be obtained through the use of competitive procedures.[11] The competition requirements of CICA articulated in 10 U.S.C. § 2304 (for DoD agencies, NASA, and Coast Guard) and 41 U.S.C. § 3301 (for civilian agencies) are nearly identical, and the sections are implemented concurrently by FAR Part 6. FAR Subpart 6.1 provides that, "with certain limited exceptions, . . . contracting officers shall promote and provide for full and open competition in soliciting offers and awarding Government contracts."

FAR Subparts 6.2 and 6.3 identify the limited exceptions under which an agency may procure goods and services through other than full and open competition. FAR Subpart 6.2 provides for full and open competition after certain sources have been properly excluded, for example, competitions involving set asides for small businesses. FAR Subpart 6.3, on the other hand, is broader and more commonly implicated in bid protests. Within Subpart 6.3, the FAR identifies the seven circumstances under which an agency may award a contract through other than full and open competition and sets forth the requirements it must meet in order to do so. Subsections 6.302-1 through 6.302-7 identify the various bases upon which an agency may forego full and open competition. These exceptions to full and open competition are:

- FAR 6.302-1—Only One Responsible Source
- FAR 6.302-2—Unusual and Compelling Urgency
- FAR 6.302-3—Industrial Mobilization
- FAR 6.302-4—International Agreement
- FAR 6.302-5—Authorized or Required by Statute
- FAR 6.302-6—National Security
- FAR 6.302-7—Public Interest

---

10. *Id.* at 520.

11. Coulson Aviation (USA) Inc., B-409356.2, Mar. 31, 2014, 2014 CPD ¶ 106, at 10 ("CICA's overriding mandate is for 'full and open competition' in government procurements, obtained through the use of competitive procedures.") (citing 41 U.S.C. § 3301(a)(1)); *see also* Innovation Dev. Enters. of Am., Inc. v. United States, 108 Fed. Cl. 711, 727 (2013) ("Congress mandated that unless a statutory exception applies, federal agencies must purchase products and services based upon 'full and open competition through the use of competitive procedures.'") (citations omitted).

If an agency seeks to rely on one of these exceptions (other than the public interest exception) to use a noncompetitive procurement procedure, it must execute a Justification & Approval (J&A).[12] The J&A must contain "sufficient facts and rationale to support the use of the cited authority" relied upon to forego competition.[13] The J&A, in turn, must meet the specific requirements prescribed by FAR 6.303 (Justifications) and FAR 6.304 (Approval of the Justification). If the agency intends to rely on the public interest exception under FAR 6.302-7, it must execute a written Determination & Finding (D&F) in accordance with FAR 1.7.

A D&F is a "special form of written approval by an authorized official" needed for various types of contract actions (e.g., if the contracting officer wants to issue a time-and-materials contract under FAR 16.601), whereas a J&A applies only to the Subsection 6.302-1 through -6 exceptions to CICA just listed.[14] The D&F must identify the nature of the action being approved and set forth the "[f]indings that detail the particular circumstances, facts, or reasoning essential to support the determination," and a "determination, based on the findings, that the proposed action is justified under the applicable statute or regulation."[15] For bid protest purposes, there is little practical difference between a J&A and a D&F, and most sole-source awards rely on one of the other exceptions listed under Section 6.302 of the FAR, so the issue does not arise very often.

When a protester challenges an agency's decision to forego competition under one of the exceptions to CICA, GAO will focus its review of the decision on the "adequacy of the agency's rationale and conclusions set forth in the [J&A]."[16] GAO will deny such a challenge if "the J&A sets out reasonable justifications for the agency's actions."[17] To this end, what follows is a discussion of protests challenging the use of noncompetitive procedures based on the specific exceptions noted earlier.

a. Only One Responsible Source

One of the most commonly used—and commonly protested—exceptions to full and open competition is the "sole-source" exception set forth in FAR 6.302-1. Under this provision, an agency may forego competition and issue award to a single source if it is the only responsible source or, for DoD, NASA, and the Coast Guard, the only

---

12. *See* 41 U.S.C. § 3304(e)(1)(A)–(B); 10 U.S.C. § 2304(f)(1)(A)–(B).
13. Career Sys. Dev. Corp., B-416021, May 18, 2018, 2018 CPD ¶ 176, at 6.
14. FAR 1.701.
15. FAR 1.704.
16. EBSCO Indus., Inc., B-414150, Mar. 2, 2017, 2017 CPD ¶ 83, at 4 (citing Camden Shipping Corp., B-406171, Feb. 27, 2012, 2012 CPD ¶ 76, at 6).
17. *Id.* (citing Piedmont Propulsion Sys., LLC, B-410914.2, Mar. 17, 2015, 2015 CPD ¶ 119, at 13).

source or one of a limited number of sources, and no other type of supplies or services will satisfy the agency's requirements.[18]

In addition to the J&A, FAR 6.302-1(d)(2) requires that an agency pursuing a sole-source award under FAR 6.302-1 publish a notice and synopsis of the proposed procurement on an official government website in order "to provide potential competitors the opportunity to challenge the agency's intent to procure without full and open competition."[19] Prior to 2019, the notice and synopsis had to be posted on the Federal Business Opportunity website (FBO). The government has since migrated to https://beta.sam.gov. The synopsis, as articulated by GAO,

> must provide an "accurate description" of the property or services to be purchased and must be sufficient to allow a prospective contractor to make an informed business judgment as to whether to request a copy of the solicitation. 41 U.S.C. sect. 416(b); 15 U.S.C. sect. 637(f). . . . In addition, the FAR requires that the description of the supplies or services be "clear and concise." FAR sect. 5.207(c), (d). Moreover . . . a synopsis must provide prospective alternative sources a meaningful opportunity to demonstrate their ability to provide what the agency seeks to purchase. . . . In short, the fundamental purpose of these notices, including in the circumstance where an agency contemplates a sole-source award, is to enhance the possibility of competition.[20]

The FAR identifies three specific situations in which supplies or services may be considered available from only one or a limited number of sources sufficient to justify the use of sole-source procedures:

- "**Supplies or services** may be considered to be available from only one source *if the source has submitted an unsolicited research proposal* that (A) Demonstrates a unique and innovative concept (see definition at 2.101), or, demonstrates a unique capability of the source to provide the particular research services proposed; (B) Offers a concept or services not otherwise available to the Government; and (C) Does not resemble the substance of a pending competitive acquisition."[21]
- "**Supplies** may be deemed to be available only from the original source in the case of a follow-on contract for the *continued development or production of a major system or highly specialized equipment*, including major components

18. FAR 6.302-1(a).

19. Career Sys. Dev. Corp., B-416021, May 18, 2018, 2018 CPD ¶ 176; FAR 6.302-1(d)(2) ("For contracts awarded using this authority, the notices required by [FAR] 5.201 shall have been published and any bids, proposals, quotations, or capability statements must have been considered.").

20. M.D. Thompson Consulting, LLC, B-297616, Feb. 14, 2006, 2006 CPD ¶ 41, at 3 (citations omitted).

21. FAR 6.302-1(a)(2)(i) (citing 10 U.S.C. § 2304(d)(1)(A); 41 U.S.C. § 3304(b)(1)) (emphasis added).

thereof, when it is likely that *award to any other source would result in* (A) *Substantial duplication of cost* to the Government that is not expected to be recovered through competition; or (B) *Unacceptable delays* in fulfilling the agency's requirements."[22]

- **Services**—only for DoD, NASA, and the Coast Guard—"may be deemed to be available only from the original source in the case of follow-on contracts for the *continued provision of highly specialized services* when it is likely that award to any other source would result in (A) *Substantial duplication of cost* to the Government that is not expected to be recovered through competition; or (B) *Unacceptable delays* in fulfilling the agency's requirements."[23]

Supplies and services may be available from only one source because of intellectual property rights restrictions. FAR 6.302-1(b)(2) provides that the authority in FAR 6.302-1(a)(2) to procure through other than full and open competition may be used when "[t]he existence of limited rights in data, patent rights, copyrights, or secret processes . . . make the supplies and services available from only one source. . . ."[24] A sole-source award based on limited data rights still requires a J&A that reasonably justifies the procurement. One of the justifications used frequently is that an unacceptable delay would arise if an agency were required to use a different source. In *Wamore, Inc.*,[25] for example, where the Army did not possess adequate data rights, it justified a sole-source award because awarding the contract to another source would have resulted in five years' worth of delays and an additional $17 million for testing, validating, and calibrating systems.

Because they are the antithesis of competed procurements, GAO "will closely scrutinize sole-source procurements."[26] Protests challenging a sole-source procurement often turn on whether the J&A satisfies the multifaceted and largely unde-

22. FAR 6.302-1(a)(2)(ii) (citing 10 U.S.C. § 2304(d)(1)(B); 41 U.S.C. § 3304(b)(2)) (emphasis added).

23. FAR 6.302-1(a)(2)(iii) (citing 10 U.S.C. § 2304(d)(1)(B)) (emphasis added).

24. *See, e.g.*, Wamore, Inc., B-417450, July 9, 2019, 2019 CPD ¶ 253 (denying protest of sole-source award for highly specialized equipment for foreign military sales purposes where only one firm possessed the necessary data rights to produce the item and any other source would have unreasonably delayed fulfilling agency requirements); MFVega & Assocs., LLC, B-291605.3, Mar. 25, 2003, 2003 CPD ¶ 65, at 4 ("An agency may properly take into account the existence of software data rights and licenses when determining whether only one responsible source exists.").

25. B-417450, July 9, 2019, 2019 CPD ¶ 253; *see also* Humanetics Innovative Sols., B-416979.3, May 15, 2019, 2019 CPD ¶ 183 (proposed sole-source acquisition of follow-on contract for highly specialized equipment where government had only limited data rights found unobjectionable where agency reasonably determined that award to any other source would cause unacceptable delays in fulfilling the agency's requirements).

26. Career Sys. Dev. Corp., B-416021, May 18, 2018, 2018 CPD ¶ 176 (citing Sabreliner Corp., B-288030, Sept. 13, 2001, 2001 CPD ¶ 170, at 5); *see also* Julie Research Labs., Inc., B-218593, Aug. 29, 1985, 85-2 CPD ¶ 246 ("Since procurements must be conducted on a competitive basis to the

fined requirements set forth in FAR 6.302-1. For example, neither CICA nor the FAR define the term "highly specialized equipment," under the sole-source exception of FAR 6.302-1(a)(2)(ii). GAO, however, has applied this term in various contexts and has "concluded that equipment specially developed for the agency was 'highly specialized' notwithstanding that the underlying technology was mature and had been in production for a number of years," and also "that commercial equipment specially modified to meet the agency's specific needs was 'highly specialized.'"[27] In *FN America*, GAO denied a protest asserting that rifles the military sought to procure on a sole-source basis from another manufacturer were not "specialized." GAO noted that the agency had already procured thousands of rifles from the intended awardee and concluded that the need for a standard rifle reasonably justified the sole-source award. GAO and COFC also assess whether the agency performed reasonable market research and documented its efforts.[28] The "substantial duplication of costs" component found in two of the three justifications for the sole-source exception has also formed the basis of protests at GAO and COFC. For example, in *Innovation Development*,[29] COFC found the J&A's reliance on the agency's "calculations as to the 'substantial duplication of costs' of the transition to a new contractor" to be arbitrary and capricious given the lack of a "credible explanation" for the estimate upon which the calculations were based.[30]

Brand name procurements are a close cousin to sole-source procurements. FAR 6.302-1 expressly states that a solicitation that requires offerors to provide a brand name product or feature peculiar to one manufacturer necessarily involves other than full and open competition.[31] Procurements using brand name restrictions must be supported by a J&A pursuant to FAR 6.303 and 6.304. A brand name J&A also "should indicate that the use of such descriptions in the acquisition or portion of an acquisition is essential to the Government's requirements, thereby precluding consideration of a product manufactured by another company."[32] Protests challenging an

---

maximum extent practicable, once a protester contends that it is a potential supplier of the items, the burden is on the agency to show that its sole source procurement is properly justified.").

27. FN Am., LLC, B415261, Dec. 12, 2017, 2017 CPD ¶ 380, at 7 (citing Magnavox Elec. Sys. Co., B-258076.2, Dec. 30, 1994, 94-2 CPD ¶ 266, at 6; Unitron LP, B-406770, Aug. 14, 2012, 2012 CPD ¶ 247, at 3).

28. *See* Innovation Dev. Enters. of Am., Inc. v. United States, 108 Fed. Cl. 711, 730 (2013) ("the Air Force did not conduct any significant market research . . . the lack of market research to support this sole-source procurement violates FAR Part 10"); Desktop Alert, Inc., B-408196, July 22, 2013, 2013 CPD ¶ 179, at 4, 8 ("We also conclude that the justification is deficient because the agency failed to document adequately its market research of other vendors' similar products.").

29. 108 Fed. Cl. 711 (2013).

30. *Id.* at 728–29.

31. FAR 6.302-1(c).

32. FAR 6.302-1(c)(ii)(B).

agency's reliance on this exception to full and open competition typically argue that the brand name feature or product is not essential to meeting the agency's needs.[33]

Agencies also employ a variant of the "brand name" requirement that calls for a specified brand name or its "equal." These less restrictive solicitation requirements allow contractors to propose alternative brands that meet the "salient physical, functional, or performance characteristics of the brand name item."[34] Agencies including a "brand name or equal" requirement in their solicitation must provide both the brand name and a general description of the salient characteristics of the brand name that represent "firm requirements."[35] These salient characteristics must be reasonably related to the agency's minimum needs and must not be unduly restrictive of competition.[36] GAO has consistently held that under a brand name or equal solicitation, offerors must provide sufficient descriptive detail regarding the salient characteristics of the offered product for an agency to make a meaningful comparison of the offered product to the brand name product.[37]

b. Unusual and Compelling Urgency

FAR 6.302-2 allows the government to procure through other than full and open competition where an "agency's need for the supplies or services is of such an unusual and compelling urgency that the Government would be seriously injured unless the agency is permitted to limit the number of sources from which it solicits bids or proposals."[38] Notably, an agency may *not* rely on the "only one responsible source" exception to full and open competition where the "unusual and compelling urgency" exception may be applied. As COFC explained:

---

33. *See, e.g.*, Harris IT Servs. Corp., B-411699, Oct. 2, 2015, 2015 CPD ¶ 293 (protest sustained where, among other things, "agency's attempt to acquire Motorola-specific equipment appear[ed] fundamentally inconsistent" with agency's need for interoperable equipment).

34. FAR 11.104(b).

35. *Id.*

36. T-Mobile USA, Inc., B-418394, Apr. 8, 2020, 2020 CPD ¶ 142 (denying protest where solicitation provisions adequately identified salient characteristics of the brand name or equal requirement and were not unduly restrictive of competition); Hesco Bastion Ltd. v. United States, 136 Fed. Cl. 146, 154 (2018) ("As with any specifications, the salient characteristics set forth in a 'brand name or equal' procurement must be reasonably related to the agency's minimum needs and must not be unduly restrictive of competition."); G.H. Harlow Co., Inc., B-266049, Jan. 26, 1996, 96-1 CPD ¶ 95, at 2 ("When a protester challenges a salient characteristic included in a brand name or equal solicitation as unduly restrictive of competition, we will review the record to determine whether the restrictions imposed are reasonably related to the contracting agency's minimum needs.").

37. *See, e.g.*, Logistics Network, Inc., B-408995, Jan. 6, 2014, 2014 CPD ¶ 24 ("Under a brand name or equal solicitation such as the one here, firms offering equal products must submit sufficient descriptive literature to permit the contracting agency to assess whether the equal product meets all the salient characteristics specified in the solicitation."); OnSite Sterilization, LLC, B-405395, Oct. 25, 2011, 2011 CPD ¶ 228; Am. Gov't Mktg., Inc., B-294895, Nov. 22, 2004, 2005 CPD ¶ 109.

38. FAR 6.302(a)(2).

> One logical reason for this prohibition is that under FAR 6.302–2, the government is permitted in appropriate circumstances to "limit [but not automatically reduce to one] the number of sources from which it solicits bids or proposals." FAR 6.302–2(a)(2); *see also* FAR 6.302–2(c)(2) ("This statutory authority requires that agencies shall request offers from as many potential sources as is practicable under the circumstances."). Under FAR 6.302–1, however, the government is permitted in appropriate circumstances to solicit an offer from one source only. See FAR 6.302–1(b)(1). In essence, the prohibition in FAR 6.302–1(b) forces the agency to solicit offers from as many sources as is practicable, in situations of unusual and compelling urgency, before resorting to soliciting offers from only a single source, in circumstances which may also present unusual and compelling urgency.[39]

Unusual and compelling urgency solicitations must be limited to address only the urgency identified. FAR 6.302-2(d) limits the period of performance of a contract awarded under its authority to one year unless "exceptional circumstances apply." Agencies invoking the "unusual and compelling urgency" exception must still comply with other policies designed to protect the integrity of the procurement process.[40] As noted earlier, the exception for unusual and compelling urgency permits agencies to limit the number of sources from which it solicits bids or proposals. However, agencies are required to achieve the maximum level of competition possible under the circumstances and may not simply ignore the potential for competition.[41] The urgency of an agency's procurement cannot be caused by the agency's own failure to engage in adequate advance planning.[42]

c. Industrial Mobilization

FAR 6.302-3 permits agencies to forego competition when it "is necessary" to award to a particular source to "maintain a facility, producer, manufacturer, or other supplier available for furnishing supplies or services in case of a national emergency or to achieve industrial mobilization."[43] In *Coulson Aviation (USA) Inc.*,[44] GAO sustained a protest challenging a noncompetitive procurement under this authority for airtankers to perform firefighting functions. There, the agency represented that it grounded its decision on the belief that without the contract, the proposed source would cease

39. Innovation Dev. Enters. of Am., Inc. v. United States, 108 Fed. Cl. 711, 729 (2013) (alteration in original).

40. *See, e.g.*, Filtration Dev. Co., LLC v. United States, 59 Fed. Cl. 658 (2004) (agency's invocation of the "unusual and compelling urgency" exception did not preclude challenge to procurement based on allegation that agency violated OCI regulations).

41. Bausch & Lomb, Inc., B-298444, Sept. 21, 2006, 2006 CPD ¶ 135.

42. Major Contracting Servs., Inc., B-401472, Sept. 14, 2009, 2009 CPD ¶ 170.

43. FAR 6.302-3(a)(2)(i).

44. B-409356.2, Mar. 31, 2014, 2014 CPD ¶ 106.

to remain a vital supplier after its predecessor contract expired. GAO held that the record did not contain any analysis of the supplier's financial condition after the expiration of its contract, and explained that agencies are "not permitted to make a noncompetitive award for industrial mobilization reasons where . . . there has been no showing that the award is presently necessary to maintain a supplier even if deemed vital."[45]

By contrast, in *Ridgeline Industries, Inc.*,[46] GAO denied a protest where the Defense Logistics Agency (DLA) properly invoked the industrial mobilization exception. A study commissioned by the DLA had found that tent production required specialized skill and production lines. Domestic manufacturers had experienced difficulty in increasing production to meet the military's requirements. DLA funded a tent manufacturer with a "minimum sustaining rate of production" to preserve the domestic supply chain to meet wartime needs for tents. DLA successfully explained that the award was needed to keep the manufacturer's production line in operation while the military assessed its requirements for tents and the other firms in the study did not require a minimum sustaining order. GAO concluded that "[d]ecisions as to which producers should be included in the mobilization base, and which restrictions are required to meet the needs of industrial mobilization, involve complex judgments that must be left to the discretion of the military agencies."[47]

d. International Agreement

FAR 6.302-4 permits agencies to forego competition

> when precluded by the terms of an international agreement or a treaty between the United States and a foreign government or international organization, or the written directions of a foreign government reimbursing the agency for the cost of the acquisition of the supplies or services for such government.

Agencies are still required to submit a J&A for this exception.[48] In *Hyperion, Inc. v. United States*,[49] the Kingdom of Jordan provided the U.S. Army with nonrepayable foreign military funds for a contract to install and perform infrastructure upgrades to fiber optic cable networks in Jordan. The Kingdom of Jordan requested a sole-source award, which the Army executed pursuant to the "International Agreement" exception of CICA. Because the contract was ultimately being paid for by a foreign

45. *Id.* at 15.

46. B-402105, Jan. 7, 2010, 2010 CPD ¶ 22.

47. *Id.* at 2; *see also* Outdoor Venture Corp., B-405423, Oct. 25, 2011, 2011 CPD ¶ 241.

48. FAR 6.302-4(c); Kollsman, a Div. of Sequa Corp. v. United States, 25 Cl. Ct. 500 (1992) (foreign military sale sole-source contracts required conformance to written justification and approval requirement).

49. 120 Fed. Cl. 504 (2015).

nation (Kingdom of Jordan), the sole-source award was proper under the "International Agreement" exception.[50]

e. Authorized or Required by Statute

The exception to full and open competition under CICA contained in FAR 6.302-5 provides agencies with the authority to forego competition requirements when statutes "expressly authorize or require that acquisition be made from a specified source or through another agency." The FAR provision provides a nonexhaustive list including acquisitions from Federal Prison Industries, qualified nonprofit agencies for the blind or other severely disabled people, and sole-source awards under the HUBZone Act of 1997, Veterans Benefits Act of 2003, and the WOSB Program.[51] The "expressly" language is interpreted literally, requiring agencies to point to explicit provisions of statutes that authorize or require other than full and open competition. This was illustrated in *National Government Services, Inc. v. United States*,[52] where the Centers for Medicare and Medicaid Services interpreted provisions of the Medicare Modernization Act, Pub. L. No. 108-173, as creating an "award limit" for contractors. The award limit precluded a contractor from winning an award when the award combined with its current contracts would have put it over the award limit. The Federal Circuit held that the agency's contract award limit did not provide for full and open competition and was not justified under the "expressly authorized by statute" exception because the statute cited by the agency did not expressly provide an exception to the competition requirement.

f. National Security

The national security exception to CICA, found in FAR 6.302-6, allows agencies to forego full and open competition "when the disclosure of the agency's needs would compromise the national security"; it also may be used in any acquisition where "disclosure of the Government's needs would compromise the national security (e.g., would violate security requirements)." The authority, though, cannot be used simply because the acquisition is classified or access to classified material is required for offerors to submit proposals or perform the contract.[53] In addition, agencies are strongly

50. *Id.* at 513–14; *see also* L-3 Commc'ns Corp. v. United States, 99 Fed. Cl. 283 (2011) (Air Force sole-source contract for procurement of flight simulators to train Egyptian pilots fell within international agreement exception because Egypt qualified as "foreign government" reimbursing agency).

51. FAR 6.302-5(b).

52. 923 F.3d 977 (Fed. Cir. 2019).

53. FAR 6.302-6(b).

encouraged to solicit offers from "as many potential sources as is practicable under the circumstances."[54]

The Air Force successfully used this exception in *The Boeing Co.; Bombardier, Inc.*[55] The Air Force issued a classified J&A for a sole-source award to L3 for a weapons system called the Compass Call re-host. The Air Force's rationale submitted to Congress was that "national security interests prevent[ed] disclosure of highly classified information required to build, integrate, and operate the COMPASS CALL capability to any source other than L–3."[56] Boeing challenged the Air Force's use of the national security exception on the grounds that FAR 6.302-6(b) does not allow the exception to be used merely because the acquisition is classified. GAO, however, found the Air Force's rationale went beyond the "mere fact of classification." Instead, the agency had determined that national security concerns precluded "the clearance of additional contractors for the purpose of solicitation and performance of tasks, even to those contractors that might possess access to information classified at the TS/SCI level on other programs."[57] GAO explained that "[a]n agency's decision whether to grant a firm security clearance for a particular acquisition, however, is not a matter our Office will generally review."[58]

g. Public Interest

The public interest exception at FAR 6.302-7 is a catchall provision used "when none of the other authorities in 6.302 apply."[59] But it comes with several limitations: (1) it requires written authorization by the Secretary of Defense, the Secretary of the Army, the Secretary of the Navy, the Secretary of the Air Force, the Secretary of Homeland Security for the Coast Guard, the Administrator of NASA, or the "head of any other executive agency"; (2) unlike the other exceptions to CICA's requirement for full and open competition, the authority to invoke this exception may not be delegated; (3) Congress must be notified of such a determination in writing within 30 days before award of the contract; and (4) as mentioned earlier, the exception requires a D&F.[60] The D&F is required to set out "facts and circumstances that clearly and convincingly justify [the agency head's] determination of the public interest."[61]

---

54. FAR 6.302-6(c).
55. B-414706, Aug. 25, 2017, 2017 CPD ¶ 274.
56. *Id.* at 13.
57. *Id.* at 15.
58. *Id.* at 16.
59. FAR 6.302-7(b).
60. FAR 6.302-7(c).
61. Spherix, Inc. v. United States, 58 Fed. Cl. 351, 356 (2003) (holding that Secretary of Agriculture's determination that it was necessary in the public interest to make a sole-source modification to incumbent's contract was clearly and convincingly justified).

GAO addressed the use of this exception in *Sikorsky Aircraft Corp.*,[62] where the Acting Secretary of the Navy issued a determination that restricted competition to obtain 21 Russian-made Mi-17 helicopters for the Afghanistan Air Force. The D&F explained that the Afghanistan Air Force's familiarity with flying and maintaining the Mi-17 warranted the exception because it would otherwise take at least three years to recruit and re-train Afghan pilots on a new aircraft, which would "result in unacceptable delays and significantly impact the mission . . . and long-term success of the [Afghanistan Air Force]."[63] GAO upheld the use of the public interest exception on the basis that the D&F set forth enough facts and circumstances to clearly and convincingly justify the specific determination made by the Acting Secretary of the Navy.

3. Restricting Competition Based on Lack of Advance Planning

CICA explicitly prohibits agencies from awarding contracts on an other than full and open competition basis to address their own failure to engage in advance planning:

> In no case may the head of an agency—(A) enter into a contract for property or services using procedures other than competitive procedures on the basis of the lack of advance planning or concerns related to the amount of funds available to the agency for procurement functions.[64]

In *Major Contracting Services*,[65] the protester challenged the Army's extension of a sole-source contract for portable chemical toilet services. The contract had originally been issued as a set aside for Service-Disabled Veteran Owned Small Businesses (SDVOSBs). The protester successfully challenged the awardee's SDVOSB status at SBA, but the Army declined to terminate the contract. Instead, when the base period ended, the Army decided to extend the contract for an additional four months. In response to the protest, the Army argued that the sole-source extension met the requirements for an exception to full and open competition due to an unusual and compelling urgency as it did not have a contract in place for services during the summer months when the portable chemical toilet services would be most used. GAO agreed that the Army had an urgent and compelling need for toilet services over the summer. But GAO concluded that the urgency arose from the Army's failure to adequately plan for the procurement in advance, and that other firms were interested in and capable of meeting the agency's needs: "[W]e do not think that the agency could

62. B-403471, Nov. 5, 2010, 2010 CPD ¶ 271.
63. *Id.* at 2.
64. 10 U.S.C. § 2304(f)(4)(A); *see* 41 U.S.C. § 3304(e)(5)(A).
65. B-401472, Sept. 14, 2009, 2009 CPD ¶ 170.

sit idly by in the face of the circumstances here and not take action to obtain more competition for its requirements."[66]

The principle that an agency cannot bootstrap its own lack of advance planning into an excuse for avoiding competition is well enshrined in the case law. Where a contracting officer could reasonably take steps to encourage competition but fails to do so, the procurement will not be considered full and open competition under CICA.[67] Additionally, a lack of advance planning is never an excuse for contracting officials to use noncompetitive procedures.[68] Although there is no requirement that planning must be successful or free of errors, advance planning must be reasonable.[69]

As part of their advance planning, contracting agencies should expect protests and should build in time for the protest process during each procurement.[70] An unusually long string of protests, however, could be sufficient to show that urgency is not due to lack of planning.[71] In *eAlliant, LLC*, GAO denied a protest against the Navy's award of a one-month sole-source bridge contract where the procurement was protested, award was cancelled, and the Navy took corrective action three times over two years. GAO held that "an immediate need for services that arises as a result of an agency's implementation of corrective action in response to a protest does not constitute a lack of advance planning."[72]

4. *Restricting Competition for Administrative Convenience*

GAO has long recognized that agencies may not restrict competition for administrative convenience: "It is well-established that administrative expediency or convenience by itself provides no basis for restricting competition, and an agency must reasonably attempt to ascertain the existence of alternative sources."[73]

---

66. *Id.* at 7.

67. eFedBudget Corp., B-298627, Nov. 15, 2006, 2006 CPD ¶ 159, at 7–8 (citing VSE Corp., Johnson Controls World Servs., Inc., B-290452.3, May 23, 2005, 2005 CPD ¶ 103, at 8; HEROS, Inc., B-292043, June 9, 2003, 2003 CPD ¶ 111, at 7; Nat'l Aerospace Grp., Inc., B-282843, Aug. 30, 1999, 99-2 CPD ¶ 43, at 8; *see also* S. Rep. No. 98–50 at 18 (1984), *reprinted in* 1984 U.S.C.C.A.N. 2174, 1983 WL 25395, at 2191 (stating that CICA requires agencies to "make an affirmative effort to obtain effective competition")).

68. *See, e.g.*, eFedBudget Corp., B-298627, Nov. 15, 2006, 2006 CPD ¶ 159, at 7–8; Signals & Sys., Inc., B-288107, Sept. 21, 2001, 2001 CPD ¶ 168, at 9.

69. Cherokee Nation Techs., LLC v. United States, 116 Fed. Cl. 636 (2014); eFedBudget Corp., B-298627, Nov. 15, 2006, 2006 CPD ¶ 159, at 6.

70. *See Cherokee Nation Techs.*, 116 Fed. Cl. at 640 (finding agency's failure to adequately plan for transition of procurement including protests did not justify use of sole-source bridge contract).

71. *See* eAlliant, LLC, B-407332.4, Dec. 23, 2014, 2015 CPD ¶ 58.

72. *Id.* at 7.

73. W.H. Mullins, B-207200, Feb. 16, 1983, 83-1 CPD ¶ 158, at 5; *see also* EDP Enters., Inc., B-284533.6, May 19, 2003, 2003 CPD ¶ 93 ("Administrative convenience is not a legal basis to justify bundling of requirements, if the bundling of requirements restricts competition[.]"); Nat'l Customer

Indeed, "CICA and its implementing regulations require that the scales be tipped in favor of ensuring full and open competition, whenever concerns of economy or efficiency are being weighed against ensuring full and open competition."[74] This particular ground is most often seen in protests where the agency has decided to "bundle" into a single procurement supplies or services that had previously been separately competed and procured.

5. Failure to Provide Fair Opportunity to Win Task or Delivery Orders Placed under Multiple Award IDIQ Contracts

Orders placed under IDIQ contracts are not subject to the competition requirements of FAR Part 6 (i.e., the competition is held at the IDIQ level) or the source selection requirements in FAR Part 15. For example, the requirements for discussions set forth in FAR 15.306(d) do not apply. Nevertheless,

> [w]hile FAR § 16.505 does not establish specific requirements regarding the conduct of discussions under a task or delivery order competition, exchanges occurring with contract holders of multiple award contracts in a FAR § 16.505 procurement, like other aspects of such a procurement, must be fair.[75]

An awardee under a multiple award IDIQ contract may protest the ordering agency's failure to provide it with a "fair opportunity" to compete for an order.[76]

An agency may dispense with the "fair opportunity" process only if one of the statutory exceptions listed in FAR 16.505(b)(2) applies, and it must justify in writing the basis for such an exception. These exceptions are as follows:

- The agency need for the supplies or services is so urgent that providing a fair opportunity would result in unacceptable delays;
- Only one awardee is capable of providing the supplies or services required at the level of quality required because the supplies or services ordered are unique or highly specialized;

Eng'g, B-251135, Mar. 11, 1993, 93-1 CPD ¶ 225, at 136 ("mere administrative convenience cannot justify restricting competition"); 15 U.S.C. § 644(e)(2)(c) (reduction of administrative or personnel costs alone are not a sufficient justification for restricting competition).

74. EDP Enters., Inc., B-284533.6, May 19, 2003, 2003 CPD ¶ 93, at 2 (citing cases); Better Serv., B-265751, Jan. 18, 1996, 96-1 CPD ¶ 90 (citing Nat'l Customer Eng'g, B-251135, Mar. 11, 1993, 93–1 CPD ¶ 225).

75. Jacobs Tech., Inc., B-416314, July 31, 2018, 2018 CPD ¶ 271 (citing Engility Corp., B413120.3, Feb. 14, 2017, 2017 CPD ¶ 70, at 6).

76. *See* FAR 16.505(b)(1) ("The contracting officer must provide each awardee a fair opportunity to be considered for each order exceeding $3,500 issued under multiple delivery-order contracts or multiple task-order contracts, except as provided for in paragraph (b)(2) of this section[.]").

- The order must be issued on a sole-source basis in the interest of economy and efficiency because it is a logical follow-on to a previously issued order, provided that all awardees were given a fair opportunity to be considered for the original order;
- The order is needed to satisfy a minimum guarantee;
- For orders exceeding the simplified acquisition threshold, a statute expressly authorizes or requires that the purchase be made from a specified source; and
- Small business set asides.

An IDIQ contract holder dissatisfied with an agency's decision not to use the fair opportunity process should first determine whether the agency sought to invoke one of the statutory exceptions just listed. If not, such failure constitutes a valid ground of protest. If the agency has invoked one of the statutory exceptions, the protest should focus on the adequacy of the agency's rationale for such exception.

6. *Orders That Exceed the Scope of the Underlying Umbrella Contract*

Even where a task or delivery order–based protest may not be brought (i.e., at COFC regardless of dollar amount, or at GAO if the order falls below jurisdictional thresholds), a protester may challenge a solicitation seeking to award a task or delivery order that exceeds the scope, period of performance, or maximum value of the contract under which the order will issue.[77] Most such protests allege that the proposed order exceeds the scope of the underlying contract.

To sustain a protest based on allegations that the planned task order would exceed the scope of the contract under which it is to issue, the protester must show there is a material difference between the task order and the underlying contract.[78] Such material differences may arise from the type of work or supplies to be ordered, the order's performance period, and costs between the contract as awarded and task or delivery order. As explained by GAO, "[t]he overall inquiry is whether the task order is of a nature that potential offerors would reasonably have anticipated."[79] In *Onix Networking Corp.*,[80] for example, GAO sustained a protest alleging that the Peace Corps issued an improper, out-of-scope, sole-source delivery order where the record showed that the order contemplated the acquisition of cloud-based services never sought during the original acquisition of software update services and technical support, and there was no reasonable basis for firms to know that the Peace Corps would use the delivery order to acquire such services.

---

77. FAR 16.505(10)(i)(A).
78. *See, e.g.*, Threat Mgmt. Grp., LLC, B-413729, Dec. 21, 2016, 2017 CPD ¶ 9, at 3.
79. *Id.* (quoting DynCorp Int'l LLC, B-402349, Mar. 15, 2010, 2010 CPD ¶ 59).
80. B-411841, Nov. 9, 2015, 2015 CPD ¶ 330.

7. *Failure to Observe Set-Aside Requirements*

Among the exceptions to CICA's mandate for full and open competition are various socioeconomic preferences that agencies may be obligated to address in their procurement decision-making process. These include government-wide directives for setting aside contracts for small businesses, generally, as well as for entities that qualify under the different socioeconomic assistance programs managed by the SBA (e.g., the "HUBZone" program). In addition, the law directs specific agencies to consider certain preferences; for example, the Department of Veterans Affairs (VA) has set-aside requirements for veteran-owned small businesses. An agency's failure to comply with these requirements may be protested.

Although a detailed discussion of socioeconomic preferences and set-aside requirements is beyond the scope of this book, a look at one of the more typical grounds of protest—a failure to set aside for small business—serves to illustrate how this ground operates.

The FAR sets forth the set-aside requirements underlying the small business socioeconomic programs.[81] Specifically, in determining whether a procurement must be set aside, the FAR directs contracting officers to the expected contract value based on the simplified acquisition and micro-purchase thresholds:[82]

- If between $3,500 and $150,000, the procurement "shall be set aside for small business unless the contracting officer determines there is not a reasonable expectation of obtaining offers from two or more responsible small business concerns that are competitive in terms of fair market prices, quality, and delivery."[83]
- If over $150,000, the procurement must "be set aside for exclusive small business participation when there is a reasonable expectation that offers will be received from at least two responsible small business concerns, and award will be made at a fair market price."[84]

---

81. FAR Part 19 addresses the set-aside preferences for small businesses, generally, as well as for small businesses under the 8(a) Program (FAR Subpart 19.8), HUBZone Program (FAR Subpart 19.13), SDVOSB Procurement Program (FAR Subpart 19.14), and the Women-Owned Small Business (WOSB) Program (FAR Subpart 19.15). *See also* FAR 19.203 (addressing relationship among small business programs).

82. As of this publication, FAR 2.101 defines the micro-purchase threshold as $3,500 and the simplified acquisition threshold as $150,000, the amounts referenced herein. In October 2019, the FAR Council issued a proposed rule that would increase the two thresholds to $10,000 and $250,000, respectively. *See* Federal Acquisition Regulation: Increased Micro-Purchase and Simplified Acquisition Thresholds; 2018-004, 84 Fed. Reg. 52420 (Oct. 2, 2019).

83. FAR 19.502-2(a).

84. Alpine Cos., Inc., B-416104.2, Aug. 23, 2018, 2018 CPD ¶ 289 (citing FAR 19.502-2(b)). In addition, where over $150,000 the FAR also requires that contracting officers "first consider an

The requirement to set aside the procurement if there are at least two small businesses reasonably expected to submit competitive offers is known as the "rule of two." GAO affords contracting agencies discretion in deciding whether to set aside a procurement, reviewing such decisions under a reasonableness standard.[85]

Although GAO will not hear a protest challenging whether an offeror qualifies as a small business concern because such protests fall within the exclusive province of the SBA, GAO will sustain a protest where an agency has attempted to determine a business concern's size or socioeconomic status rather than referring the matter to the SBA. Where a small business that would otherwise win the award is rejected by the contracting officer because of concerns regarding the firm's ability to perform the contract, the small business may appeal through the SBA's certificate of competency (COC) program. Through the COC program, SBA industrial and financial specialists review the firm's capabilities and make a final determination.[86] If the COC affirms the small business's ability to perform the contract, the agency must award the contract to the small business.[87]

Set-aside protests may arise from contractors excluded from competition because of an agency determination to set aside a procurement, as well as from contractors challenging an agency's decision not to set aside a procurement. An example of the former is *Triad Isotopes, Inc.*[88] In *Triad*, GAO sustained a protest challenging an agency's decision to set aside a procurement exclusively for small business where the market research conducted did not provide a reasonable basis for the "agency's conclusion that it would receive viable quotations from at least two responsible small business concerns." Conversely, in *Aerosage, LLC*,[89] GAO sustained a protest of an agency's decision not to set aside a procurement where the agency failed to consider that certain line items fell between $3,500 and $150,000 and were therefore required to be set aside under FAR 19.202-2(a).

The socioeconomic preferences attending procurements by the VA have been a subject of high-profile litigation in recent years. In 2016, the U.S. Supreme Court addressed whether the "rule of two" analysis imposed on the VA by the Veterans

---

acquisition for the small business socioeconomic contracting programs (i.e., 8(a), HUBZone, SDVOSB, or WOSB programs) before considering a small business set-aside (see 19.502-2(b))." FAR 19.203(c).

85. *Alpine Cos.*, B-416104.2, at 2 ("No particular method of assessing the availability of capable small businesses is required; rather, the assessment must be based on sufficient facts so as to establish its reasonableness.").

86. SBA Certificates of Competency, https://www.sba.gov/node/4808 (last visited July 13, 2020).

87. *Id.; see* Singleton Enters.-GMT Mech., A Joint Venture, B-310552, Jan. 10, 2008, 2008 CPD ¶ 16 (GAO sustained a protest where the agency determined a bidder was nonresponsive under a solicitation set-aside for SDVOSB because the agency determined on its own that the bidder did not qualify as a SDVOSB instead of referring the matter to the SBA for a COC).

88. B-411360, July 16, 2015, 2015 CPD ¶ 220.

89. B-416381, Aug. 23, 2018, 2018 CPD ¶ 288.

Benefits, Health Care, and Information Technology Act of 2006 (VBA) applied to all VA procurements, or whether the VA could disregard the requirement for procurements made under the FSS, or if the VA had already met its small business contracting goals for the year.[90] Specifically, the Supreme Court examined the VBA's provision that the VA "'shall award' contracts to veteran-owned small businesses when there is a 'reasonable expectation' that two or more such businesses will bid for the contract at 'a fair and reasonable price that offers best value to the United States.'"[91] The protester challenged the VA's award of multiple FSS orders without first conducting the VBA's rule of two analysis. The Supreme Court held that the VA had "to apply the Rule of Two to all contracting determinations," adding that the statutory requirement for set-aside preferences "does not allow the [VA] to evade the Rule of Two on the ground that it has already met its contracting goals or on the ground that the [VA] has placed an order through the FSS."[92]

8. *Improper Bundling*

Bundling occurs when the government consolidates two or more "procurement requirements for goods or services previously provided or performed under separate smaller contracts into a solicitation of offers for a single contract that is likely to be unsuitable for award to a small-business concern."[93] In this context, separate smaller contracts are contracts that were performed by small business concerns or were suitable for award to small business concerns.[94] If an agency decides to engage in bundling, it must justify its decision in light of its impact on small business participation. To this end, FAR 7.107-3(a) provides: "[T]he agency shall make a written determination that the bundling is necessary and justified in accordance with 15 U.S.C. 644(e)."

The decision to bundle will be upheld in the face of a protest if the agency demonstrates that such an approach will provide substantial benefits to the government compared to the benefits available through the use of separate contracts.[95] The reduc-

---

90. *See* Kingdomware Techs., Inc. v. United States, 136 S. Ct. 1969, 195 L. Ed. 2d 334 (2016).

91. *Id.* at 1972 (quoting 38 U.S.C. § 8127(d)).

92. *Id.* at 1976. The Supreme Court further cemented the nondiscretionary nature of the rule of two analysis required for VA procurements in January 2020, when it declined a petition for certiorari to review the Federal Circuit's opinion in *PDS Consultants, Inc. v. United States*, 907 F.3d 1345 (Fed. Cir. 2018), *cert. denied sub nom. Winston-Salem Indus. for Blind v. PDS Consultants, Inc.*, 140 S. Ct. 909 (2020). In *PDS Consultants,* the Federal Circuit affirmed a COFC ruling that the VA must prioritize the VBA's rule of two for veteran-owned businesses over the government-wide statutory preference for entities included on the "AbilityOne" list of products and services produced by nonprofits employing disabled individuals.

93. 15 U.S.C. § 632(o)(2).

94. *Id.* § 632(o)(3).

95. TRS Research, B-290644, Sept. 13, 2002, 2002 CPD ¶ 159 (protest sustained where agency failed to demonstrate that bundling was justified and failed to coordinate its anticipated consolidated procurement with the SBA).

tion of administrative or personnel costs alone, however, is not a sufficient justification for bundling contract requirements "unless the cost savings are expected to be substantial in relation to the dollar value of the procurement requirements to be consolidated."[96]

In *National Customer Engineering*,[97] GAO made clear that administrative convenience, in and of itself, is an insufficient reason to bundle. The Bureau of Land Management sought to procure hardware and software maintenance services to maintain certain legacy systems. The agency decided to bundle both services to avoid "finger pointing" among different contractors over any technical problems that might arise during performance, and to save "some amount of time as well as some additional expense."[98] The protester argued that by bundling these services, the agency unduly restricted competition. GAO sustained this ground of protest, explaining that "when concerns of economy or efficiency are being weighed against maximizing competition, CICA and the implementing regulations require that the scales be tipped in favor of maximizing competition," and held that "[w]hile having one contractor handle both hardware and software may be administratively convenient for the agency, mere administrative convenience cannot justify restricting competition."[99]

GAO echoed this principle in *EDP Enterprises, Inc.*,[100] when it addressed the Army's attempt to bundle a contract for food services with a contract for base, vehicle, and aircraft maintenance services. In that case, the Army argued that grouping food services with other logistical services aligned with its minimum needs because regulations required that they be grouped together. GAO distinguished between the need to administer various services from one office and the need to procure them from one source. The Army further argued that de-coupling these services would "lead inevitably to the dismemberment" of the logistics functions and deprive it "of any meaningful efficiencies derived from management techniques such as cross-utilization and cross-training of personnel."[101] GAO disagreed, observing that "the agency's reason for bundling [the various services] in a solicitation seems to merely reflect the belief that it is administratively more convenient to manage one entity performing all of the requirements . . . as opposed to two entities."[102] Administrative convenience, GAO explained, "is not a legal basis to justify bundling of requirements, if the bundling of requirements restricts competition" as GAO found it did in *EDP*.[103] While noting

96. 15 U.S.C. § 644(e)(2)(C).
97. B-251135, Mar. 11, 1993, 93-1 CPD ¶ 225.
98. *Id.* at 4.
99. *Id.* at 136 (citing Burton Myers Co., B-190791, May 10, 1978, 78-1 CPD ¶ 354).
100. B-284533.6, May 19, 2003, 2003 CPD ¶ 93.
101. *Id.* at 4.
102. *Id.* at 3.
103. *Id.*

that management efficiencies could, in certain circumstances, justify bundling, GAO noted that in *EDP* the Army had not demonstrated that bundling food services with other unrelated services would lead to cross-training or cross-utilization efficiencies.

9. Solicitation Terms That Conflict with Statutory or Regulatory Requirements

Protestors can challenge solicitations containing terms that conflict with federal statutes or regulations.[104]

For example, in *Intertribal Bison Cooperative*,[105] GAO sustained a pre-award protest where the solicitation permitted non–Native American cooperative organizations to submit proposals to supply bison to a Native American food program in violation of a statute that required the purchase of bison from "Native American producers and cooperative organizations without competition." In *Harris IT Services Corp.*,[106] GAO sustained a protest against an FBI procurement for radios in part because the FBI sought to award a purported delivery order under another agency's IDIQ contract without meeting FAR requirements regarding delivery orders. The FBI's solicitation for the so-called delivery order failed to identify the quantity sought, the place of delivery, or delivery dates. As GAO explained, "while the agency has significant discretion to tailor the procedures that it will use in placing delivery orders, it does not have discretion to use instruments that do not satisfy the requirements of FAR § 16.505(a)(7)."[107]

10. Unreasonable Evaluation Methodology

Agencies have broad discretion to select the methods by which they will evaluate proposals; however, prospective offerors can challenge solicitations on the basis that the evaluation methods are unreasonable. Such protests are distinct from post-award challenges in which offerors claim the agency failed to adhere to the evaluation methods set forth in the solicitation. Although the rationale behind pre-award protests

104. *See, e.g.*, Crane & Co., Inc., B-297398, Jan. 18, 2006, 2006 CPD ¶ 22 (sustaining protest where an agency's solicitation for distinctive currency paper provided for the award of a contract with a six-year term in violation of 31 U.S.C. § 5114(c), which limited contracts for currency paper to periods of not more than four years); Puerto Rico Marine Mgmt., Inc., B-247975, Oct. 23, 1992, 92-2 CPD ¶ 275 (sustaining protest where agency failed to include an evaluation preference for domestic vessels under the Buy American Act, 41 U.S.C. §§ 10a–10d (1988), as required by FAR 25.109); U.S. Def. Sys., Inc., B-244653, Dec. 23, 1991, 92-2 CPD ¶ 179 (sustaining protest where solicitation failed to include a domestic preference provision required by statute).

105. B-288658, Nov. 30, 2001, 2001 CPD ¶ 195.

106. B-411699, Oct. 2, 2015, 2015 CPD ¶ 293.

107. *Id.* at 8.

challenging an agency's stated evaluation methods would largely be the same regardless of the evaluation factor at issue—the chosen method will not result in a reasonable assessment of the offerors' proposals—such protests often involve challenges to the agency's planned approach for evaluating cost or price proposals.

For example, in *CACI Inc.-Federal*,[108] the solicitation contemplated cost-reimbursable task orders but did not require offerors to propose cost-reimbursable labor rates. GAO sustained the protest on the grounds that the solicitation precluded the agency from meaningfully evaluating proposed costs.[109]

11. Unreasonable Evaluation Criteria

Protesters face a high hurdle if they challenge the agency's selection of evaluation criteria. "Agency acquisition officials have broad discretion in the selection of the evaluation criteria that will be used in an acquisition, and [GAO] will not object to the absence or presence of a particular evaluation criterion so long as the criteria used reasonably relate to the agency's needs in choosing a contractor or contractors that will best serve the government's interests."[110] Simply put, GAO is reticent to object to an agency's selection of evaluation criteria so long as they reasonably relate to the agency's needs in choosing a contractor that will best serve the government's interests.[111]

For example, although the FAR directs agencies to evaluate past performance in "all source selections for negotiated competitive acquisitions expected to exceed the simplified acquisition threshold," the FAR also provides that past performance need not be evaluated if the contracting officer documents why it would not be an appropriate evaluation factor.[112] GAO shows great deference to the agency's judgment of its needs.[113]

---

108. B-413028, Aug. 3, 2016, 2016 CPD ¶ 238.

109. *Id.*; *see also* AirTrak Travel, B-292101, June 30, 2003, 2003 CPD ¶ 117 (sustaining protest where agency's pricing model did not account for the fact that certain travel systems would be phased in at various locations over time); S.J. Thomas Co., Inc., B-283192, Oct. 20, 1999, 99-2 CPD ¶ 73 (sustaining protest where the solicitation scheme planned to only evaluate offerors' pricing based on proposed mark-up rates, not on the cost to the government as required under FAR 15-304(c)).

110. Crewzers Fire Crew Transp., Inc., B-402530, May 17, 2010, 2010 CPD ¶ 117 (citing King Constr. Co., Inc., B-298276, July 17, 2006, 2006 CPD ¶ 110, at 3).

111. *See* SML Innovations, B-402667.2, Oct. 28, 2010, 2010 CPD ¶ 254, at 2 (denying protest where it was deemed reasonable for Army to limit the examination of past performance to contracts over $2 million because small business awardees would likely be required to manage multiple concurrent task orders in excess of $2 million).

112. *Compare* FAR 15.304(c)(3)(i) *with* FAR 15.304(c)(3)(iii).

113. *See* Data Monitor Sys., Inc., B-415761, Mar. 6, 2018, 2018 CPD ¶ 79 (denying protest where agency officials identified and documented reasonable basis for decision not to include past performance as an evaluation factor).

Where the criteria fail to provide a meaningful basis for award selection, however, GAO will sustain the protest. In *PWC Logistics Services Co.*,[114] the DLA issued a solicitation for two IDIQ contracts to provide meals to personnel in Kuwait, Iraq, and Jordan. The agency's RFP divided the requirement for food distribution into two geographic zones and contemplated an award to two different offerors. One zone's contract was worth almost five times more than the other zone. The RFP, however, did not contain a description of the factors the government would use to determine which zone would be awarded to an offeror whose proposal could be found most advantageous for both zones. GAO held that the RFP evaluation criteria were "inconsistent with the requirement in CICA that agencies identify the bases upon which offerors' proposals will be evaluated."[115]

12. Lack of Mutual Consideration

GAO will sustain a protest if the protester can establish that the solicitation would not result in an enforceable contract due to a lack of mutual consideration. This arises in two different areas: (1) a requirements contract that does not obligate the government to purchase all its requirements from a particular contract, or (2) an IDIQ contract that fails to specify the guaranteed minimum quantity.

A requirements contract obligates an agency to purchase all its requirements for supplies or services during a specified period from a specific contractor and the contractor is required to provide all the specific supplies or services the agency requires.[116] These mutual obligations serve as consideration for the contract.[117] The absence of an obligation to perform by either party constitutes a lack of consideration, rendering the contract unenforceable.[118] For example, in *Satellite Services, Inc.*,[119] GAO sustained a protest where the requirements contract solicitation allowed the agency to order work from other contractors whenever "otherwise determined to be in the best interest of the Government."

The other successful protest scenario based on lack of mutual consideration arises where an IDIQ contract fails to guarantee a minimum quantity. An enforceable IDIQ contract "must require the Government to order and the contractor to furnish at least a stated minimum quantity of supplies or services" that is more than nominal.[120] "There is no 'magic number' that the FAR or [GAO's] decisions

114. B-400660, Jan. 6, 2009, 2009 CPD ¶ 67.
115. *Id.* at 7.
116. *See* FAR 16.503; Modern Sys. Tech. Corp. v. United States, 979 F.2d 200, 205 (Fed. Cir. 1992).
117. *See* Sea-Land Serv., Inc., B-266238, Feb. 8, 1996, 96-1 CPD ¶ 49.
118. *Id.* at 4.
119. B-280945, Dec. 4, 1998, 98-2 CPD ¶ 125.
120. FAR 16.504(a)(1)–(2).

set as adequate consideration for a contract; instead, the determination of whether a stated minimum quantity is 'nominal' must consider the nature of the acquisition as a whole."[121] GAO, however, accords agencies latitude in determining the minimum amount. To this end, GAO's Appropriations Law Division has advised agencies that, "[f]rom an appropriations standpoint," a guaranteed minimum quantity of as little as $500 for an IDIQ contract was not objectionable.[122]

Guaranteed minimum values necessary to establish consideration for IDIQ contracts are not tied to minimum order amounts. In *CW Government Travel, Inc.*,[123] GAO denied a protest where the protestor argued that the $2,500 guaranteed minimum was unreasonable because it was "so far out of line with the $15,000,000 minimum order amount." As GAO explained,

> [i]n light of the purpose of FAR 16.504(a) to establish a binding minimum—in effect, consideration for the ID/IQ contract—we do not believe that a contract's minimum order establishes the minimum guarantee or serves as a firm target against which the reasonableness of the minimum guarantee must be evaluated. Instead, the minimum guarantee must be evaluated in the context of all of the specific facts and circumstances of the procurement.[124]

13. *Improper Disclosure of Proprietary Information*

A protester can challenge the improper disclosure of proprietary information in a pre-award protest.[125] Although the government may attempt to defend against such a claim by asserting that the protester waived its proprietary rights, a waiver of proprietary rights "must be a voluntary, knowing and intelligent act done with sufficient awareness of the relevant circumstances and likely consequences."[126] Such a waiver "need not be express, but may be inferred from a pattern of conduct."[127] In *DynCorp International*,[128] an incumbent contractor filed a pre-award bid protest challenging an agency's decision to continue soliciting bids after publicly disclosing the incumbent

---

121. CW Gov't Travel, Inc., B-295530, Mar. 7, 2005, 2005 CPD ¶ 59 (citing Carr's Wild Horse Ctr., B-285833, Oct. 3, 2000, 2000 CPD ¶ 210, at 3; ABF Freight Sys., Inc., B-291185, Nov. 8, 2002, 2002 CPD ¶ 201, at 4; Sea–Land Serv., Inc., B-278404, Feb. 9, 1998, 98–1 CPD ¶ 47, at 12); *accord* Library of Cong.-Obligation of Guaranteed Minimums for Indefinite-Delivery, Indefinite-Quantity Contracts Under the Fedlink Program, B-318046, July 7, 2009, 2009 WL 1978719 (appropriations decision).

122. Library of Cong.-Obligation of Guaranteed Minimums for Indefinite-Delivery, Indefinite-Quantity Contracts Under the Fedlink Program, B-318046, July 7, 2009, 2009 WL 1978719.

123. B-295530, Mar. 7, 2005, 2005 CPD ¶ 59.

124. *Id.* at 2.

125. *See* DynCorp Int'l, LLC v. United States, 125 Fed. Cl. 1, 2 (2016); Sec'y of the Air Force, B-165542, July 11, 1969, 1969 CPD ¶ 47.

126. *See* DynCorp Int'l, LLC v. United States, 125 Fed. Cl. 446, 452 (2016).

127. *Id.* (citing Am. Airlines, Inc. v. United States, 77 Fed. Cl. 672, 681 (2007)).

128. 125 Fed. Cl. 446 (2016).

contractor's proprietary cost and pricing data. COFC granted the agency's motion for judgment on the administrative record, finding that DynCorp

> consistently failed to mark its indirect cost and profit data as "proprietary," and did not even object when the Air Force inquired whether the life cycle management reports could be posted as part of the new solicitation. DynCorp thereby waived its right to assert that the data was "proprietary," and the Air Force did nothing wrong by disclosing the data as part of the new solicitation.[129]

Regardless of markings, information that can be "independently obtained from publicly available literature or common knowledge" will not be deemed proprietary.[130] In *Digital Healthcare, Inc.*,[131] GAO denied the protest because a significant amount of the protester's alleged proprietary data was available to the public on the protester's website.

When the protester prevails on the merits, GAO or COFC may recommend the government award a sole-source contract to the aggrieved offeror, or, "if possible, cancel the solicitation and resolicit without using the [protester's] proprietary data."[132]

14. *Improper Cancellation of Solicitation*[133]

Agencies have "broad authority to decide whether to cancel a solicitation, and to do so, need only establish a reasonable basis."[134] But,

---

129. *Id.* at 448; *see* Del Mar Avionics-Request for Reconsideration, B-231124, Feb. 9, 1989, 89-1 CPD ¶ 131, at 2 ("a company might waive objections to the disclosure of its proprietary data by failing to protest the data's inclusion in an earlier solicitation") (citing Litton Applied Tech., B-227090, Sept. 3, 1987, 87–2 CPD ¶ 219).

130. Digital Healthcare, Inc., B-296489, Aug. 24, 2005, 2005 CPD ¶ 166.

131. *Id.*

132. Sentel Corp., B-244991, Dec. 6, 1991, 91-2 CPD ¶ 519, at 2; *see also* Sec'y of the Air Force, B-165542, July 11, 1969, 1969 CPD ¶ 47 (same).

133. Although this section discusses pre-award protests, post-award protests challenging an agency's decision to cancel a solicitation may also be brought, for example, as a corrective action in response to a disappointed offeror's protest. *See, e.g.*, FMS Inv. Corp. v. United States, 139 Fed. Cl. 221, 225, *amended*, 139 Fed. Cl. 439 (2018) (holding that the agency's corrective action canceling solicitation for student loan debt consolidation services in favor of a new "enhanced services" program was irrational where the cancellation notice constituted the first public announcement of the new program, the agency admitted the program had yet to be reviewed for compliance with applicable laws and regulations, and the Administrative Record lacked critical information regarding the program, including a timeline for implementation or a source of funding).

134. *See* Computer World Servs. Corp., B-416042, May 22, 2018, 2018 CPD ¶ 191 (denying protest alleging that agency improperly cancelled the solicitation where the agency reasonably determined that the solicitation's statement of work no longer met its needs). With respect to Invitations for Bids (IFB) for sealed bidding acquisitions under FAR Part 14, an agency must have a "compelling reason" to cancel after bids have been opened. FAR 14.404-1 ("Preservation of the integrity of the competitive bid system dictates that, after bids have been opened, award must be made to that responsible bidder who

> where a protester has alleged that an agency's rationale for cancellation is but a pretext, that is, the agency's actual motivation is to avoid awarding a contract on a competitive basis or to avoid resolving a protest, [GAO] will closely examine the reasonableness of the agency's actions in canceling the acquisition.[135]

GAO has sustained protests alleging the improper cancellation of a solicitation where the agency:

- Failed to provide GAO with its rationale for canceling the solicitation;[136]
- Sought to avoid awarding a lease for office space to the next-in-line offeror after its preferred offeror failed to return a signed lease;[137]
- Erroneously believed it was required to procure janitorial services in a manner not called for by the solicitation;[138]
- Concluded that the integrity of the procurement had been compromised without first determining whether the alleged irregularities could have compromised the award;[139] and
- Asserted that its needs had materially changed although the changes requested by the agency "would have only an inconsequential effect, if any, on the overall producibility of the required item."[140]

15. Insourcing Decisions

Government decisions to insource work present a challenge for protesters because COFC, GAO, and U.S. District Courts have each, at one time or another, disavowed the power to review such protests on either jurisdictional or standing grounds. Although an agency presumably has the purview to entertain an agency-level protest against an insourcing decision, such a route probably has a low likelihood of success. Recently, however, a COFC judge exercised jurisdiction and found standing for a

---

submitted the lowest responsive bid, unless there is a compelling reason to reject all bids and cancel the invitation."); *see* Veterans Elec., LLC, B-415064.2, Feb. 1, 2018, 2018 CPD ¶ 42, at 3 ("The standard requiring a compelling reason for cancellation applies to IFB procurements because of the potential adverse impact on the competitive bidding system of cancelation after bid prices have been exposed at a public bid opening." (citing United Contracting LLC, B-407417, Jan. 2, 2013, 2013 CPD ¶ 1, at 2)). But even under the "compelling reason" standard applicable to the cancellation of an IFB, an agency's decision is assessed on a "reasonableness" basis: "The agency has the discretion to determine whether a compelling reason exists to cancel a solicitation, and we will review the decision to ensure that it was reasonable." *Veterans Elec., LLC,* B-415064.2.

135. Superlative Techs., Inc., B-310489, Jan. 4, 2008, 2008 CPD ¶ 12, at 3.
136. Walker Dev. & Trading Grp., Inc., B-413924, Jan. 12, 2017, 2017 CPD ¶ 21.
137. JER 370 Third Street, LLC, B-402025.2, June 1, 2010, 2010 CPD ¶ 120.
138. Aleman & Assocs., Inc., B-287275.2, July 2, 2001, 2001 CPD ¶ 120.
139. R. & W. Flammann Gmbh, B-278486, Feb. 4, 1998, 98-1 CPD ¶ 40.
140. Pro-Fab, Inc., B-243607, Aug. 5, 1991, 91-2 CPD ¶ 12, at 3.

protester that challenged an insourcing decision. Thus, COFC offers the most promising avenue for relief. Each of the three forums for which publicly available decisions are available—U.S. District Court, GAO, and COFC—are discussed next.

a. U.S. District Courts

In *Fisher-Cal Industries, Inc. v. United States,*[141] the plaintiff brought suit under the APA to enjoin the Air Force from proceeding with a decision to insource multimedia services. Plaintiff alleged that it sought to challenge only the government's compliance with its own insourcing guidelines and procedures, and that its claims therefore did not involve a procurement. The court disagreed, explaining that the definition of procurement

> includes all stages of the process of acquiring property or services, beginning with the process for determining a need for property or services and ending with contract completion and closeout. . . . *As numerous other courts, including the Fifth, Eleventh, and Federal Circuits, have noted, insourcing necessarily involves determining a need for property or services* and whether there was a need to perform such functions through private contractors.[142]

Because the court determined that insourcing met the definition of "procurement," it dismissed plaintiff's claims as falling exclusively within COFC's jurisdiction. Similarly, in *Vero Technical Support, Inc. v. United States,*[143] the Eleventh Circuit explained that because the decision to insource a government contract involves the process of determining a need for property or services, it occurs in connection with a procurement or proposed procurement and may be challenged only at COFC.[144]

b. GAO

GAO appears disinclined to accept jurisdiction over protests challenging an agency's decision to insource.[145] In contrast to the *Fisher-Cal* court's conclusion that an

141. 839 F. Supp. 2d 218 (D.D.C. 2012).

142. *Id.* at 222 (emphasis added) (internal citations and quotations omitted).

143. 437 F. App'x 766 (11th Cir. 2011).

144. *See also* Colo. Building & Constr. Trades Council v. United States, No. 12–cv–632–AP, 2012 WL 3609824, at *1 (D. Colo. Aug. 22, 2012) (protest challenging DoD insourcing decision dismissed for lack of jurisdiction, as COFC has "exclusive jurisdiction over the specific insourcing decision-making process at issue here"); Roth Dev., Inc. v. United States, No. SA–10–CV–743–XR, 2010 WL 4595824, at *9 (W.D. Tex. Nov. 3, 2010), *aff'd,* 666 F.3d 336 (5th Cir. 2011) (challenge to insourcing decision dismissed as "exclusive jurisdiction over such challenges is vested in the COFC").

145. Prior to their moratorium, A-76 procurements could be protested at GAO. A-76 procurements originated with OMB Circular A-76, which provided that, whenever possible, the federal government should conduct competitions between public agencies and the private sector to determine who should perform the work. *See* Valerie Ann Bailey Grasso, *Circular A-76 and the Moratorium on DoD*

agency's failure to comply with its insourcing guidelines involved a procurement, GAO disclaimed jurisdiction on that basis. In *Aleut Facilities Support Services, LLC*,[146] Aleut protested the Air Force's decision to cancel a solicitation for fuel and transportation services so that it could perform the work in-house. Aleut alleged that the Air Force had failed to comply with its own guidelines for determining whether to insource the work. GAO dismissed the protest:

> Although we review agency decisions to cancel solicitations to determine whether those decisions are reasonably based, we generally do not review them when the work in question is to be performed in-house because such decisions are generally a matter of executive branch policy.[147]

c. Court of Federal Claims

In *Loomacres, Inc. v. United States*,[148] COFC concluded that the protester had the right to challenge an insourcing decision because it had previously won a contract to provide the services at issue and was poised to offer those same services following the end of its contract. Although acknowledging that the Federal Circuit has not yet addressed whether a prospective bidder has standing to contest an insourcing decision, the *Loomacres* court relied on analogous cases in which prospective bidders deprived of the opportunity to compete were deemed interested parties with standing to challenge the government's actions.

The *Loomacres* court acknowledged that two previous COFC cases—*Triad Logistics Services Corp. v. United States*[149] and *Elmendorf Support Services Joint Venture v. United States*[150]—concluded that protesters lacked standing to challenge insourcing

---

Competitions: Background and Issues for Congress, Cong. Rsch. Serv., R40854 (Jan. 16, 2013), https://fas.org/sgp/crs/misc/R40854.pdf. Congress passed a government-wide moratorium on A-76 competitions in its 2008 NDAA, which is still in place at the writing of this book. *Id.*

146. B-401925, Oct. 13, 2009, 2009 CPD ¶ 202.

147. *Id.* at 2; *see also* Desktop Alert, Inc., B-417170, Jan. 24, 2019, 2019 CPD ¶ 29 ("Our Office generally does not review agency decisions to perform requirements in-house rather than to contract for them, because such decisions are a matter of executive branch policy. . . . We will review such decisions only where a competitive solicitation has been issued to compare the costs of contracting out with in-house performance and it is alleged that the resulting comparison is faulty or misleading."); Triad Logistics Servs. Corp., B-403726, Nov. 24, 2010, 2010 CPD ¶ 279 (protest based on agency's failure to comply with internal guidance for insourcing services dismissed as not based on a procurement statute or bearing directly on a procurement). GAO acknowledged that it would review the cancelation of a solicitation under certain limited circumstances, namely: whether the solicitation required a cost comparison that was not performed; whether a statute or regulation required such a cost comparison; or whether the protest alleged the cancelation was a pretext. Aleut Facilities Support Servs., LLC, B-401925, Oct. 13, 2009, 2009 CPD ¶ 202, at 2.

148. 134 Fed. Cl. 779 (2017).

149. No. 11-43C, 2012 WL 5187846 (Fed. Cl. Feb. 29, 2012).

150. No. 12-346C, 2012 WL 3932774 (Fed. Cl. Sept. 10, 2012).

decisions but distinguished those decisions as having turned on the lack of meaningful relief. In each of those prior cases, the work had progressed so far along that injunctive relief was impractical. It is worth noting that in all three cases, there had been a contract for the work at issue prior to the government's insourcing decision.

In contrast, COFC declined jurisdiction over an insourcing decision in *VFA, Inc. v. United States*,[151] where

> DoD never contemplated or initiated a procurement process. The Government did not issue an RFI, did not receive information from vendors, and did not plan to award any contract. From the DoD's standpoint, it already possessed the SMS program it wanted to use, and there was no reason to acquire anything.

COFC noted that VFA sought a competitive procurement in order to sell to the government something the government already possessed. As COFC explained, "CICA's competition requirements may well have applied when the DoD originally developed the various SMS modules, but that development occurred long ago and is not before the Court."[152] Similarly, in *Desktop Alert Inc. v. United States*,[153] COFC dismissed a protest challenging the Army's decision to utilize an alert system it already owned rather than holding a competition to meet the requirement through commercial offerings. The court found instead of protesting "an actual procurement," the commercial system provider objected "to the *lack* of a procurement."[154] Because 28 U.S.C. § 1491(b)(1) "speaks 'exclusively' to 'procurement solicitations and contracts,'" and neither existed, the court dismissed the matter for a lack of subject matter jurisdiction.[155]

In *PDS Consultants v. United States*,[156] COFC exercised jurisdiction over a protest challenging the VA's decision to shift the fabrication of eyeglasses from a private contractor to the VA Optical Lab, only to deny the protest on the merits. The court explained that an agency's decision to cease procuring goods from the private sector and to instead use its own employees "may properly be challenged in a bid protest." COFC further held, however, that the "Rule of Two" analysis required for VA contract awards did not apply. "While a decision not to procure might be enough to implicate our jurisdiction over a bid protest, a decision not to award any contract cannot implicate the Veterans Benefits Act provision relied upon by PDS. Thus, the government is correct on the merits of this protest."

151. 118 Fed. Cl. 735, 741 (2014).
152. *Id.*
153. 146 Fed. Cl. 298 (2020).
154. *Id.* at 300 (underline in original).
155. *Id.* at 302 (internal citations omitted).
156. 2020 WL 5887550 (Fed. Cl. 2020).

16. Commercial Item Procurements

The Federal Acquisition Streamlining Act of 1994 (FASA) "requires that federal agencies, to the maximum extent practicable, procure commercially available technology to meet their needs."[157] Thus, the provider of a commercial item capable of meeting a procuring agency's needs may have grounds to protest that agency's decision to forego a commercial solution.

In *Palantir USG, Inc. v. United States*, the Federal Circuit affirmed COFC's decision that the Army violated FASA by seeking to procure a data management platform through a sole-source developmental contract without assessing whether its needs could be met using the protester's commercially available technology. The Federal Circuit explained that "[d]espite repeated notice that commercial products might well be available and could be modified to meet the Army's needs, the Army concluded that [the required system] could not be procured as a commercial product with scant explanation."[158]

In acquiring commercial items, procuring agencies may not

> tailor any clause or otherwise include any additional terms or conditions in a solicitation or contract for commercial items in a manner that is inconsistent with customary commercial practice for the item being acquired unless a waiver is approved in accordance with agency procedures.[159]

If a protester alleges that the solicitation's terms are inconsistent with customary commercial practice, the agency must demonstrate that it conducted adequate market research (pursuant to FAR Part 10) to show that the protested requirement is indeed customary, or that it obtained a waiver to tailor the FAR commercial item provision to meet the needs of the government.[160] In *Smelkinson Sysco Food Servs.*, the offeror protested the RFP requirement that offerors disclose, among other things, profit and freight costs exceeding actual costs related to interorganizational transfers among affiliates, alleging such disclosures were contrary to customary practice in the food distribution industry. GAO sustained the protest:

---

157. Palantir USG, Inc. v. United States, 904 F.3d 980, 983 (Fed. Cir. 2018) (citing Federal Acquisition Streamlining Act of 1994, Pub. L. No. 103-355, § 8104, 108 Stat. 3243 (1994) (codified as amended at 10 U.S.C. § 2377)).

158. *Id.* at 992–93.

159. FAR 12.302(c); *see* Crescent Helicopters, B-284706, May 30, 2000, 2000 CPD ¶ 90, at 2 ("FAR part 12 was intended to establish acquisition policies more closely resembling those of the commercial marketplace as well as other considerations necessary for proper acquisition planning, solicitation, evaluation, and award of contracts for commercial items.").

160. *See* Smelkinson Sysco Food Servs., B-281631, Mar. 15, 1999, 99-1 CPD ¶ 57.

> Given the lack of any meaningful market research showing that the challenged terms are consistent with customary commercial practice, we conclude that the agency violated the requirement in FAR § 12.302(a) to conduct appropriate market research prior to tailoring the regulatory provision. In the alternative, given the agency's apparent concession that there is no customary commercial practice calling for the type of disclosure required by the RFP clause, we conclude that the agency improperly tailored the standard clause at FAR § 52.212-4 without obtaining the requisite waiver to do so under FAR § 12.302(c).[161]

Where an agency has conducted market research, GAO assesses that research for reasonableness.[162] In *Red River Waste Solutions, LP*, the protester challenged the Army's solicitation for commercial waste management services. The Army's market research relied primarily upon other federal *government* contracts as a basis for establishing customary *commercial* practice. GAO concluded that the Army's determination that its provisions were consistent with commercial practices was not reasonable "since contracts with the federal government are not generally considered to be part of the commercial marketplace."[163] Accordingly, GAO sustained the protest.[164]

To obtain a waiver, the agency must

> describe the customary commercial practice found in the marketplace, support the need to include a term or condition that is inconsistent with that practice, and include a determination that the use of the customary commercial practice is inconsistent with the needs of the government.[165]

GAO further stated in the *Verizon Wireless* decision:

> We note . . . that decisions by our Office and the Court of Federal Claims stand for the proposition that agencies must, even in the event of a valid waiver, set forth a reasonable basis for the use of particular clauses or terms that deviate from customary commercial practice.[166]

---

161. *Id.* at 4.

162. *See* Red River Waste Sols., LP, B-411760.2, Jan. 20, 2016, 2016 CPD ¶ 4.

163. *Id.* at 4.

164. *See also* Dep't of the Army-Reconsideration & Request for Modification of Recommendation, B-411760.3, June 15, 2016, 2016 CPD ¶ 162, at 8–10; CW Gov't Travel, Inc. v. United States, 99 Fed. Cl. 666, 679–80 (2011) (agency's market research as to whether 15-year contract term was consistent with commercial practice "revealed nothing about whether setting the price for each option period at the outset of a 15–year contract is consistent with customary commercial practice").

165. Verizon Wireless, B-406854, Sept. 17, 2012, 2012 CPD ¶ 260, at 4 (citing FAR § 12.302(c)).

166. *Id.* at 12 n.4 (citing, among other cases, U.S. Foodservice, Inc. v. United States, 100 Fed. Cl. 659, 681–83 (2011) and CW Gov't Travel, Inc. v. United States, 99 Fed. Cl. 666, 679–80 (2011)).

B. Post-Award Protest Issues

1. Mis-Evaluations

One of the most common grounds of protest is that an agency mis-evaluated an offeror's proposal. The challenge in winning this ground is that GAO and COFC consider the evaluation of proposals to fall squarely within an agency's discretion. As a result, neither GAO nor COFC will substitute its judgment for the agency's and determine de novo what ratings, strengths, or weaknesses a proposal should have received. Instead, they will examine the record to determine whether the evaluation was reasonable and consistent with the terms of the solicitation and the requirements of law. In other words, if reasonable minds could disagree over whether the agency's or the protester's preferred conclusion was more appropriate, the agency will get the benefit of the doubt. A protester's "mere disagreement" with the agency's evaluation and source selection decision is not, on its own, a valid basis for sustaining a protest.

A corollary to this "reasonableness standard" is that GAO generally will not delve into the minutiae of technical issues about which subject-matter experts may disagree. When an evaluation rests on the "considered judgments of the agency's technical experts," GAO will defer to the agency unless the protester can demonstrate that the experts' conclusions are "arbitrary or otherwise unreasonable."[167] This usually means that a protester can win a battle of "dueling experts" only if its own expert conclusively shows that the agency's experts were objectively wrong. Simply providing a contrary "second opinion" by a different expert will not be enough. And, if the protester's "rebuttal" of the agency experts' scientific or engineering judgment consists only of "statements furnished by legal counsel," the protester probably should not make the argument at all.[168]

The deference afforded to an agency's technical evaluation does not mean that all challenges to that evaluation must fail—it merely means that the protest must be based on clear, objective errors in the agency's evaluation rather than subjective disagreements with the agency's judgment. For example, if agency evaluators ignore or fail to consider salient information in an offeror's proposal, the evaluation is likely to be found unreasonable.[169]

---

167. Boeing Co., B-412441, Feb. 16, 2016, 2016 CPD ¶ 269, at 15.

168. *See id.* at 13.

169. *See* Irving Burton Assocs., Inc., B-401983.3, Mar. 29, 2010, 2010 CPD ¶ 92, at 5–6 (concluding that the agency's rating and assessment of weaknesses lacked a rational basis where the evaluators had ignored relevant information included in the protester's proposal); *see also* Kellogg Brown & Root Servs., Inc., B-298694, Nov. 16, 2006, 2006 CPD ¶ 160, at 7–8 (agency's assertion that offeror's proposed contingency plan lacked detail unreasonably failed to credit information in the proposal, which—contrary to the agency's assertion—was not "more limited or general than the awardees' plans"); Locus Tech., Inc., B-293012, Jan. 16, 2004, 2004 CPD ¶ 16.

Likewise, if the record fails to support the agency's evaluation, the award decision is likely to be found unreasonable.[170] In *Kaman Dayron*,[171] the solicitation placed "particular importance" on the offerors' experience producing parts comparable in complexity to the part being procured, with different levels of "similar" and "nearly identical" used to assess the degree to which the parts previously produced by the offerors matched the part being procured by the agency. Although the record showed that the awardee's parts were less complex than the part being procured, the agency described them as "nearly identical." GAO sustained the protest, finding that the record did not support this determination:

> Since this finding [of near identicality] was one of the bases underlying [the awardee's] excellent rating under the technical factor, it follows that this rating, and the overall determination that the offerors were relatively equal under the non-cost factors, were unreasonable.[172]

In addition, if the agency evaluates a proposal in an internally inconsistent or contradictory manner, for example, by assigning both a strength and weakness to an offer for the same issue, the evaluation may be considered unreasonable. For example, in *T-C Transcription, Inc.*,[173] GAO deemed an evaluation unreasonable where it simultaneously assigned a deficiency for failing to "mention skill with ESL (English as second language)" and a strength to the same subfactor for requiring personnel to "have experience with ESL." Similarly, in *Honeywell Technology Solutions, Inc.; Wyle Laboratories, Inc.*,[174] GAO found an evaluation unreasonable where the agency failed to explain an inconsistency between the "strength" assigned to the awardee's proposed staffing level and the determination in the cost realism evaluation that the proposed staffing level was "significantly inadequate."[175]

An agency's evaluation must be consistent with solicitation requirements. GAO has long held that "it is improper for an agency to depart in any material way from the evaluation plan described in the solicitation without informing the offerors and

---

170. *See, e.g.*, Kaman Dayron, Inc., B-292997, Jan. 15, 2004, 2004 CPD ¶ 101.

171. *Id.*

172. *Id.* at 5.

173. T-C Transcription, Inc., B-401470, Sept. 16, 2009, 2009 CPD ¶ 172.

174. Honeywell Tech. Sols., Inc.; Wyle Labs., Inc., B-292354, Sept. 2, 2003, 2003 CPD ¶ 107.

175. The mere fact that an agency's cost realism analysis leads to an upward adjustment does not, however, necessarily mandate a negative technical evaluation. *See, e.g.*, The Aegis Techs., Inc., B-412884, June 28, 2016, 2016 CPD ¶ 175, in which GAO stated: "The RFP's description of the agency's intended cost realism evaluation provided that '[a] significant difference between the Offeror's proposed Cost/Price for the cost type CLINs and the GEMPC will be considered an indicator that the Offeror does not understand the requirement. . . .' However, this language pertains to the cost realism evaluation only; that is, it does not address the agency's technical evaluation. . . . There is no language in the RFP providing that an upward cost adjustment under the cost realism evaluation must result in a negative technical evaluation."

giving them an opportunity to structure their proposals with the new evaluation scheme in mind."[176] In *Fluor International, Inc. v. United States*,[177] the plaintiff succeeded on the merits where COFC found that "the record demonstrates that the Agency chose not to comply with the [solicitation] requirement and instead conducted irrational price reasonableness evaluations based on a newly devised evaluation method."

Consistent with the requirement that evaluations adhere to the solicitation criteria, an agency must also interpret the solicitation in a reasonable manner. Where an agency's evaluation of the solicitation is incorrect or unreasonable, its evaluation will also be considered unreasonable.[178] This also means that an agency may not double count an aspect of an evaluation in such a manner as to exaggerate its importance beyond that called for by the solicitation. In *J.A. Jones Management, Inc.*,[179] GAO explained that

> an agency may not double count, triple count, or otherwise greatly exaggerate the importance of any one listed factor; stated differently, where an RFP lists a number of evaluation factors of stated importance, a single one cannot be accorded more than the weight prescribed in the RFP's evaluation methodology by the agency repeatedly considering the same factor in conjunction with the other major factors.

Finally, GAO and COFC have concluded that an agency's evaluation must be well documented. This means that the contemporaneous documentation of the agency's evaluation decisions must be sufficient to allow GAO to review the evaluation and understand the agency's rationale. Without adequate documentation, the evaluation could be considered unreasonable.[180] The agency's obligation to document its source selection decision also applies to simplified acquisitions, such as those conducted under FAR Part 8.[181]

---

176. Arltec Hotel Grp., B-213788, Apr. 4, 1984, 84-1 CPD ¶ 381, at 2.

177. Fluor Intercontinental, Inc. v. United States, 147 Fed. Cl. 309, 337 (2020).

178. IAP-Hill, LLC, B-406289, Apr. 4, 2012, 2012 CPD ¶ 151, at 7 (finding that where the "RFP instructions to offerors were unequivocal," it is unreasonable to read in a different definition).

179. *See also* Arctic Slope Mission Servs., LLC, B-410992.5, Jan. 8, 2016, 2016 CPD ¶ 39 (protest sustained where agency overemphasized and thereby exaggerated the importance of corporate experience subfactor in evaluating proposals).

180. *See, e.g.*, Deployable Hosp. Sys., Inc., B-260778, July 21, 1995, 95-2 CPD ¶ 65, at 8 ("Implicit in the requirement that the agency's judgment in conducting a technical evaluation be reasonable is the requirement that these judgments be documented in sufficient detail to show that they are not arbitrary."); A1 Procurement, JVG, B-404618, Mar. 14, 2011, 2011 CPD ¶ 53, at 4 ("Where an agency fails to provide documentation of its evaluation, it bears the risk that there may not be adequately supporting rationale in the record for [GAO] to conclude the agency had a reasonable basis for the selection decision.").

181. *See* Language Select LLP, d.b.a. United Language Grp., B-415097, Nov. 14, 2017, 2017 CPD ¶ 359 (In "FAR subpart 8.4 acquisitions that require a statement of work . . . the record of the source

2. *Latent Ambiguities*

Latent ambiguities are more subtle than patent ambiguities, which as previously discussed are obvious, gross, or glaring errors.[182] As GAO has explained, when "there is a latent ambiguity, both parties' interpretation of the provision may be reasonable, and the appropriate course of action is to clarify the requirement and afford offerors an opportunity to submit proposals based on the clarified requirement."[183]

To prevail on a protest that the solicitation had a latent ambiguity, the protestor must demonstrate that (1) two or more reasonable interpretations of a provision exist, (2) the ambiguity was not obvious on the face of the solicitation, (3) the protester relied on its own interpretation in formulating its proposal, and (4) its reliance resulted in competitive prejudice.[184]

The rationale underlying a latent ambiguity protest is that an "agency must provide offerors with a sufficiently detailed solicitation that enables them to compete intelligently and on a relatively equal basis."[185]

"[A] party's particular interpretation need not be the most reasonable to support a finding of ambiguity; rather, a party need only show that its reading of the solicitation provisions is reasonable and susceptible of the understanding that it reached."[186] For example, in *Millennium Corp., Inc.*,[187] GAO sustained a protest where both the protester and the agency offered reasonable interpretations of the provision at issue. The solicitation instructed offerors to self-score their past performance based on the ratings they had received in their referenced Contractor Performance Assessment Reports (CPARs) and included a list of standard CPAR categories. The agency deducted points from the protester for calculating its score using a CPAR category not found in the solicitation's list of standard categories, asserting that the standard list was also an exclusive list. The protester asserted that the solicitation did not restrict offerors to only the CPAR categories listed in the solicitation, but instead called for self-scoring "based on each CPAR criteria" in the offerors' referenced CPARs. GAO found that both interpretations were defensible and that a latent ambiguity existed.

---

selection must document the rationale for any tradeoffs made in the selection," and the "rationale, or source selection decision documentation, must include *sufficient detail* to show that it is reasonable." (citing Harmonia Holdings Grp., LLC, B-413464, Nov. 4, 2016, 2017 CPD ¶ 62)).

182. *See* Harper Constr. Co., Inc., B-415042, Nov. 7, 2017, 2018 CPD ¶ 47.

183. *Id.* at 3.

184. *See* Millennium Corp., Inc., B-416485.2, Oct. 1, 2018, 2018 CPD ¶ 329; *Harper Constr. Co., Inc.*, B-415042.

185. Docmagic, Inc., B-415702, Feb. 16, 2018, 2018 CPD ¶ 96, at 2 (citing CWTSatoTravel, B-404479.2, Apr. 22, 2011, 2011 CPD ¶ 87, at 12).

186. The Arora Grp., Inc., B-288127, Sept. 14, 2001, 2001 CPD ¶ 154, at 4.

187. B-416485.2.

COFC similarly looks to ensure that (1) the protestor's interpretation and the agency's interpretation differ and (2) each falls within a "zone of reasonableness."[188] Although GAO and COFC employ what is nominally the same standard, they do not always reach the same result. For example, in *Guzar Mirbachako*,[189] the protester originally filed at GAO, arguing that the solicitation's electronic submission requirements were latently ambiguous as it did not expressly preclude offerors from submitting their proposals via zip files. GAO dismissed the protest as untimely because the Army notified GMT five hours before proposals were due that zip files were unacceptable. COFC took a different view and determined that the latent ambiguity precluded GMT from timely submitting its proposal and ordered the agency to review GMT's proposal and evaluate it for award.

For the protester to prevail, the parties' differing interpretations had to bear on the award decision. In *Docmagic, Inc.*,[190] GAO denied a protest where the record did not reflect that the agency and the protestor interpreted the solicitation differently at any time through award. *Docmagic* arose from a solicitation for software licenses. The solicitation stated that the agency sought the software as a service or as a solution hosted by the awardee. Docmagic claimed that a latent ambiguity existed because the contracting officer said—during the course of the protest—that the agency would host the software. The contracting officer, however, retracted her statement. GAO denied the protest because "the contemporaneous record reveal[ed] no evidence that, at any time prior to the contracting officer's 'mistaken' statements . . . the parties held differing interpretations of the solicitation."[191]

GAO and COFC both use a plain language approach to determine if a solicitation is ambiguous.[192] COFC interprets a solicitation as it would a contract, beginning with the "language of the written agreement," and giving "meaning to all of its parts."[193] As

188. NVT Techs., Inc. v. United States, 370 F.3d 1153, 1159 (Fed. Cir. 2004); *see also* Archura LLC v. United States, 112 Fed. Cl. 487, 500 (2013) ("A contract is ambiguous only when its language is susceptible to more than one reasonable interpretation.").

189. Guzar Mirbachakot Transp. v. United States, 104 Fed. Cl. 53, 68–69 (2012).

190. B-415702.

191. *Id.* at 3.

192. *See, e.g.*, Point Blank Enters., Inc., B-411839, Nov. 4, 2015, 2015 CPD ¶ 345, at 3; *NVT Techs.*, 370 F.3d at 1159 (citing Foley Co. v. United States, 11 F.3d 1032, 1034 (Fed. Cir. 1993)). GAO resolves questions of interpretation by reading the solicitation as a whole and in a manner that gives effect to all provisions. "[T]o be reasonable, and therefore valid, an interpretation must be consistent with such a reading." Desbuild Inc., B-413613.2, Jan. 13, 2017, 2017 CPD ¶ 23, at 4; CTIS, Inc., B-414852, Oct. 3, 2017, 2017 CPD ¶ 309 ("[W]e will resolve the matter by reading the solicitation as a whole and in a manner that gives effect to all of its provisions; to be reasonable, and therefore valid, an interpretation must be consistent with the solicitation when read as a whole and in a reasonable manner.").

193. *NVT Techs.*, 370 F.3d at 1159; Furniture by Thurston v. United States, 103 Fed. Cl. 505, 512 (2012) ("In determining whether rival interpretations of a solicitation are reasonable, the court must

noted earlier, to prevail the protestor must demonstrate that it relied on its own interpretation in preparing its proposal.[194]

Finally, the protester must establish that "but for" the ambiguity, the protester had a substantial chance of contract award.[195]

3. *Disparate Treatment*

A core principle in government procurement is the requirement that agencies treat offerors equally. In *BAE Technical Services, Inc.*,[196] GAO defined the principle as follows: "[I]t is fundamental that the contracting agency must treat all offerors equally, which includes providing a common basis for the preparation and the submission of proposals and not disparately evaluating offerors with respect to the same requirements."[197]

This means, inter alia, that an agency cannot apply stricter scrutiny to one offeror's proposal than it does to another's. In *BAE Technical Services*,[198] GAO concluded that even though the agency's concerns with the protester's proposal were reasonable, the evaluation was not because it applied a more stringent standard to the protester's offer:

> It appears to us that, while the agency viewed [protester]'s proposal with reasonable skepticism, it abandoned this skepticism in evaluating [awardee]'s proposal. This constituted application of different evaluation standards—one stricter than the other—to the two proposals, and was unreasonable.[199]

'begin with the plain language of the document.'") (quoting Banknote Corp. of Am., Inc. v. United States, 365 F.3d 1345, 1353 (Fed. Cir. 2004)).

194. *See NVT Techs.*, 370 F.3d at 1162 (protester must show reliance); Harper Constr. Co., Inc., B-415042, Nov. 7, 2017, 2018 CPD ¶ 47 (protester's understanding of latently ambiguous term caused it to submit a proposal agency found technically unacceptable); *see also* Maint. Engineers, Inc. v. United States, 21 Cl. Ct. 553 (1990) (protest failed where, contrary to protester's assertions, record showed that it had not calculated its proposed price based on the interpretation of the solicitation it advanced during the protest).

195. *See* SunGard Data Sys., Inc., B-410025, Oct. 10, 2014, 2014 CPD ¶ 304, at 6 ("We will not sustain a post-award protest against an ambiguous solicitation provision where there is no evidence that any offeror was prejudiced by the ambiguity."); AEgis Techs. Grp., Inc., B-412884, June 28, 2016, 2016 CPD ¶ 175 (protest denied despite presence of latent ambiguity where protester's inferior technical and past performance rating precluded possibility of award).

196. B-296699, Oct. 5, 2005, 2006 CPD ¶ 91, at 5.

197. *See also* Cubic Applications, Inc., B-411305, July 9, 2015, 2015 CPD ¶ 218 (same); 2M Research Servs., LLC v. United States, 139 Fed. Cl. 471 (2018) (judgment entered for protester where record showed agency failed to treat offerors fairly and equally and evaluate their proposals evenhandedly).

198. B-296699.

199. *Id.* at 9.

This means that not only must an agency refrain from applying a stricter level of scrutiny to one offeror's proposal than it does to another's, it must also treat offerors' proposals the same with respect to evaluated strengths and weaknesses, evaluation of costs, and, as addressed later, during the conduct of discussions.

Practically speaking, disparate treatment arguments often are raised as supplemental protest grounds rather than in the initial protest. This is because debriefings and other information an offeror will have as a result of the award decision often do not provide the relevant facts necessary to form the basis of a disparate treatment argument. Rather, these facts often only come to light during the review of the agency record, for example, by analyzing the awardee's proposal or conducting a side-by-side comparison of the evaluations of each offeror. With that said, if the protester has information prior to submitting its initial protest that might suggest disparate treatment of some kind, it should raise it at that time rather than waiting for the Agency Report to confirm the information. Not only could the disparate treatment argument be considered untimely if it is not raised based on the initial information, but the allegation could also serve as a basis upon which to request the documents necessary to validate this ground of protest.

4. Unstated Evaluation Criteria/Waived Requirements

Two additional protest arguments that often arise—unstated evaluation criteria and waived requirements—are, in effect, two sides of the same coin and are often alleged in the alternative. In each, the focus of the protest is on what was required (or not required) by the solicitation and whether the agency's evaluation was consistent with the information provided to offerors by the solicitation. These arguments may be advanced as a complement to a latent ambiguity ground of protest.

a. Unstated Evaluation Criteria

Under an unstated evaluation criteria theory, the protester must show that it was faulted for a weakness, or the awardee was credited with a strength, that has no logical relation to the stated evaluation criteria. GAO has long stated that agencies are "required to evaluate proposals based solely on the factors identified in the solicitation."[200] The agency, however, is not limited to a strict interpretation of the factors identified in the solicitation; rather, the agency "may properly apply evaluation considerations that are not expressly identified in the RFP if those considerations are reasonably and logically encompassed within the stated evaluation criteria, so long as there is a clear nexus linking them."[201] An agency may not, however, "give impor-

200. Intercon Assocs. Inc., B-298282, Aug. 10, 2006, 2006 CPD ¶ 121, at 4.
201. Phoenix Air Grp., B-412796.2, Sept. 26, 2016, 2016 CPD ¶ 308, at 9.

tance to specific factors, subfactors, or criteria beyond that which would reasonably be expected by offerors."[202] Thus, GAO's (and COFC's) analysis in these protests often focuses on the "nexus" between the express solicitation language and the way in which the agency evaluated proposals and whether offerors could have reasonably recognized that nexus.

For example, in *Risk Analysis and Mitigation Partners*,[203] GAO sustained a protest in which the protester was assessed a weakness for, among other things, a failure to address certain standards that were not specifically referenced in the solicitation (but were listed in a document on the agency's website containing approximately 400 standards). In response, the agency pointed out (and GAO acknowledged) that the solicitation required offerors to ensure "compliance with FEMA standards" in responding to a performance objective. GAO concluded, however, that the mere reference to the standards did not "reasonably advise[ ] offerors of the agency's view that offerors were required to specifically address their experience" with the specific standards for which the protester was given a weakness.[204] Moreover, GAO noted that the agency did not assess weaknesses for the protester's failure to address every standard listed on the website, but only for specific standards that were not specifically called out in the solicitation; thus offerors "could not have known that the agency expected the offerors to focus their proposals on a particular number of the numerous standards listed" on the website.[205]

Similarly, in *Apex-MBM, Joint Venture*,[206] GAO concluded that the agency had used unstated evaluation criteria in rejecting an offeror's proposal because it failed to propose site-specific staff deployments and supplies. In reaching this conclusion, GAO noted that the solicitation required only that offerors describe their "proposed plans, processes, procedures, and systems, and provide all supporting data and documentation," and did not specifically require site-specific staff deployments.[207] Moreover, the solicitation provided offerors only 15 pages in which to describe their technical solutions and included a performance work statement stating that *after award* offerors would submit schedules and a list of supplies and equipment needed. Thus, GAO concluded that an offeror could not "reasonably understand that it was required to propose staff deployments . . . as well as tools, supplies and equipment" for each of the sites.[208]

---

202. *Id.*

203. B-409687, July 15, 2014, 2014 CPD ¶ 214.

204. *Id.* at 7.

205. *Id.* at 8.

206. B-405107.3, Oct. 3, 2011, 2011 CPD ¶ 263.

207. *Id.* at 1.

208. *Id.* at 4; *see also* Coburn Contractors, B-408279.2, Sept. 30, 2013, 2013 CPD ¶ 230 (protest sustained where agency assigned weakness to proposal for failing to include a list of subcontractors, when the RFP required only the successful contractor to provide such a list).

In contrast, in *Micro Technologies, LLC*,[209] GAO concluded that an agency's evaluation of the specific tasks necessary for performance of overall sample tasks was reasonably related to the stated evaluation criteria. In that case, the solicitation required offerors to respond to three sample task orders that would be evaluated to determine "whether the offeror understood the problem and had a feasible approach to solving it."[210] In evaluating the responses, the agency "prepared a list of key focus and lower level focus areas that it believed an offeror would have to address to demonstrate that it understood the task[.]"[211] GAO held that this evaluation was reasonably related to the solicitation requirements, noting that "understanding and feasibility . . . are not factors that can be evaluated on their own, without reference to the work to be accomplished" and that the sample task order attachment to the RFP stated that offerors should describe all tasks necessary for the effort.[212] As a result, GAO concluded that offerors were reasonably on notice that the agency would consider the tasks it believed were necessary to perform the sample task and denied the protest.

b. Waived or Relaxed Requirements

While an unstated evaluation criteria protest looks to whether the evaluators relied on a requirement not found in the solicitation, the waived or relaxed requirement protest ground asserts that the agency *failed* to apply a solicitation or specification requirement to the awardee's proposal. According to GAO, "it is a fundamental principle in a negotiated procurement that a proposal that fails to conform to a material solicitation requirement is technically unacceptable and cannot form the basis for award."[213] Thus, where an offeror is awarded a contract despite failing to meet material solicitation requirements, a protester may allege that the agency has waived or relaxed such requirements and has evaluated proposals in a manner inconsistent with the solicitation. For example, in *J Square, Inc. dba University Loft Co.*,[214] GAO held that the agency had relaxed a material solicitation requirement associated with the procurement of barracks furniture. In particular, the solicitation called for beds with a tool-free assembly. The protester alleged that the agency had failed to evaluate the technical acceptability of the offeror's proposal to ensure that its beds could be assembled without tools and thus improperly relaxed this requirement. GAO first concluded that "clearly stated technical requirements are considered material to the

209. B-403713.6, June 9, 2012, 2012 CPD ¶ 131.
210. *Id.* at 3.
211. *Id.* at 2.
212. *Id.* at 3.
213. Trandes Corp., B-411742, Oct. 13, 2015, 2015 CPD ¶ 317, at 4.
214. B-407302, Dec. 17, 2012, 2013 CPD ¶ 9.

needs of the government," then sustained the protest, finding that the agency had failed to reasonably evaluate the awardee's technical acceptability.[215]

Similarly, in *S.M. Stoller Corp.*,[216] the protester contended that the agency had waived or relaxed a material solicitation requirement in its evaluation of the awardee's technical proposal. In that procurement, offerors were required to submit a corrective action investigation plan and a corrective action decision document related to each of several corrective action units associated with environmental remediation service locations. In its proposal, the awardee consolidated three of the corrective action units into a single corrective action unit for purposes of its technical approach. The protester alleged that the agency's acceptance of this technical approach, which deviated from the requirements of the solicitation in a way that other offerors could not have foreseen, was improper. GAO agreed, sustaining the protest and concluding that the agency had waived or relaxed the requirement to respond to each of the corrective action units separately and did not put offerors on notice that it would accept an offer consolidating the units.

As with any protest ground, an offeror must show not only that the agency waived or relaxed a material solicitation requirement, but also that it was prejudiced. In the context of a waived or relaxed requirement, this does *not* mean that an offeror must show that the waiver benefited the awardee. Rather, the protester must demonstrate that it "would have submitted a different proposal or quotation or that it could have done something else to improve its chances for award had it known that the agency would waive the requirement."[217] When an offeror cannot demonstrate what it would have done differently, its protest will be denied.[218] This is an important prac-

215. *Id.* at 4.

216. B-400937, Mar. 25, 2009, 2009 CPD ¶ 193.

217. Glock, Inc., B-414401, June 5, 2017, 2017 CPD ¶ 180.

218. This test for prejudice likely does not apply in situations where the agency simply discards a solicitation requirement, even though the awardee complied with it. GAO has previously held that under such circumstances, the agency has not "waived" the offerors' obligation to comply with the requirement; rather, the agency simply failed to adhere to the solicitation's stated evaluation criteria. *See, e.g.*, Tribalco, LLC, B-414120, Feb. 21, 2017, 2017 CPD ¶ 73, at 10 n.7 (refusing to apply "the principle that where an agency waives a requirement, the question of prejudice turns on whether the protester would have submitted a different offer with a reasonable possibility of being selected for award had it known the requirement would be waived" because the agency had not waived requirements); *see also* 2M Research Servs., LLC v. United States, 139 Fed. Cl. 471, 479 (2018) (agency's failure to comply with terms of solicitation constitutes "a quintessential example[] of conduct which lacks a rational basis"); Fluor Intercontinental, Inc., 147 Fed. Cl. 309, 337–38 (2020) (court rejected government's argument that failure to comply with solicitation requirement was nothing more than permissible waiver and therefore did not require plaintiff to prove it would have submitted a different proposal; instead, court concluded that prejudice was presumed, and that in any event, plaintiff demonstrated prejudice by showing that agency's reliance on improper evaluation method was "significant to the protestor's chance of being awarded the contract").

tice note for drafting protests concerning relaxed or waived solicitation requirements that a protester should include in its initial protest all aspects and allegations forming the basis of its protest, including its basis for prejudice.

5. Unequal or Misleading Discussions

The term "discussions" refers to communications with offerors after receipt of initial proposals and following establishment of a competitive range. The underlying purpose of discussions is to determine the acceptability of an offeror's proposal or to allow offerors to strengthen their proposals so that the procuring agency obtains a better offering (e.g., an improved technical solution and/or a lower price).

a. Discussions versus Other Types of Informational Exchanges

i. Discussions

GAO has long held that the "acid test" for determining if a particular exchange constitutes discussions is "whether the agency has provided an opportunity for proposals to be revised or modified,"[219] or "when an agency communicates with an offeror for the purpose of obtaining information essential to determine the acceptability of the proposal."[220] This may be an actual pen-and-paper change to the proposal or any other exchange the agency needs to determine the acceptability of a proposal.[221]

Exchanges other than discussions (such as "clarifications") generally do not allow for the submission of proposal revisions. The regulations governing discussions—as well as other types of exchanges after receipt of initial proposals—are found at FAR 15.306.

The idea behind discussions is fairly straightforward: informational exchanges between offerors and the procuring agency may help offerors improve the quality of their proposals—and improve the bargains they offer to the government. At the same time, certain initial proposals may be so inferior to competing proposals that the procuring agency decides they are not worth the time and expense to pursue further. The process by which the agency separates the wheat from the chaff is known as establishing the "competitive range." Ordinarily, the competitive range needs to include only "the most highly rated proposals," although the agency may reserve its right within the solicitation to reduce the range further for economy's sake.[222] Thus, the competitive range may comprise all the submitted proposals or consist only of a competitive

219. Raytheon Co., B-404998, July 25, 2011, 2011 CPD ¶ 232, at 4.
220. Global Language Ctr., B-413503.8, June 1, 2017, 2017 CPD ¶ 238, at 4–5.
221. *See* Int'l Waste Indus., B-411338, July 7, 2015, 2015 CPD ¶ 196.
222. FAR 15.306(c).

range of one. As previously discussed, offerors excluded from the competitive range may protest their exclusion in a pre-award protest.

Discussions may be oral, written, or some combination thereof. Agencies often issue Evaluation Notices (ENs), advising offerors of their initial evaluation results and areas they should consider revising. Under FAR 15.306(d)(3), if an agency holds discussions, it must, at a minimum, raise with each offeror in the competitive range all significant weaknesses, deficiencies, and adverse past performance information to which they have not yet had the opportunity to respond.[223] Although GAO will take note of the label the agency attaches to a particular defect, it also will consider the context of the evaluation to determine whether the defect was so significant it should have been raised in discussions.[224]

Importantly, once the agency has addressed an issue in discussions, it need not address it again. Thus, if the agency explains its concern to an offeror and the offeror makes revisions that do not solve the problem, the agency is under no obligation to point this fact out. Nor is the agency required to reopen discussions to address problems the offeror first introduces after discussions have closed—for example, when an offeror's final proposal revisions correct one problem but inadvertently cause a new one.[225]

ii. Clarifications and Communications

Clarifications, unlike discussions, are "limited exchanges that do not allow offerors to revise their proposals but may allow them to clarify certain aspects of their proposals or resolve minor clerical errors."[226] Clarifications may occur after a competitive range has been established, or even when discussions and proposal revisions are not contemplated at all. Clarifications "cannot be used to cure proposal deficiencies or material omissions, materially alter the technical or cost elements of the proposal, and/or otherwise revise the proposal."[227]

223. The "opportunity to respond" need not arise in the course of discussions. For example, this requirement may be met if an offeror had an opportunity to respond to a negative past performance rating during the administration of the contract giving rise to that negative review. *See, e.g.*, Erickson Helicopters, Inc., B-409903, Sept. 5, 2014, 2014 CPD ¶ 288 (protest ground regarding unequal discussions denied where the protester "was provided the opportunity to address its performance of the incumbent contract, given that this adverse past performance information was contained in CPARS to which the protester was provided an opportunity to comment"); *see also* Torres-Advanced Enter. Sols., LLC, B-412755.2, June 7, 2016, 2016 CPD ¶ 167. Also, under FAR 15.306(a)(2), even if the agency decides not to hold discussions, it still may give offerors the opportunity to address adverse past performance information to which the offeror has not had an opportunity to respond.

224. *See* AT&T Corp., B-299542.3, Nov. 6, 2007, 2008 CPD ¶ 65.

225. TASC, Inc., B-412674.2, Aug. 25, 2016, 2016 CPD ¶ 230, at 5.

226. FAR 15.306(a)(1), (2).

227. STG, Inc., B-411415, July 22, 2015, 2015 CPD ¶ 240, at 7.

Communications are a third category of exchanges and occur before the competitive range has been established.[228] Like clarifications, they do not allow offerors "to cure proposal deficiencies or material omissions, materially alter the technical or cost elements of the proposal, and/or otherwise revise the proposal."[229] Communications are intended only to permit the government to improve its understanding of proposals or past performance information and address minor issues before a competitive range is established. When adverse past performance information to which the offeror has not yet had an opportunity to respond would be the "determining factor" in excluding the offeror from the competitive range, the agency must open communications with the offeror to address that information.[230] For all other issues, the agency may hold communications if an offeror's "exclusion from, or inclusion in, the competitive range is uncertain."[231] Because communications occur prior to establishment of the competitive range, they do not come up often in the context of post-award protests concerning discussions.

b. Why the Distinction Matters

Discussions, when they are conducted, must be meaningful, equal, and not misleading. Generally speaking, an agency may conduct clarifications with an individual offeror without having to conduct exchanges of any sort with the other offerors. However, as discussed further later, when an agency opens discussions with one offeror, it must treat the other offerors equally and open discussions with all offerors in the competitive range.[232] That is why the distinction between discussions and clarifications matters: Because the dividing line between clarifications and discussions is not always obvious, it sometimes is possible to argue that an agency's borderline exchange with one offeror was actually a discussion, even though the agency may not have intended to conduct discussions at all. It does not matter how the agency characterizes the exchange; rather, the key question is whether an offeror was afforded the opportunity to revise its proposal.[233]

---

228. *See* FAR 15.306(b).

229. FAR 15.306(b)(2).

230. FAR 15.306(b)(1)(i).

231. FAR 15.306(b)(1)(ii).

232. Cascadian Am. Enters., B-412208.3, Feb. 5, 2016, 2016 CPD ¶ 29.

233. *See, e.g.*, Standard Commc'ns, Inc., B-406021, Jan. 24, 2012, 2012 CPD ¶ 51 (because the agency's exchanges with the awardee allowed it to materially revise its quote, discussions had been opened, thereby requiring agency to conduct discussions with protester); JWK Int'l Corp., 52 Fed. Cl. at 661 (Clarifications "are not to be used to cure proposal deficiencies or material omissions, materially alter the technical or cost elements of the proposal, or otherwise revise the proposal.").

It should be noted, however, that exchanges directed at determining an offeror's responsibility are not subject to the rules regarding discussions. *See* Engility Corp., B-413202, Sept. 2, 2016, 2016 CPD ¶ 251 ("the rules relating to clarifications and discussions have no application to possible inquiries regarding

Having a protest sustained on this ground can result in an opening of discussions as corrective action, which may be all the protester needs to correct the weaknesses that prevented it from award the first time around. An unfortunate side-effect posed by the risk that an agency's attempt to clarify an issue will be deemed "discussions" is that agencies sometimes refrain from engaging in legitimate clarifications and end up awarding the contract to an offeror that submitted an inferior proposal. GAO and COFC differ on the deference accorded to an agency's decision to refrain from clarifications. GAO has long held that such decisions are purely within agency discretion.[234] COFC has taken a stricter view of an agency's exercise of its discretion in this regard. For example, in *Level 3 Communications, LLC v. United States*,[235] the court concluded that the agency's decision not to seek clarifications was arbitrary and capricious where the protester's price was much lower than that of the awardee.[236]

c. Challenging the Agency's Conduct of Discussions

A protest arising from an agency's improper conduct of discussions may rest on one or more of three bases: (1) the discussions were not meaningful, (2) the discussions were misleading, and/or (3) the discussions were unequal.

i. Were the Discussions Not Meaningful?

Discussions are not meaningful if the agency has serious concerns about the evaluated proposal but does not clearly raise them with the offeror. Agencies are not required to raise mere weaknesses in discussions. Nor are they required to advise an offeror that its price is too high, provided that the agency has not determined that the price is so high as to be unreasonable. If, on the other hand, the evaluators have identified

---

matters of responsibility. Simply stated, an agency's exchanges with an offeror regarding matters of responsibility do not constitute discussions.") (citing McKissack+Delcan JV II, B-401973.2, Jan. 13, 2010, 2010 CPD ¶ 28).

234. Cubic Simulation Sys., Inc., B-410006, Oct. 8, 2014, 2014 CPD ¶ 299, at 7 (holding that agency was within its rights to refuse to conduct clarifications and refusing to apply COFC case law); PN & A, Inc., B-406368, Apr. 23, 2012, 2012 CPD ¶ 145, at 3 (holding that agency was not required to conduct clarifications); *see also* CJW—Desbuild JV, LLC, B-414219, Mar. 17, 2017, 2017 CPD ¶ 94, at 4 n.2 (refusing to apply COFC case law and holding that failure to submit proof of a joint venture agreement was not a minor clerical error).

235. 129 Fed. Cl. 487 (2016).

236. *See also* BCPeabody Constr. Servs., Inc. v. United States, 112 Fed. Cl. 502 (2013) (holding that contracting officer abused her discretion when refusing to seek clarification from disappointed bidder regarding clerical error in its offer); *but see* Bd. of Regents of Nevada Sys. of Higher Educ. on Behalf of Desert Research Inst. v. United States, 132 Fed. Cl. 435 (2017), *redacted opinion issued*, No. 16-376C, 2017 WL 2856416 (Fed. Cl. July 5, 2017) (holding that DOE was not required to seek clarification from bidder regarding workbook where DOE treated missing workbook as material omission rather than clerical error eligible for clarification).

significant weaknesses, deficiencies, and adverse past performance information to which the offeror has not had the opportunity to respond, those must be raised.[237]

An agency need not spoon-feed an offeror or explain the evaluated problems in great detail, but it must at least lead the offeror into "the areas of its proposal requiring amplification or revision in a manner to materially enhance the offeror's potential for receiving the award."[238] Protests alleging lack of meaningful discussions often end up in a fight over whether general concerns the agency raised in discussions were clear enough to lead the protester to specific deficiencies that the agency had identified but did not expressly address.[239]

ii. Were the Discussions Misleading?

Discussions are misleading if they prejudicially communicate (whether by statements, questions, or silence) a problem that is not there, fail to communicate a problem, assure an offeror that a problem has been resolved when it has not been, or otherwise induce acts or omissions that are competitively prejudicial to the offeror. For example, if an agency tells an offeror that its price is unrealistically low (when it really is not), and the offeror raises the price, only to lose the contract in part because its price was too high, there may be a viable protest ground on the basis of misleading discussions.[240]

iii. Were the Discussions Unequal?

Unequal discussions are a form of disparate treatment. Discussions need not be identical—an offeror with numerous weaknesses, for example, naturally will receive "more" discussion attention than an offeror with fewer weaknesses. But the basis upon which they are conducted must be equal.

At the most basic level, if an agency conducts discussions with one offeror, it must do so with all offerors that have not been excluded from the competitive range. To do otherwise is unequal treatment.[241] Likewise, if an agency follows up with an

---

237. Crowley Logistics, Inc., B-412628.3, Apr. 19, 2016, 2016 CPD ¶ 120 (discussions were not meaningful where the agency cited a concern with the protestor's proposal in award decision but did not raise that concern during discussions).

238. Lewis-Price & Assocs., Inc., B-409851, Aug. 26, 2014, 2014 CPD ¶ 263, at 7.

239. *See* West Sound Servs. Grp., B-406583.2, July 3, 2013, 2013 CPD ¶ 276.

240. Vencore Servs. & Sols., Inc., B-412949, July 18, 2016, 2016 CPD ¶ 346; *see also* Mission Essential Personnel, B-407493, Jan. 6, 2013, 2013 CPD ¶ 22, at 3–4 (discussions misleading where agency identified three reasons for assigning the protestor a "no-go" rating but raised only one of its concerns during discussions).

241. Rotech Healthcare, Inc., B-413024, Aug. 17, 2016, 2016 CPD ¶ 225 ("Where, as here, an agency conducts discussions with one offeror, it must conduct discussions with all offerors in the competitive range.") (citing Gulf Copper Ship Repair, Inc., B-293706.5, Sept. 10, 2004, 2005 CPD ¶ 108); SRA Int'l, Inc., B-410973, Apr. 8, 2015, 2016 CPD ¶ 32.

offeror that did not resolve a concern on the first round of discussions (despite having no obligation to do so), the agency must treat other offerors in the same way.[242]

By their nature, allegations of unequal discussions tend to be supplemental protest grounds that generally are apparent only after the agency record has been produced.

d. What about Prejudice?

As previously explained, prejudice is an essential element of every viable protest. This is the "so what?" question. It is the protester's responsibility to articulate how the alleged procurement error prevented the protester from having a substantial chance of contract award. In the context of discussions, this generally entails explaining what the protester would have done differently if its discussions had been meaningful, not misleading, or equal, and why those changes reasonably could have put the protester in line for award. Although GAO resolves doubts about prejudice in favor of the protester, the wider the competitive gap between the protester and the awardee, the more closely GAO will scrutinize prejudice.[243]

e. Agency Discretion to Conduct Discussions

As a general rule, in negotiated procurements under FAR Part 15, agencies have nearly unfettered discretion to conduct or not conduct discussions and clarifications. Although GAO has held that this discretion is not absolute, and therefore is subject to the rule of reason, one is hard put to find a single GAO decision that has sustained a protest on the grounds that the agency abused its discretion by not opening discussions or conducting clarifications in a Part 15 procurement. In short, even if a proposal contains an obvious, easily correctable error that could be fixed with a simple clarification, the agency has the discretion to evaluate the proposal as written and not seek a clarification.

That said, there are a couple of wrinkles in the rule. The first involves DoD procurements valued at more than $100 million. The DFARS currently provides: "For acquisitions with an estimated value of $100 million or more, contracting officers *should conduct discussions*."[244] In two recent decisions, GAO has suggested that this fairly new regulation establishes a default expectation that discussions will occur on all DoD procurements valued at more than $100 million, unless the procuring agency

242. Front Line Apparel Grp., B-295989, June 1, 2005, 2005 CPD ¶ 116 (agency's actions amounted to disparate treatment when it improperly held second round of discussions with awardee but not protester).

243. *See* DynCorp Int'l LLC, B-411465, Aug. 4, 2015, 2015 CPD ¶ 228.

244. DFARS 215.306(c)(1) (emphasis added).

can explain why discussions should not be conducted.[245] Although GAO has not, as of this writing, sustained a protest on this ground, one suspects it is only a matter of time before it happens. Protesters will face interesting timeliness hurdles and can expect agencies (and awardees) to argue that any challenges based on this regulation should be raised as pre-award protests.

While clarifications are always discretionary under FAR Part 15 negotiated procurements, they can be obligatory under a FAR Part 14 sealed-bid procurement. In a sealed-bid acquisition, contracting officers "shall" allow a bidder "an opportunity to cure any deficiency resulting from a minor informality or irregularity in a bid or waive the deficiency, whichever is to the advantage of the Government."[246] The FAR provides a nonexclusive list of minor bid informalities and irregularities that may be rectified after bid opening.[247] None of these rules apply to negotiated procurements through competitive proposals, however.

Finally, as noted earlier, agencies are required to conduct "communications" with an offeror prior to establishing the competitive range if there is adverse past performance information to which the offeror has not had the opportunity to respond (for example, in regular past performance reviews), and that information would be determinative in excluding the offeror from the competitive range.[248]

6. Out of Scope Contract Modifications

Before modifying a previously awarded contract, the contracting officer must first determine that the planned modification falls within the scope of the contract, that is, it could have been reasonably anticipated by competitors at the time of contract award. Such in-scope modifications are permissible, and, as a general matter, GAO will not entertain protests of contract modifications, treating them as related to contract administration and beyond the scope of its bid protest function.[249]

But "[a]n agency may not modify a contract by changing or relaxing requirements where the resulting work is fundamentally different from the work anticipated by the original solicitation."[250] GAO will, therefore, entertain protests alleging that a modification changed the scope of the contract such that the original and modified

---

245. *See* McCann-Erickson USA, Inc., B-414787, Sept. 18, 2017, 2017 CPD ¶ 300, at 9 n.10; Sci. Applications Int'l Corp., B-413501, Nov. 9, 2016, 2016 CPD ¶ 328, at 8–11.

246. FAR 14.405.

247. *Id.*

248. FAR 15.306(b)(1)(i).

249. *See* Zodiac of N. Am., Inc., B-414260, Mar. 28, 2017, 2017 CPD ¶ 107 ("Once a contract is awarded, however, our Office will generally not review modifications to that contract because such matters are related to contract administration and are beyond the scope of our bid protest function.") (citing 4 C.F.R. § 21.5(a)).

250. Poly-Pacific Tech., Inc., B-296029, June 1, 2005, 2005 CPD ¶ 105, at 4.

contracts are materially different. In determining whether a modification is within or outside the scope of the original contract, GAO looks to the

> extent of any changes in the type of work, performance period, and costs between the modification and the underlying contract. Where an agency has relaxed a contract's performance requirements, [GAO] also looks to whether the change in requirements was the type that reasonably would have been anticipated under the solicitation, and whether the modification materially changed the field of competition for the requirement.[251]

A similar analysis is applied at COFC.[252]

7. Organizational Conflicts of Interest

FAR Subpart 9.5 addresses Organizational Conflicts of Interest (OCIs), and requires contracting officers "to avoid, neutralize, or mitigate potential significant conflicts of interest so as to prevent an unfair competitive advantage or the existence of conflicting roles that might impair a contractor's objectivity."[253] Protests based on alleged OCIs are typically brought either by a disappointed offeror claiming that the awardee had an OCI, or by an offeror eliminated from competition because the contracting officer concluded it had an unmitigated (or unmitigable) OCI. OCIs arise under one or more of three categories: "biased ground rules, unequal access to information, and impaired objectivity."[254]

The contracting officer has the responsibility for determining whether an OCI exists, and his or her judgment is entitled to deference. As GAO explained in *C2C Innovative Solutions*:

> We review the reasonableness of a contracting officer's OCI investigation and, where an agency has given meaningful consideration to whether a significant conflict of interest exists, we will not substitute our judgment for the agency's, absent clear evidence that the agency's conclusion is unreasonable. In this regard, the identification

251. *Id.* at 3.

252. *See* Cardinal Maint. Serv., Inc. v. United States, 63 Fed. Cl. 98, 109 (2004) ("Where, as here, the amount of additional work nearly doubles the price of the contract that was awarded, and the nature of the work was so substantially increased that the change provision of the contract had to be deleted to accomplish the modifications, the originally awarded contract has been materially changed.").

253. Vion Corp., B-409985.4, Apr. 3, 2015, 2015 CPD ¶ 141 (citing FAR 9.504(a), 9.505).

254. C2C Innovative Sols., Inc., B-416289, July 30, 2018, 2018 CPD ¶ 269 (citing McConnell Jones Lanier & Murphy, LLP, B–409681.3, Oct. 21, 2015, 2015 CPD ¶ 341, at 13). OCIs are different from personal conflicts of interest, which are addressed in FAR Subpart 3.11 and involve a "situation in which a covered employee has a financial interest, personal activity, or relationship that could impair the employee's ability to act impartially and in the best interest of the Government when performing under the contract." BAE Sys. Tech. Sols. & Servs., Inc., B-411810.3, June 24, 2016, 2016 CPD ¶ 174 (citing FAR 3.1101).

of conflicts of interest is a fact-specific inquiry that requires the exercise of considerable discretion. A protester must identify "hard facts" that indicate the existence or potential existence of a conflict; mere inference or suspicion of an actual or potential conflict is not enough. Nonetheless, once it has been determined that an actual or potential OCI exists, the protester is not required to demonstrate prejudice; rather, harm from the conflict is presumed to occur.[255]

It is not unusual for a protester to include an OCI ground in a supplemental protest upon receipt of the Agency Report that includes the protester's technical proposal identifying, among other things, the awardee's key personnel and/or subcontractors and their backgrounds. In responding to an OCI ground of protest, the agency may conduct an investigation and include the results in the Agency Report, or, if circumstances warrant, conduct an investigation as a corrective action and request that the protest be dismissed as academic.[256]

a. Biased Ground Rules

OCIs arising from biased ground rules involve "situations in which a firm, as part of its performance of a government contract, has in some sense set the ground rules for another government contract by, for example, writing the statement of work or the specifications."[257] In such cases, GAO has explained, "the primary concern is that the firm could skew the competition, whether intentionally or not, in favor of itself," or "that the firm, by virtue of its special knowledge of the agency's future requirements, would have an unfair advantage in the competition for those requirements."[258]

International Business Machines Corp.[259] provides an illustrative example of a biased ground rules OCI. GAO held that the contracting officer reasonably eliminated the protester from the competition where a subcontractor of one of its subcontractors "[a]ssisted in the development of the RFP, the performance work statement,

---

255. B-416289, July 30, 2018, 2018 CPD ¶ 269 (internal citations omitted).

256. The investigation of an OCI is one of the few instances where a post hoc, noncontemporaneous analysis by the agency is permitted and not uncommon. *See, e.g.*, Sci. Applications Int'l Corp., B-406899, Sept. 26, 2012, 2012 CPD ¶ 282 ("both [GAO] and the Court of Federal Claims have recognized that an agency may investigate possible OCIs after the filing of bid protests") (citing PÇCP Constructors, JV, B-405036, Aug. 4, 2011, 2011 CPD ¶ 156, at 16; NETSTAR-1 Gov't Consulting, Inc. v. United States, 101 Fed. Cl. 511, 521 (2011)).

257. Aetna Gov't Health Plans, Inc., Found. Health Fed. Servs., Inc., B-254397, July 27, 1995, 95-2 CPD ¶ 129, at 8.

258. *Id.* (citing FAR 9.505–1, 9.505–2); *see also* BAE Sys. Tech. Sols. & Servs., Inc., B-411810.3, June 24, 2016, 2016 CPD ¶ 174 ("the relevant concern for a biased ground rules OCI is not simply whether a firm drafted specifications that were adopted into the solicitation, but, rather, whether a firm was in a position to affect the competition, intentionally or not, in favor of itself") (citing L-3 Servs., Inc., B-400134.11, Sept. 3, 2009, 2009 CPD ¶ 171, at 8).

259. B-410639, Jan. 15, 2015, 2015 CPD ¶ 41.

the [independent government cost estimate], the solicitation amendments, and the responses to questions submitted by interested firms."[260] GAO explained that neither the indirect nature of the OCI, nor the protester's mitigation efforts, rendered the OCI determination unreasonable:

> Given the extensive involvement of [the employee] in drafting and advising on the ground rules of this procurement, and given that there is no basis to distinguish between a firm and its affiliates, at least where concerns about potentially biased ground rules are at issue, we find that the protester has not shown the contracting officer's OCI determination to be unreasonable. In this regard, although [the protester] responded to the contracting officer's OCI inquiries by asserting that [the employee] was firewalled from BAH, and stating that BAH would end its employment of [the employee], we believe that the contracting officer reasonably concluded that IBM had failed to mitigate the potential OCI here. As our Office has previously noted, due to the ultimate relationship of one entity to another, including an identity of interests between the entities, a firewall does not resolve an organizational conflict of interest involving biased ground rules. Further, as noted by the contracting officer, termination of [the employee's] employment after he had influenced the ground rules for the procurement in no way avoided any potential harm in this regard.[261]

b. Unequal Access to Information

An unequal access to information OCI arises from a contractor's ability to access nonpublic information as a result of its performance of a government contract, where such access may provide it with a competitive advantage in future competitions. As GAO explained in *Absolute Business Solutions*:

> As relevant to the allegation here, an unequal access to information OCI exists where a firm has access to nonpublic information as part of its performance of a government contract, and where that information may provide the firm an unfair competitive advantage in a later competition for a government contract. FAR §§ 9.505(b), 9.505-4; *Cyberdata Techs., Inc.*, B-411070 *et al.*, May 1, 2015, 2015 CPD ¶ 150 at 6.[262]

In short, an unequal access to information OCI accounts for the fact that certain contractors, by the very nature of the work they perform, are in a position to access and leverage competitively useful information not available to their competitors. These contractors are paid for the work they perform, but they also pay a price—potential preclusion from competitions for related work.

260. *Id.* at 7.
261. *Id.* (internal citations omitted).
262. B-418184, Jan. 21, 2020, 2020 CPD ¶ 35, at 4.

To preserve the integrity of the procurement process, GAO has made clear that even if only a "*potential* OCI exists, the protester is not required to demonstrate prejudice; rather, harm from the conflict is presumed to occur."[263]

A contractor's hiring of a former government official presents concerns closely analogous to an unequal access to information OCI. Indeed, as GAO has recognized, an allegation of an "unfair competitive advantage analysis stemming from a firm's use of a former government employee is virtually indistinguishable from the concerns and considerations that arise in protests where there is an allegation that a firm has gained an unfair competitive advantage arising from its unequal access to information as a result of an organizational conflict of interest."[264] In such instances, GAO determines "whether any action of the former government employee may have resulted in an unfair competitive advantage for, or on behalf of, the awardee during the award selection process."[265] GAO will sustain a protest where that official had access to nonpublic, competitively useful information—"even if no actual impropriety can be shown, so long as the determination of an unfair competitive advantage is based on facts and not on mere innuendo or suspicion."[266]

> In determining whether an offeror obtained an unfair competitive advantage in hiring a former government employee based on the individual's knowledge of non-public information, our Office has considered a variety of factors, including whether the non-public information was in fact available to the protester, whether the non-public information was the protester's proprietary information, and whether the non-public information was competitively useful.[267]

c. Impaired Objectivity

"[A]n impaired objectivity OCI exists where a firm's ability to render impartial advice to the government will be undermined by the firm's competing interests, such as a relationship to the product or service being evaluated."[268]

---

263. Dell Servs. Fed. Gov't, Inc., B-414461.3, June 19, 2018, 2018 CPD ¶ 213 (citing McCarthy/Hunt JV, B-402229.2, Feb. 16, 2010, 2010 CPD ¶ 68).

264. Health Net Fed. Servs., LLC, B-401652.3, Nov. 4, 2009, 2009 CPD ¶ 220, at 29 n.15.

265. Liquidity Servs., Inc., B-409718, July 23, 2014, 2014 CPD ¶ 221 (citing Creative Mgmt. Tech., Inc., B-266299, Feb. 9, 1996, 96–1 CPD ¶ 61, at 7).

266. Int'l Res. Grp., B-409346.2, Dec. 11, 2014, 2014 CPD ¶ 369, at 7 (sustaining protest where awardee of USAID Office of Water contract gained unfair competitive advantage by employing former director of USAID Office of Water); *see also* Health Net Fed. Servs., LLC, B-401652.3 (sustaining protest where awardee employed former chief of staff of procurement activity).

267. Northrop Grumman Sys. Corp., B-412278.7, Oct. 4, 2017, 2017 CPD ¶ 312. As discussed later, however, one critical distinction between an unequal access to information OCI and an allegation of unfair competitive advantage from the hiring of a former government official is the agency's ability to waive the OCI.

268. C2C Innovative Sols., Inc., B-416289, July 30, 2018, 2018 CPD ¶ 269, at 5 (citing FAR 9.505–3; Alion Sci. & Tech. Corp., B-297022.3, Jan. 9, 2006, 2006 CPD ¶ 2).

A recent GAO decision illustrates the type of facts that give rise to an impaired objectivity OCI. In *Leidos, Inc.*,[269] the protester challenged the agency's determination that it was ineligible for a follow-on contract award because of an OCI created by its proposed subcontractor (which served as a subcontractor on a related advisory and assistance services (A&AS) contract). The agency determined that an OCI existed because the two contracts were managed by the same leadership, their teams consistently interacted with each other, and they shared numerous tasks and issues in common. As a result, the agency concluded that the subcontractor's ongoing obligations as an A&AS subcontractor meant that it could provide "direct input to the overall . . . strategy . . . and has the ability . . . to influence" decisions about the contract for which Leidos sought to compete.[270] As GAO explained,

> the agency was concerned that if Subcontractor A served as the primary subcontractor under the CCE follow-on, the agency would not receive objective advice regarding the Air Force's transformation strategy because Subcontractor A would have a vested interest in ensuring that the CCE follow-on was maximized and that option years are exercised.[271]

In deciding that the agency reasonably determined that an OCI existed, GAO noted that an impaired objectivity OCI "is not limited to situations in which a contractor is evaluating its own or a competitor's work. Rather, an impaired objectivity OCI is concerned with whether the contractor's performance on one contract can affect other interests of the contractor."[272]

d. Waiver

One issue confronting protesters is the agency's ability to waive an OCI even after a protest has been filed. Under FAR 9.503, the agency head or a designee may waive an OCI as defined under FAR Part 9 by determining that its application in a particular situation would not be in the government's interest. GAO limits its review of such a waiver to consideration of whether the waiver complies with the requirements of the FAR, that is, whether it is in writing, sets forth the extent of the conflict, and is approved by the appropriate individual within the agency.[273]

In *AT&T Government Solutions, Inc.*,[274] GAO dismissed a post-award protest alleging a failure to investigate unequal access to information and impaired objectivity OCIs as academic after the agency issued a waiver three days before GAO's

---

269. B-417994, Dec. 17, 2019, 2019 WL 7019036.
270. *Id.* at 7.
271. *Id.*
272. *Id.* at 8.
273. *See* AT&T Gov't Sols., Inc., B-407720, Jan. 30, 2013, 2013 CPD ¶ 45.
274. *Id.*

decision. GAO informed the parties in an outcome prediction conference that it would likely sustain the protest, but the agency declined to take corrective action. Instead, three days before the GAO decision was to issue, the agency advised that it waived any OCIs regarding the challenged award. As a result, GAO dismissed the protest as academic, explaining:

> The FAR authority here permits waiver of any general rule or procedure within FAR Subpart 9.5. The issues in dispute in this case arise from the rules and procedures in Subpart 9.5, and . . . the application of these rules and procedures have been waived for this procurement by the Marine Corps, which renders the protest academic.[275]

Such waivers typically arise in the context of unequal access or impaired objectivity OCIs. GAO's decisions suggest that biased ground rules OCIs are much more difficult to mitigate, with traditional mitigation methods such as firewalls, termination of employees, severance of communication between affiliates, the absence of direct financial interest by those performing the evaluation of proposals, and a "clean break" between the requirements and solicitation phases regularly deemed inadequate. In *Aetna Government Health Plans, Inc.*,[276] GAO cited to two potential OCIs illustrated in FAR 9.508 that "cannot be mitigated." Specifically, GAO pointed to paragraphs (e) and (f) of FAR 9.508, which provide examples of cases in which companies involved in developing requirements for solicitations are thereafter excluded from the following acquisition. The usual remedy for biased ground rules OCI cases "is the elimination of that competitor from the competition."[277]

It is also important to note the distinction between an unequal access to information OCI arising under FAR Part 9 and an "unfair competitive advantage" arising under FAR Part 3 based on the hiring of a former government official. Although the two issues present similar concerns, GAO made clear that for purposes of waiver, it distinguishes between them:

> We acknowledge that our Office has issued decisions which generally describe allegations concerning the hiring of former government employees as an unequal access to information OCI. *E.g., Liquidity Servs., Inc.*, B–409718 *et al.*, July 23, 2014, 2014 CPD ¶ 221 at 7–8; *Science Applications Int'l Corp.*, B–406921, B–406921.2, Oct 1, 2012, 2012 CPD ¶ 267 at 10–11. However, as the FAR and our decisions regarding unequal access to information OCIs make clear, such OCIs arise where a contractor has access to non-public information as part of its performance of a government contract, or where the contractor possesses information improperly provided by a government employee. FAR §§ 9.505(b), 9.505–4; *CapRock Gov't Solutions, et al.*,

275. *Id.* at 3.

276. B-254397, July 27, 1995, 95-2 CPD ¶ 129, GAO cited FAR 9.508(e), (f).

277. L-3 Servs., Inc., B-400134.11, Sept. 3, 2009, 2009 CPD ¶ 171 (citing The Jones/Hill Joint Venture, B-286194.4, Dec. 5, 2001, 2001 CPD ¶ 194, at 22 n.26).

> B-402490 *et al.,* May 11, 2010, 2010 CPD ¶ 124 at 25. In contrast, an unfair competitive advantage arising from the hiring of a former government employee does not implicate the contractor's access to information through that contractor's performance of a government contract or from a current government employee. For this reason, our decisions have distinguished between the concerns arising under FAR subpart 3.1 and FAR subpart 9.5. To the extent any of our prior decisions suggest a contrary conclusion, we clarify that because FAR subpart 3.1 does not permit the agency to waive concerns arising under that subpart, a waiver executed pursuant to FAR § 9.503 does not warrant dismissal of an argument that the hiring of a former government employee violates the principles of FAR subpart 3.1.[278]

8. *Procurement Integrity Act*

The procurement integrity provisions of the Office of Federal Procurement Policy Act, as amended, 41 U.S.C. §§ 2101–2107—referred to as the Procurement Integrity Act (PIA)—prohibit disclosing or obtaining source selection and contractor bid or proposal information, regulate nonfederal employment offers to procurement officials, and contain certain restrictions on the ability of former federal officials to accept compensation from contractors. The FAR implements the PIA in FAR 3.104 *et seq.* Although an in-depth examination of the PIA falls beyond the scope of this volume, a brief discussion of the statute and implementing regulations is important to understanding when the PIA can, and when it cannot, serve as a ground of protest.

a. History of the PIA

The PIA was born in the wake of Operation Ill Wind, a three-year multi-agency investigation led by the FBI that started in 1986 as a small bid rigging investigation and culminated in the prosecution of more than 60 contractors, consultants, and government officials and resulted in $622 million in fines, recoveries, restitutions, and forfeitures.[279] The investigation started when a Virginia-based defense contractor alerted the FBI that he had been approached by a military consultant who offered to provide him with a competitor's proprietary bid information in exchange for cash. The FBI monitored the contractor's calls with the consultant, confronted the consultant with the evidence, and flipped him. Armed with the consultant's cooperation and court-authorized wiretaps, the FBI and other participating agencies (including the Naval Investigative Service, the Defense Criminal Intelligence Service, the Air Force Office of Special Investigations, and the Internal Revenue Service) executed search warrants on defense contractors, consultants, and government officials in

278. Northrop Grumman Sys. Corp., B-412278.7, Oct. 4, 2017, 2017 CPD ¶ 312, at 7.

279. *Operation Illwind*, FBI History: Famous Cases & Criminals, https://www.fbi.gov/history/famous-cases/operation-illwind (last visited July 9, 2020).

Washington DC and 12 other states. Indictments and convictions followed. Among the convicted were Melvyn Paisley, Assistant Secretary of the Navy, who pled guilty to accepting hundreds of thousands of dollars in bribes and served four years in prison; James Gaines, the Deputy Assistant Secretary of the Navy, who took over for Paisley only to be convicted of accepting an illegal gratuity and sentenced to six months in prison; and Victor Cohen, Deputy Assistant of the Air Force, who pled guilty to accepting bribes and conspiring to defraud the government.[280]

The public outcry was so great that Congress took swift action. On November 17, 1988—just five months after the search warrants were executed—the original version of the PIA was enacted.

b. Disclosing or Obtaining Procurement Information

Most protests involving alleged PIA violations assert that source selection or contractor bid or proposal information was wrongfully disclosed or obtained to the prejudice of the protester. Under 41 U.S.C. § 2102(a), a present or former federal official or a person who has had access to contractor bid or proposal information or source selection information cannot, except as provided by law, knowingly disclose that information before the award of a federal agency procurement contract to which the information relates. Under 41 U.S.C. § 2102(b), no person may, except as provided by law, knowingly obtain such information before the award of such a contract. Notably, the proscription applies to government and contractor personnel who knowingly obtain such information.[281]

---

280. *See* Douglas Frantz, *Paisley Gets 4-Year Term in Ill Wind Case: Pentagon: He Is the Highest-Ranking Target and His Sentence Is the Stiffest Yet in the Defense Procurement Scandal*, L.A. Times (Oct. 19, 1991, 12:00 AM), https://www.latimes.com/archives/la-xpm-1991-10-19-mn-526-story.html; AP, *Ex-Official Sentenced*, N.Y. Times (June 1, 1992), https://www.nytimes.com/1992/06/01/business/ex-official-sentenced.html?src=pm; Carolyn Skorneck, *Former Air Force Official Pleads Guilty in Ill Wind Probe*, AP (Aug. 22, 1991), https://apnews.com/d4c941ccfa8a2f51761aae4aaf5856f3.

281. In one matter, COFC expressed a contrary view. In *The GEO Group, Inc. v. United States*, 100 Fed. Cl. 223, 227 (2011), the court opined that the "knowingly obtain" provision, "[r]ead in context . . . appears to apply only to current or former officials of the United States or persons who are acting or have acted on such an individual's behalf. . . . [T]hat conclusion is not apparent from the statutory language, which merely refers generically to a 'person.' But, this conclusion is supported by the overall structure of the statute, including the definitions therein of 'bid and proposal information' and 'source selection information,' both of which talk in terms of specific information obtained by a Federal agency." The *GEO Group* case does not cite to any other cases for this proposition, nor are the authors of this volume aware of any such cases. To the contrary, as discussed further later, the cases that discuss the "knowingly obtain" prong of the PIA assume that contractors can violate the PIA and focus instead on whether the information falls within the purview of the statute or whether the savings provision renders the statute inapplicable.

i. Contractor Bid or Proposal Information

Contractor bid or proposal information means any of the following information submitted to a federal agency as part of or in connection with a bid or proposal, so long as the information has not previously been made available to the public or publicly disclosed:

- Cost or pricing data (as defined in 10 U.S.C. § 2306a(h)(1))[282] with respect to procurements subject to that section, and 41 U.S.C. § 3501(a)(2)[283] with respect to procurements subject to that section;
- Indirect costs and direct labor rates;
- Proprietary information about manufacturing processes, operations, or techniques marked by the contractor in accordance with applicable law or regulation;
- Information marked by the contractor as contractor bid or proposal information in accordance with applicable law or regulation; and
- Information marked in accordance with FAR 52.215-1(e).[284]

ii. Source Selection Information

Source selection information means any of the following information that is prepared for use by an agency for the purpose of evaluating a bid or proposal to enter into an agency procurement contract, if that information has not been previously made available to the public or disclosed publicly:

- Bid prices submitted in response to a federal agency invitation for bids, or lists of those bid prices before bid opening;
- Proposed costs or prices submitted in response to a federal agency solicitation, or lists of those proposed costs or prices;
- Source selection plans;
- Technical evaluation plans;

282. 10 U.S.C. § 2306a(h)(1) defines cost or pricing data as "all facts that . . . a prudent buyer or seller would reasonably expect to affect price negotiations significantly. Such term does not include information that is judgmental, but does include the factual information from which a judgment was derived."

283. 41 U.S.C. § 3501(a)(1) defines cost or pricing data as "all facts that . . . a prudent buyer or seller would reasonably expect to affect price negotiations significantly. The term does not include information that is judgmental, but does include factual information from which a judgment was derived."

284. 41 U.S.C. § 2101(2); FAR 3.104-1. FAR 52.215-1 provides "Instructions to Offerors—Competitive Acquisition." FAR 52.215-1(e) instructs offerors that include in their proposals data they do not want disclosed to the public for any purpose, or used by the government except for evaluation purposes, to mark the title page with a prescribed legend and to mark each sheet of data they wish to restrict with a legend advising that the use or disclosure of data on that sheet is subject to the restriction on the title page.

- Technical evaluation of proposals;
- Cost or price evaluations of proposals;
- Competitive range determinations that identify proposals that have a reasonable chance of being selected for award of a contract;
- Rankings of bids, proposals, or competitors;
- Reports and evaluations of source selection panels, boards, or advisory councils; and
- Other information marked as "source selection information" based on a case-by-case determination that disclosure would jeopardize the integrity or successful completion of the procurement to which the information relates.[285]

c. The PIA's Savings Provision

Notably, the PIA contains a "savings provision" at 41 U.S.C. § 2107 that identifies a list of items to which the PIA does not apply. As discussed in more detail later, the savings provision has sounded the death knell of a number of protests based on alleged PIA violations. Specifically, the savings provision states that the PIA does not

- Restrict disclosure of information to, or its receipt by, persons authorized, in accordance with agency regulations or procedures, to receive that information;
- Restrict a contractor from disclosing its own bid or proposal information or the recipient from receiving that information;
- Restrict the disclosure or receipt of information relating to a federal agency procurement canceled before award unless the agency plans to resume the procurement;
- Prohibit meetings between federal agency officials and offerors or potential offerors so long as no unauthorized disclosure or receipt of contractor bid or proposal information or source selection information occurs;
- Authorize the withholding of information from, nor restrict its receipt by, Congress, a committee or subcommittee of Congress, the Comptroller General, a federal agency, or an inspector general of a federal agency;
- Authorize the withholding of information from, nor restrict its receipt by, the Comptroller General in the course of a protest against the award or proposed award of a federal agency procurement contract; or
- Limit the applicability of a requirement, sanction, contract penalty, or remedy established under another law or regulation.

---

285. 41 U.S.C. § 2101(7); FAR 2.101.

d. Reporting Requirement

A contractor that becomes aware that a competitor has or may have obtained its proprietary information must be mindful of the deadline for reporting the potential PIA violation. Indeed, no protest ground based on a violation of the PIA may be filed unless the protester first reported to the agency responsible for the procurement the information the protester believed constituted evidence of the violation. The report must be made within 14 days of the discovery of the possible violation.[286]

Under FAR 3.104-7, a contracting officer who receives information of a violation or possible violation of the PIA must determine whether it has any impact on the pending award or selection of the contractor. COFC and GAO grant broad deference to the contracting officer's decision as to whether a PIA violation occurred and treat the decision as to whether to exclude the party violating the PIA as a responsibility determination.[287]

Given the discretion afforded contracting officers, contractors concerned that their proprietary information has been obtained by a competitor should provide the contracting officer with sufficient details to help guide and frame the investigation. If the contracting officer determines that there is an impact, he or she must promptly forward the information to the head of the contracting activity (HCA). If the contracting officer concludes there is no impact, he or she must forward the information received and documentation supporting the "no impact" determination for second level review. If the second level review concurs that there is no impact, the contracting officer may proceed with the procurement. If the second level reviewer does not concur, he or she must promptly forward the information and documentation to the HCA and advise the contracting officer to withhold award.

The HCA reviews the information and may adopt any one or more of several courses of action, including advising the contracting officer to continue with the procurement, investigating the allegation, and referring the matter to criminal

286. *See* 41 U.S.C. § 2106; 4 C.F.R. § 21.5(d) (GAO will dismiss any protest ground based on procurement integrity "where the protester failed to report the information it believed constituted evidence of the offense to the Federal agency responsible for the procurement within 14 days after the protester first discovered the possible violation."); Concurrent Techs. Corp., B-412795.2, Jan. 17, 2017, 2017 CPD ¶ 25, at 8 (GAO "will not review an alleged violation of [the PIA] where the protester failed to report the information it believed constituted evidence of the offense to the Federal agency responsible for the procurement within 14 days after the protester first discovered the possible violation.").

287. *See* IBM Corp., B-415798.2, Feb. 14, 2019, 2019 CPD ¶ 82; DynCorp Int'l, LLC v. United States, 757 F. App'x 927 (2018) (Federal Circuit affirmed judgment for government on protest alleging that awardee was not responsible contractor because it had obtained and used protester's proprietary information, stating, "[c]ontracting officers are vested with authority to exercise discretion on a wide range of procurement issues, including determinations regarding whether a particular offeror is a responsible offeror.").

investigative agencies. If the HCA concludes that a violation has occurred, and the contract has not yet been awarded, then the HCA may direct the contracting officer to cancel the procurement, disqualify an offeror, or take other appropriate action. If the contract has been awarded, the HCA may direct the contracting officer to employ contractual remedies (including profit recapture or fee adjustment), void or rescind the contract, and/or refer the matter to the agency suspension and debarment official.

e. Information Must Relate to the Current Procurement

The PIA prohibits the release of information that is relevant to the contract being awarded. *S&K Aerospace, LLC*[288] reflects a rather stark example of this limitation. In *S&K Aerospace*, an offeror deliberately unlocked a government password on a pricing matrix included in the RFP so that it could more easily import data from the matrix. Unlocking the matrix revealed previously hidden tabs that contained fee data from the incumbent contract. The offeror removed the employee responsible for unlocking the matrix from the proposal team and reported the incident to the agency. The agency investigated, found additional disclosures of the incumbent's fee information on its publicly accessible website, and removed all such information. S&K protested that the agency's disclosures violated the PIA. GAO denied the protest, stating that "the release of information regarding a prior incumbent contract does not meet [the] definition" of information released "before the award of a . . . contract to which the information relates."[289]

Conversely, in *Dell Services Federal Government, Inc.*,[290] GAO sustained a PIA protest arising from the disclosure of historical information. In *Dell Services*, an offeror alerted the contracting officer that it had come into possession of two of its competitor's proposals from prior procurements. The agency limited its investigation to a comparison of how its IT requirements on those prior procurements compared to the current procurement and concluded that the differences rendered the historical information "stale." GAO, however, noted among other things that one of the proposals contained detailed information as to the protester's ten-year labor rate history, and that such information could provide "significant insight" into the protester's "current and historical pricing and labor rates" that would provide a competitive advantage to the offeror that had received it.[291]

---

288. B-411648, Sept. 18, 2015, 2015 CPD ¶ 336.
289. *Id.* at 5.
290. B-414461, June 21, 2017, 2017 CPD ¶ 192.
291. *Id.* at 4.

f. Information Must Be "Knowingly" Disclosed or Obtained

The PIA prohibits government officials from knowingly disclosing, or persons from knowingly obtaining, source selection or contractor bid or proposal information. It is not directed at the inadvertent or negligent disclosure or receipt of such information. In *S&K Aerospace*,[292] GAO explained that the agency's negligent posting of the incumbent contractor's fee information on the agency's publicly accessible website did not meet the "knowingly" standard. Nor did GAO find the ten-day delay between the date the agency learned of the inadvertent disclosure and the removal of the information from the website as triggering the PIA. Rather, GAO characterized the agency as having "diligently pursued the deletion of the pricing matrix from the FBO website."[293]

Agencies do, however, have an obligation to investigate the potential disclosure of PIA-covered information. *Satellite Tracking of People, LLC*[294] is a rather bizarre example of circumstances that give rise to the duty to investigate. Satellite Tracking (STOP) protested the award of a task order to BI Incorporated (BI) for GPS equipment and monitoring services for criminal offenders. The agency argued that STOP had an unmitigable OCI problem and was therefore ineligible for award. Specifically, the contracting officer represented that after reviewing STOP's proposal, she determined that it contained BI's proprietary information. This conclusion led the agency to look further into the matter, whereupon it learned that its own program manager for the procurement was a former STOP employee who had a continuing financial interest in STOP. STOP countered that the program manager was a disgruntled former employee who tried to steer the award away from STOP. Thus, according to STOP, it was the agency that had the conflict of interest problem.

---

292. B-411648, Sept. 18, 2015, 2015 CPD ¶ 336.

293. *Id.* at 5. Contractors on the receiving end of an inadvertent disclosure must not misuse such information. For example, MCR Federal, LLC was suspended after it obtained source selection information. MCR Federal, LLC v. JB&A, Inc., 808 S.E.2d 186, 189–90 (Va. 2017). One could reasonably argue that MCR Federal did not "knowingly" obtain the information because it arrived in an unsolicited e-mail inadvertently sent by the Air Force. *Id.* at 189. The MCR Federal employee who received the information forwarded it to six other employees on the proposal team. *Id.* The Air Force tried to recall the information soon after forwarding, but later found that four employees had held meetings to discuss the information after they had been notified that such information was inadvertently disclosed. *Id.* at 190. The Air Force also found that, despite possessing information about a competitor's bid, the employees helped prepare MCR Federal's final bid. *Id.* The Air Force suspended MCR Federal and the four employees, and in subsequent Administrative Agreements, MCR Federal agreed, among other things, to replace the CEO and the General Counsel, establish a new position of Chief Compliance Officer, add a Board member with ethics expertise, implement a new training program for all employees, hire an outside consultant to review its compliance programs, and send a letter to all its suppliers regarding its commitment to integrity.

294. B-411845, Nov. 6, 2015, 2015 CPD ¶ 347.

GAO sustained STOP's protest given the program manager's apparent conflict of interest (regardless of which way it cut) and recommended that the agency terminate the task order, cancel the RFP, and begin the acquisition anew. GAO also expressed its surprise that the agency had not taken any steps to investigate or resolve the possible PIA violations implied by the contracting officer's representations, stating that it did "not understand why the alleged possible PIA violation also has not been actively and thoroughly investigated by the agency."[295] As GAO explained:

> We view the contracting officer's representation that STOP's protest included its competitor's proprietary information to be a serious allegation. It may imply that one or more individuals within the agency knowingly provided STOP with BI's proprietary information, and that both STOP and its counsel may knowingly have received such information. Such activity on the part of agency personnel, STOP personnel, or STOP's counsel, could give rise to a violation of the Procurement Integrity Act (PIA), 41 U.S.C. §§ 2101–2107.[296]

The "knowingly" requirement does not, however, apply to the intentional obtaining of a contractor's competitive bid or proposal information for improper purposes if such information was voluntarily provided by the contractor—even where the recipient employs it in violation of agreed-upon restrictions as to its permitted use. Because the PIA's saving provision does not "[r]estrict a contractor from disclosing its own bid or proposal information or the recipient from receiving that information," GAO treats such situations as private disputes outside of its purview.[297]

GEO Group, Inc.[298] provides a dramatic illustration of this point.[299] GEO submitted a proposal to the Bureau of Prisons to provide correctional services, along with a letter to the agency stating that its former vice president, a Mr. Brown, suddenly resigned after transmitting confidential GEO information to his private e-mail account. By virtue of his position at GEO, Mr. Brown had access to sensitive information, including GEO's staffing plan from its prior proposal, its personnel resource plan, and other documents, including all the information GEO used in crafting its proposal. In addition, one week prior to resigning from GEO, Mr. Brown met with other GEO officials to review GEO's draft proposal line by line. GEO learned that

---

295. *Id.* at 8.

296. Satellite Tracking of People, LLC, B-411845, Nov. 6, 2015, 2015 CPD ¶ 347, at 7.

297. 41 U.S.C. § 2107. Although this book focuses on protests, it should be noted that protests are not a contractor's only recourse for obtaining relief. In fact, while GAO and COFC will expressly disclaim jurisdiction over purely private disputes such as misappropriation of trade secrets or violations of a nondisclosure agreement (*see, e.g.*, IBM Corp., B-415798.2, Feb. 14, 2019, 2019 CPD ¶ 82), an aggrieved contractor can pursue such claims in federal or state court.

298. B-405012, July 26, 2011, 2011 CPD ¶ 153.

299. Some of the facts described herein are drawn from *GEO Group, Inc. v. United States*, 100 Fed. Cl. 223 (2011).

Mr. Brown left to work at CFS, a company he had founded several years earlier. GEO submitted its proposal to BOP a few days after Mr. Brown resigned. CFS submitted its proposal shortly afterward. During his evaluation of the proposals, the contracting officer found a number of instances in which the wording of GEO's and CFS's proposals was nearly identical. He recommended that the procurement be placed on hold and that the issues in the GEO letter be investigated as a potential PIA violation. The investigation concluded that CFS's proposal had been written by a third-party proposal writer without reference to GEO's proprietary information, and the procurement continued. GEO protested the subsequent award to CFS alleging that it was "implausible that CFS did not utilize confidential GEO information obtained by the CFS CEO in preparing its proposal. . . ."[300] GAO, however, ruled that "any protected pricing materials obtained by the CFS CEO . . . are covered by the PIA's savings clause. . . ."[301] GEO argued that the PIA savings clause should not apply where the CFS CEO had concealed his interest in CFS and lied to GEO in breach of his fiduciary duties and GEO's code of ethics. GAO disagreed, stating that it has

> repeatedly determined that the PIA's savings provisions apply notwithstanding the fact that the voluntarily provided information is subsequently misused or not properly safeguarded. Here, GEO voluntarily provided its confidential information to the CFS CEO in the course of his employment with GEO. The CFS CEO's alleged misuse of that information in transferring it to CFS, [in] breach of his fiduciary duties to GEO, or breach of GEO's corporate code of ethics, are matters of a private dispute not for resolution by our Office.[302]

Similarly, in *DynCorp International, LLC*,[303] GAO found that the PIA's savings provision precluded the possibility of a PIA violation. In reviewing proposals for a logistics support contract for the Air Force's fleet of C-21 aircraft, the agency's technical evaluation team identified a number of passages in one offeror's (M1) proposal that were identical to passages in the incumbent DynCorp's proposal. The agency investigated and learned that M1 had been a subcontractor to DynCorp under the predecessor contract. DynCorp's proposal for that previous contract contained several

300. *Id.* at 3.

301. *Id.*

302. *Id.* at 3–4 (citations omitted). As previously noted, GEO subsequently filed a protest at COFC. In ruling on GEO's motion for injunctive relief, the court commented that the PIA should perhaps be read as applying only to government officials. The court stated further that even "if the court were ultimately to conclude that the Procurement Integrity Act covered conduct of an individual not associated with the United States, there is significant evidence that Mr. Brown did not have access to GEO's pricing information. . . . Such a finding would deprive plaintiff's argument of much of its vitality, as its claim is that Mr. Brown used his knowledge to craft a proposal for CFS that had price [sic] lower than that offered by GEO." 100 Fed. Cl. 223 at 227 n.4. The court did not reference the Savings provision.

303. B-408516, Oct. 29, 2013, 2013 CPD ¶ 243.

of the identical proposal passages. The agency then submitted an evaluation notice to M1 (but not to DynCorp). M1 responded to the agency by stating that it had the right to use all the information in its proposal pursuant to a teaming agreement it had executed with DynCorp. The agency concluded that the identical passages in the competing proposals belonged to each offeror independently. M1 won the award, and after DynCorp received a debriefing, it protested under the PIA. DynCorp argued that its teaming agreement with M1 expressly prohibited M1's use of any proposal language in a competitive context. GAO pointed out that M1 obtained DynCorp's proprietary information because DynCorp provided it voluntarily pursuant to that teaming agreement. GAO denied the protest, finding that the circumstances about which DynCorp complained "fit squarely within the PIA 'savings provision'" and that "[a]t base, DynCorp's complaint is that M1 failed to abide by the terms of private agreements between the two firms."[304]

9. Bad Faith and Bias

After awards are announced, it is not uncommon for rumors to work their way through the capture teams about the possible reasons for the agency's decision, including stories of unfair bias. Protests based on such grounds rarely succeed. Although on rare occasions there may be concrete evidence (as opposed to speculation) suggesting that a procurement was tainted by a government official's bad faith actions, asserting suspected bias and bad faith as a protest ground is usually a futile endeavor.

Although GAO and COFC will consider allegations of bad faith, the protester's burden of proof is almost impossibly high. GAO holds that

> government officials are presumed to act in good faith, and a protester's contention that procurement officials are motivated by bias or bad faith must be supported by convincing proof; our Office will not consider allegations based on mere inference, supposition or unsupported speculation.[305]

In addition, "[t]o establish bad faith, a protester must present convincing evidence that agency officials had a specific and malicious intent to harm the firm."[306] Or, to use an older formulation of the same high standard: "[T]he record must show 'well-nigh irrefragable proof' that the agency had a malicious and specific intent to injure the party alleging bad faith."[307]

---

304. *Id.* at 4–5.

305. Hewlett Packard Enter. Co., B-413444.4, Jan. 18, 2017, 2017 CPD ¶ 29, at 7 n.5.

306. Trailboss Enters., Inc., B-415970, May 7, 2018, 2018 CPD ¶ 171, at 11.

307. Delta Data Sys. Corp., B-213396, Apr. 17, 1984, 84-1 CPD ¶ 430 (quoting Kalvar Corp. v. United States, 543 F.2d 1298, 1301 (Ct. Cl. 1976)).

COFC applies the standard enunciated by the Federal Circuit in *Croman Corp. v. United States*:

> Government officials are presumed to "act 'conscientiously in the discharge of their duties.'" *Kalvar Corp., Inc. v. United States*, 543 F.2d 1298, 1301 (Ct. Cl. 1976) (quoting *Librach v. United States*, 147 Ct. Cl. 605, 612 (1959)). Courts have always been "loath to find to the contrary," and to induce a court to abandon the presumption of good faith dealing, "requires 'well-nigh irrefragable proof.'" *Id.* at 1301–02 (quoting *Knotts v. United States*, 128 Ct. Cl. 489, 492, 121 F. Supp. 630 (1954)). Thus, [a protester] must offer clear and convincing evidence that the [government] did not act in good faith in order to prevail on this issue.[308]

The presumption of good faith means that GAO gives procurement officials the benefit of the doubt that they were not biased and did not act in bad faith. To rebut that presumption, the protester must show evidence that agency officials specifically set out to harm it—not merely that they took an action that happened to harm the protester. And the protester's evidence must constitute "well-nigh irrefragable proof." This is substantially higher than a "more likely than not" standard.

Lockheed Martin Corp.[309] is one of the few protests sustained on the basis of bad faith and bias. Following the conviction of former Air Force Principal Undersecretary for Acquisition Darlene Druyun, for violating conflict-of-interest provisions in connection with her employment at Boeing, Druyun asserted at her sentencing that she had given Boeing favorable treatment before taking the job. Lockheed Martin thereupon protested a contract that had been awarded to Boeing years earlier. GAO found that Druyun's plea statement demonstrated bias in favor of Boeing and prejudiced Lockheed Martin (despite the agency's arguments that her involvement in the procurement was not "significant") and recommended that Phase II of Boeing's contract be competed. Similar protests based on Druyun's involvement in the C-130 avionics modernization upgrade program also resulted in victory for the protesters, years after the contract was awarded to Boeing.[310]

These rare victories are very much outliers.[311] The *Palantir* case included a protest ground asserting bad faith based on, among other things, government e-mails identifying "entrenched animosity" toward Palantir, and efforts by agency personnel "to rescind and alter" a favorable report regarding Palantir's capabilities. In addition, government officials "struggled during the depositions to remember or explain

---

308. 724 F.3d 1357, 1364 (Fed. Cir. 2013).

309. B-295402, Feb. 18, 2005, 2005 CPD ¶ 24.

310. *See* Lockheed Martin Aeronautics Co., B-295401, Feb. 24, 2005, 2005 CPD ¶ 41.

311. *See, e.g.*, Palantir USG, Inc. v. United States, 129 Fed. Cl. 218, 256 (2016), *aff'd on other grounds*, 904 F.3d 980 (Fed. Cir. 2018).

potentially unfavorable e-mails or statements about Palantir. . . ."[312] Nevertheless, the court concluded that "Palantir ha[d] not produced clear and convincing evidence of bias and/or bad faith. . . ."[313]

Apart from a situation where a procurement official has admitted to rigging procurements, and in the absence of unambiguous, objective proof of prejudicial bad faith, a protest asserting bad faith or bias has little to no chance to succeed, and may end up backfiring on an unsuccessful offeror as accusing agency personnel of bad faith can damage the relationship with that customer. In addition, alleging bad faith without the facts to back it up may undermine the credibility of other grounds of protest.

Finally, competitive prejudice is an essential element in every protest. That is, even in the unlikely event a protester can convince GAO that one or more agency officials acted in bad faith or were biased against the protester, the protester also must show that it had a substantial chance of being awarded the contract but for the bad faith. If the biased official was not in a position to alter the source selection decision, or if other issues unrelated to bias would have independently prevented the protester from winning the competition, proving bad faith alone will not lead to a sustained protest.

Notwithstanding the above, in certain situations where a government official was significantly involved with the procurement and had pervasive ties with the awardee, GAO will presume prejudice and not require the protester to prove bad faith or actual bias. In *Teledyne Brown Engineering, Inc.*,[314] GAO sustained the protest after finding that a voting member of the agency's Source Evaluation Board (whom GAO identified as Mr. X) met weekly throughout the entire procurement process with a high level employee of the awardee's major subcontractor and an employee of the awardee itself for dinner, "camaraderie," and foosball. Although the agency's ethics counsel recommended that Mr. X be removed from the board or stop attending the weekly dinners, he refused to stop the dinners and the agency refused to remove him from the board. The agency argued that its mitigation measures protected against any prejudice. GAO disagreed, and added:

> In any event, we need not resolve whether or not Mr. X's participation in the acquisition resulted in actual prejudice against the other offerors, or in favor of SGT. *In circumstances such as these, the potential harm flowing from an actual or apparent conflict of interest is, by its nature, not susceptible to demonstrable proof of bias or preju-*

312. *Id.* at 256.

313. *Id.* It is worth noting that COFC entered judgment for Palantir on a different, wholly unrelated issue that was affirmed on appeal, that is, the agency's failure to comply with 10 U.S.C. § 2377's mandate to meaningfully assess whether commercial or nondevelopmental items could meet the agency's needs.

314. B-418835, Sept. 28, 2020, 2020 CPD ¶ 303 (emphasis added) (internal citations omitted).

dice. Thus, where, as here, the record establishes that a conflict or apparent conflict of interest exists, and the agency did not resolve the issue, to maintain the integrity of the procurement process, *we will presume that the protester was prejudiced*, unless the record includes clear evidence establishing the absence of prejudice. No such evidence exists here.

10. Key Personnel

Issues related to key personnel typically arise in one of two ways. First, and most common, are issues related to the availability of key personnel after delays in the procurement process resulting, for example, from multiple rounds of protests, corrective actions, or administrative delays in the agency's selection process. In the intervening months between when an offeror submits its proposal and when award is made, proposed employees may become unavailable. In such situations, GAO has held that offerors have an obligation to notify the contracting officer of material changes in its staffing and resources after submission of bids.[315] Where an offeror fails to provide such notice, disappointed bidders may argue that the offeror materially misled the agency or failed to meet mandatory staffing or key personnel requirements. Typically, the awardee's post-award recruiting efforts—learned either through public recruiting efforts or during transition activities as the incumbent—and publicly available employment information on websites such as LinkedIn are used as evidence of the unavailability of the awardee's proposed key personnel.

For example, in *Paradigm Technologies*,[316] GAO sustained a protest in which the Missile Defense Agency awarded a task order to Booz Allen Hamilton despite having been notified that Booz Allen's proposed program manager—a required key personnel position—was no longer available. In its evaluation, rather than finding that Booz Allen failed to satisfy the material RFP requirement to propose a suitable program manager, the agency merely assigned it a weakness for its unavailable program manager. GAO concluded that "[u]nder these circumstances, MDA should have either rejected Boo [sic] Allen's proposal as technically unacceptable for failing to meet a material requirement or reopened discussions to permit the firm to correct this deficiency."[317]

Even where an offeror does provide notice regarding the unavailability of its proposed personnel, it may still be excluded from the competition. In *URS Federal Services, Inc.*,[318] GAO upheld an agency's determination that URS's proposal was unacceptable and thus unawardable as a result of the resignation of a proposed key

315. *See* Pioneering Evolution, LLC, B-412016, Dec. 8, 2015, 2015 CPD ¶ 385, at 9.
316. B-409221.2, Aug. 1, 2014, 2014 CPD ¶ 257.
317. *Id.* at 5.
318. B-413034, July 25, 2016, 2016 CPD ¶ 209.

software engineer. GAO noted that while the employee's resignation was not the fault of URS, the decision to conduct discussions to allow an offeror to amend its proposed key personnel in such circumstances falls within the agency's discretion.

The second issue related to key personnel arises when an offeror misleads the agency about its key personnel by proposing specific key personnel that it does not, in fact, intend to use should it win the contract award. In its classic form, the situation unfolds as follows: An offeror proposes to use specific, qualified, experienced, credentialed personnel for the contract. The agency credits the offeror for this aspect of its proposal in a way that contributes to its winning the contract—for example, in the form of one or more significant strengths. After award, the contractor informs the agency of something it knew all along: that the named personnel are unavailable and that lesser qualified personnel will take their place. This unscrupulous practice—which, fortunately, is quite rare—could easily cross over into a False Statements Act problem under 18 U.S.C. § 1001 and give the awardee more than a protest to worry about.

GAO has outlined the elements of a bait-and-switch protest ground:

> In order to establish an impermissible "bait and switch," a protester must show: (1) that the awardee either knowingly or negligently represented that it would rely on specific personnel that it did not have a reasonable basis to expect to furnish during contract performance, (2) that the misrepresentation was relied on by the agency, and (3) that the agency's reliance on the misrepresentation had a material effect on the evaluation results.[319]

If the offeror intended or hoped to use particular personnel that it did not include in its proposal, there would be no bait-and-switch because there was no "baiting."[320] Sometimes key personnel become unavailable through no fault of and without the advance knowledge of the offeror. This unexpected unavailability is not a misrepresentation and, consequently, does not constitute a bait-and-switch.

If the offeror learned of the unavailability only after contract award, the issue will be treated as a matter of contract administration that GAO will not review.[321] If, however, the offeror becomes aware of the unavailability of proposed key personnel before award, it must inform the agency of that fact even if proposals have been submitted already.[322] And, once the agency learns that one of the offeror's proposed key personnel is unavailable, the agency must either reject the offeror's proposal as unac-

319. Patricio Enters. Inc., B-412738, May 26, 2016, 2016 CPD ¶ 145, at 3.

320. *See* Matter of Network Innovations, Inc., B-408382, Sept. 4, 2013, 2013 CPD ¶ 220.

321. *See, e.g.*, NCI Info. Sys., Inc., B-417805.5, Mar. 12, 2020, 2020 CPD ¶ 104 (denying protest where the awardee did not learn until after award about the departure of a proposed key person employed by its subcontractor).

322. *See* Greenleaf Constr. Co., Inc., B-293105.18, Jan. 17, 2006, 2006 CPD ¶ 19.

ceptable or open discussions with all offerors (thereby allowing the offeror to propose a replacement for the unavailable key personnel).[323] If the offeror fails to tell the agency about the change, or if the agency fails either to open discussions or reject the proposal once it learns of the key personnel's unavailability, an award to that offeror is impermissible. If the agency awards to that offeror nonetheless, a protest would be sustained on the ground that the awardee's proposal was unacceptable.

Bait-and-switch protest grounds rarely succeed, presumably because most offerors do not set out to deceive the government. Often, what initially looks like a bait-and-switch to an outside observer proves to be otherwise after all the facts come to light. That said, the issue of proposed key personnel becoming unavailable before award is not all that uncommon, and negligently proposing key personnel who become unavailable can be a basis for a bait-and-switch allegation. Thus, it is usually a good idea for offerors to require signed letters of commitment from the persons they propose for key positions.

11. Cost/Price Errors

Protests based on the agency's evaluation of the offerors' cost/price proposals typically arise from alleged errors in the agency's evaluation of realism, reasonableness, and/or balanced pricing. Realism looks at whether an offeror's proposed costs are too low to accurately reflect the work that needs to be done (although a solicitation can also call for a realism analysis of an offeror's proposed pricing). Reasonableness looks at whether the offeror's proposed price is too high. The balanced pricing analysis assesses whether, regardless of the total evaluated price, any particular element is overstated or understated. Balanced pricing analysis mitigates the risk that offerors will manipulate their proposals by overpricing line items that are likely to be ordered while underpricing those that are not, such that the total evaluated price is acceptable.

a. Cost Realism

An offeror may challenge an agency's cost realism analysis of its or a competitor's proposal. A cost realism analysis

> is the process of independently reviewing and evaluating specific elements of each offeror's proposed cost estimate to determine whether the estimated proposed cost elements are realistic for the work to be performed; reflect a clear understanding of the requirements; and are consistent with the unique methods of performance and materials described in the offeror's technical proposal.[324]

323. Gen. Revenue Corp., B-414220.2, Mar. 27, 2017, 2017 CPD ¶ 106, at 17.
324. FAR 15.404-1(d)(1).

Because the government is required to pay actual and allowable costs on cost-reimbursement contracts, the FAR requires that cost realism analyses be performed for each offeror on cost-reimbursement contracts to determine the probable cost.[325] Agencies are not required to conduct an in-depth cost analysis (see FAR 15.404–1(d)(1)) or to verify costs for each line item; rather, the "evaluation requires the exercise of informed judgment by the contracting agency."[326]

As explained by GAO:

> Agencies are given broad discretion to make cost realism evaluations. *Burns & Roe Indus. Servs. Co.*, B–233561, Mar. 7, 1989, 89–1 CPD ¶ 250 at 2. . . . Consequently, our review of an agency's cost realism evaluation is limited to determining whether the cost analysis is reasonably based and not arbitrary. *Jacobs COGEMA, LLC*, B–290125.2, B–290125.3, Dec. 18, 2002, 2003 CPD ¶ 16 at 26.[327]

Similarly, at COFC, the plaintiff bears the burden of proving that the agency's cost realism analysis lacked a rational basis.[328]

b. Price Realism

The purpose of a price realism analysis is "to determine whether prices are too low, such that there may be a risk of poor performance."[329] There are no prescriptive requirements for a price realism analysis in the FAR. GAO has determined it will only find an agency was required to conduct a price realism analysis where (1) the solicitation stated it would conduct a price realism analysis or (2) in the absence of such a statement, the RFP expressly stated that the agency would review prices to determine whether they are so low that they reflect a lack of technical understanding *and* the RFP stated that a proposal could be rejected on such a basis.[330]

"Unless the agency commits itself to a particular methodology in a solicitation, the nature and extent of a price realism analysis, as well as an assessment of potential risk associated with a proposed price, are generally within the sound exercise of the agency's discretion[.]"[331] Accordingly, both GAO and COFC will assess whether the

---

325. FAR 15.305(a)(1); 15.404-1(d)(2).

326. Logc2, Inc., B-416075, June 5, 2018, 2018 CPD ¶ 204 (citing AdvanceMed Corp.; TrustSolutions, LLC, B-404910.4, Jan. 17, 2012, 2012 CPD ¶ 25).

327. Logc2, Inc., B-416075, June 5, 2018, 2018 CPD ¶ 204, at 4.

328. McConnell Jones Lanier & Murphy LLP v. United States, 128 Fed. Cl. 218, 236 (2016) (citing Westech Int'l, Inc. v. United States, 79 Fed. Cl. 272, 286 (2007)).

329. EFW Inc., B-412608, Apr. 7, 2016, 2016 CPD ¶ 304, at 11.

330. Cyberdata Techs., Inc., B-417084, Feb. 6, 2019, 2019 CPD ¶ 34; Centerra Grp., LLC, B-414800, Sept. 21, 2017, 2017 CPD ¶ 307.

331. Harmonia Holdings Grp., LLC v. United States, 136 Fed. Cl. 298, 307 (2018) (quoting Mil–Mar Century Corp. v. United States, 111 Fed. Cl. 508, 541 (2013)); *accord*, Next Tier Concepts, Inc.,

agency followed the methodology identified in the solicitation (if one was identified), and whether the agency adequately documented its decision.[332]

c. Price Reasonableness

An offeror may challenge an agency's price reasonableness analysis of its or a competitor's proposal. For procurements conducted under FAR Part 15, the FAR requires that contracting officers purchase "supplies and services from responsible sources at fair and reasonable prices."[333] Where certified cost or pricing data are not required, the FAR requires that contracting officers obtain the type and quantity of data necessary; and the FAR suggests the use of techniques such as price analysis, cost analysis, and/or cost realism analysis to determine the "fair and reasonable price" for each contract.[334]

There are a variety of methods for conducting a price reasonableness analysis, and GAO will defer to agency judgment and discretion with respect to the methodology chosen.[335] "The purpose of a price reasonableness analysis is to prevent the government from paying too high a price for a contract."[336] As a practical matter, protests on this basis are not often asserted as they are difficult to win. In *Fluor Intercontinental, Inc. v. United States*,[337] however, COFC concluded that the agency had failed to "conduct a proper price reasonableness evaluation in accordance with FAR 15.404-1(b)," because it analyzed only the lowest offeror's proposed price for reasonableness and conducted a "bare comparison" of the percentage differences between that price and those of the other offerors without any analysis of the awardee's price.

d. Unbalanced Pricing

As noted earlier, "[u]nbalanced pricing exists when, despite an acceptable total evaluated price, the price of one or more line items is significantly over or understated as indicated by the application of cost or price analysis techniques."[338] The FAR requires that, for competitive procurements, agencies analyze all offers with separately priced

---

B-414337, May 15, 2017, 2017 CPD ¶ 161, at 3 ("The nature and extent of an agency's price realism analysis largely is a matter within the agency's discretion.").

332. *See, e.g.*, Next Tier Concepts, Inc., B-414337, May 15, 2017, 2017 CPD ¶ 161, at 3 ("We will object to an agency's price realism evaluation where it is unreasonable, inconsistent with the terms of the solicitation, or inadequately documented."); Limco Airepair, Inc. v. United States, 130 Fed. Cl. 544, 552 (2017) ("the evidentiary record makes clear that the Air Force documented its price realism analysis for the Solicitation").

333. FAR 15.402(a).

334. *See* FAR 15.402(a)–(b).

335. *See* Transatlantic Lines, LLC, B-411846.3, May 18, 2016, 2016 CPD ¶ 148.

336. Technatomy Corp., B-414672.5, Oct. 10, 2018, 2018 CPD ¶ 353.

337. 147 Fed. Cl. 309, 335–36 (2020).

338. FAR 15.404-1(g)(1).

line items or subline items to determine if the prices are unbalanced.[339] This analysis is required because unbalanced pricing may "increase performance risk" and "result in payment of unreasonably high prices."[340] If an agency determines that an offer is unbalanced, the FAR requires the agency to

> (1) Consider the risks to the government associated with the unbalanced pricing in determining the competitive range and in making the source selection decision; and
>
> (2) Consider whether award of the contract will result in paying unreasonably high prices for contract performance.[341]

Once an agency conducts its risk analysis, an agency may issue an award for a proposal with unbalanced pricing, provided that "the pricing does not pose an unacceptable level of risk, and the prices the agency is likely to pay under the contract are not unreasonably high."[342] The government can also reject any offer where unbalanced pricing poses an unacceptable risk to the government.[343]

For GAO to sustain a protest alleging unbalanced pricing, "a protester must show that one or more prices in the allegedly unbalanced proposal are overstated; it is insufficient for a protester to show simply that some line item prices in the proposal are understated."[344] "This is [] because low prices (even below-cost prices) are not improper and do not themselves establish (or create the risk inherent in) unbalanced pricing."[345] Although protests alleging unbalanced prices generally concern procurements involving sealed bids, the allegations may also concern negotiated procurements where cost or price constitutes a primary basis for the source selection.[346]

12. *Past Performance Evaluations*

Disappointed offerors may protest the agency's evaluation of their own or the awardee's past performance. Such protests generally challenge whether a past performance reference is recent or similar in scope to the solicitation, or whether the evaluation fairly reflects the quality of the contractor's past performance.

---

339. FAR 15.404-1(g)(2).

340. FAR 15.404-1(g)(1).

341. FAR 15.404-1(g)(2).

342. Citywide Managing Servs. of Port Washington, Inc., B-281287.12, Nov. 15, 2000, 2001 CPD ¶ 6, at 5.

343. FAR 15.404-1(g)(3).

344. DynCorp Int'l, LLC v. United States, 125 Fed. Cl. 446 (2016); Aar Supply Chain, Inc., B-415873, Apr. 12, 2018, 2018 CPD ¶ 157, at 15 n.7 (citing First Fin. Assocs., Inc., B-415713, Feb. 16, 2018, 2018 CPD ¶ 76); Marine Terminals Corp.-East, Inc., B-410698.9, Aug. 4, 2016, 2016 CPD ¶ 212, at 8.

345. *Marine Terminals Corp., East, Inc.*, B-410698.9 at 8.

346. D & G Contract Servs., B-231453, Mar. 2, 1989, 89-1 CPD ¶ 219.

Agencies enjoy a great deal of discretion in evaluating past performance, and challenges on this ground are particularly hard to win. It is well settled that

> [t]he evaluation of past performance, including the agency's determination of the relevance and scope of a firm's performance history to be considered, is a matter of agency discretion, which [GAO] will not find improper unless unreasonable, inconsistent with the solicitation criteria, or undocumented.[347]

Consistent with this discretion and the deference afforded to an agency's past performance evaluation, GAO has explained that "while an agency is obligated to consider reasonably available, relevant past performance information, a procuring agency is not required to identify each and every piece of past performance information that may potentially exist," and there is no legal requirement that all, or any, references be contacted in order for a past performance evaluation to be deemed reasonable.[348]

COFC also defers to agency discretion, arguably to an even greater extent than GAO. At COFC, "a protestor must overcome a 'triple whammy of deference by demonstrating by a preponderance of the evidence that the [Source Selection Authority (SSA)] lacked any rational basis' to assign a given past performance rating."[349] COFC limits its review of an agency's past performance evaluation to "determining whether the evaluation was reasonable, consistent with stated evaluation criteria and complied with relevant statutory and regulatory requirements."[350] COFC will consider a past performance evaluation reasonable when the agency gave "meaningful consideration" to adverse past performance information documented in the offeror's record.[351]

GAO reviews agency determinations of the relevance of past performance references for reasonableness and consistency with the solicitation's evaluation criteria.[352] Solicitations may treat relevance of past performance references in one of two ways—references may simply be deemed relevant or nonrelevant (which is relatively rare), or the solicitation may provide for an evaluation of the *degree* of relevance. Where

---

347. Harris IT Servs. Corp., B-406067, Jan. 27, 2012, 2012 CPD ¶ 57, at 8.

348. Triple Canopy, Inc., B-310566.4, Oct. 30, 2008, 2008 CPD ¶ 207, at 6; Satellite Servs., Inc., B-295866, Apr. 29, 2005, 2005 CPD ¶ 84, at 3 ("there is no legal requirement that all, or any, references be contacted in order for a past performance evaluation to be deemed reasonable"); *see also* PCT Servs., Inc., B-279168, May 12, 1998, 98-1 CPD ¶ 152, at 3 (agency is "not required to check all references listed in each offeror's proposal").

349. Am. Auto Logistics, LP v. United States, 117 Fed. Cl. 137, 186 (2014) (emphasis omitted) (quoting Overstreet Elec. Co., Inc. v. United States, 59 Fed. Cl. 99, 117 (2003)).

350. Westech Int'l, Inc. v. United States, 79 Fed. Cl. 272, 294 (2007).

351. *See* Vanguard Recovery v. United States, 99 Fed. Cl. 81, 95–96 (2011).

352. *See, e.g.*, Spinnaker JV, LLC, B-416688, Nov. 21, 2018, 2018 CPD ¶ 398; Bevilacqua Research Corp., B-293051, Jan. 12, 2004, 2004 CPD ¶ 14; MCS of Tampa, Inc., B-288271.5, Feb. 8, 2002, 2002 CPD ¶ 52.

a solicitation calls for an evaluation of a degree of relevance, and the agency merely assesses whether the references were relevant, GAO may sustain the protest.[353]

Likewise, if an awardee receives the highest past performance rating, yet does not have any highly relevant contracts, GAO may sustain the protest. In *Health Net Federal Services, LLC*,[354] the agency assigned somewhat relevant ratings (the second highest relevancy rating available) to the awardee's contracts because of their smaller size. The agency rated each of the contracts as exceptional in terms of quality of performance. Despite the fact that the awardee had no contracts that received the highest relevancy rating, the agency assigned the awardee a high confidence rating on the basis of its exceptional quality of performance. GAO explained that

> [a]t a minimum, absent some further support in the record, it was not reasonable to give [the awardee] the highest past performance rating in reliance on the "exceptional" performance ratings associated with the prior contracts of such smaller size. On the contrary, the value of the "exceptional" ratings as predictors of [the awardee's] success on the [instant] contract is inherently diminished by their lack of relevance due to their relatively small size.[355]

The agency's evaluation as to the merits of an offeror's past performance submission will be given a great deal of discretion so long as it is reasonable and treats offerors equally.[356] But where an agency assigns past performance ratings in a mechanical fashion and fails to consider substantive differences among the offerors' underlying past performance records, GAO may find the past performance evaluation to be unreasonable. In *EFW Inc.*,[357] the agency reviewed five past performance references for each offeror and assigned relevance and quality ratings to each. The agency then used a matrix to convert the relevance/quality assessment for each reference into a confidence rating, and averaged these confidence ratings into an overall past performance confidence rating for the offeror, with no further consideration of the offerors'

---

353. *See* Clean Harbors Envtl. Servs. Inc., B-296176.2, Dec. 9, 2005, 2005 CPD ¶ 222 (protest sustained where agency failed to consider the degree of relevance of past performance information as required by solicitation).

354. B-401652.3, Nov. 4, 2009, 2009 CPD ¶ 220.

355. *Id.* at 14 (emphasis added).

356. In this regard, it should be noted that a protester is unlikely to prevail on an argument that the procuring agency evaluated its proposal unreasonably because it relied on a flawed CPAR rating. Such an argument is generally viewed by GAO and COFC as a matter of contract administration for which the protester's vehicle for relief is the Contract Disputes Act (CDA) dispute resolution process, not a bid protest. *See, e.g.*, Gen. Revenue Corp., B-414220.2, Mar. 27, 2017, 2017 CPD ¶ 106 ("Such challenges to the methodology utilized for assessing the contractors' performance on the predecessor contracts, or the findings in connection with those performance reviews, involve matters of contract administration that are not for [GAO's] review as part of [its] bid protest function.") (citing 4 C.F.R. § 21.5(a); ProActive Techs., Inc., B-412957.5, Aug. 23, 2016, 2016 CPD ¶ 244).

357. B-412608, Apr. 7, 2016, 2016 CPD ¶ 304.

underlying performance histories, or whether there were any discriminators among the offerors. GAO sustained the protest because the only past performance information the agency considered in its award decision was the mechanically generated overall confidence ratings.

Similarly, GAO may sustain a protest where an agency treats offerors' past performance unequally.[358] For example, in *CSR, Inc.*,[359] the solicitation required offerors to submit past performance reference projects and provided that the agency might also consider past performance other than that cited by the offeror. In evaluating the reference projects, the agency considered only the most recent CPARs for the protester's cited projects, but for the awardee also included a favorable CPAR from a task order the offeror did not identify in its proposal. Although an agency reasonably may "limit its review of past performance information in various ways," GAO found it "disparate and unreasonable" for the agency to consider additional, uncited projects for the awardee and not to attempt to do the same for the protester.[360]

In addition, GAO may sustain a protest where an agency fails to give meaningful consideration to all the relevant past performance information it possesses. This most obviously applies to situations where an agency ignores past performance information the offeror references in its proposal. But, in certain narrow circumstances, GAO may sustain a protest if an agency fails to consider information *not* included in a proposal. GAO has generally limited application of this principle to situations where the past performance information relates to contracts for the same services with the same procuring activity, or information personally known to the evaluators.

The first of these narrow circumstances occurs when an offeror properly includes a past performance reference in its proposal, but the agency fails to consider the related past performance record for reasons outside the offeror's control. The seminal decision for this protest ground is *International Business Systems, Inc.*[361] There, the protester included two past performance references in its proposal, but the agency refused to evaluate one because the agency official responsible for completing the evaluation form for that contract failed to do so. GAO noted that the record showed that the ignored past performance information was recent and of excellent quality, and involved "the same agency, the same services, and the same contracting officer."[362] GAO found the agency should have considered this past performance reference because "some information is simply too close at hand to require

358. *See, e.g.*, Barnes Aerospace Grp., B-298864, Dec. 26, 2006, 2006 CPD ¶ 204 (sustaining protest where record showed that agency treated offerors unequally with respect to application of its qualification requirements).

359. B-413973, Jan. 13, 2017, 2017 CPD ¶ 64.

360. *Id.* at 5–6.

361. B-275554, Mar. 3, 1997, 97-1 CPD ¶ 114.

362. *Id.* at 4.

offerors to shoulder the inequities that spring from an agency's failure to obtain, and consider, the information."[363] This was not a situation where the protester failed to submit a well-written proposal by omitting past performance references it should have included; rather, the agency unreasonably failed to obtain the information that the proposal did reference. Later protest decisions have applied this "too close at hand" rule to similar circumstances.[364]

The second scenario in which the "too close at hand" rule may apply arises when an agency ignores recent, relevant, adverse past performance information of which it is aware concerning the awardee. For example, in *Northeast Military Sales, Inc.*,[365] the agency rated the awardee's past performance as exceptional, despite the evaluators' receipt of multiple e-mails from government customers reporting a number of serious problems with the awardee's performance. Because the record did not demonstrate that the evaluators gave any consideration to the adverse information in their possession, GAO found that the exceptional rating was not reasonably supported. Likewise, in *Contrack International, Inc.*,[366] a protester objected to the awardee's excellent past performance rating following corrective action despite alleged performance problems of which the agency was aware but that it did not consider. GAO observed that although the agency may not have been aware of certain adverse information contained in an inspector general's report during the initial award decision, the protester included that report with its initial protest. Thus, in the corrective action following the initial protest, it was unreasonable for the agency not to consider the information in its new past performance evaluation.

Over the years, protesters have attempted to extend the "too close at hand" rule to other circumstances but generally have been unsuccessful. Protesters often cite news reports, inspector general reports, case dockets, and other public information in initial protests to argue that agency evaluators unreasonably failed to consider adverse past performance information about an awardee. To be successful, the protester must eventually show that the evaluators knew or should have known of the information in question at the time of the evaluation and ignored it. In *Exelis Systems Corp.*,[367] for

363. *Id.*

364. *See, e.g.*, Shaw-Parsons Infrastructure Recovery Consultants, LLC; Vanguard Recovery Assistance, Joint Venture, B-401679.4, Mar. 10, 2010, 2010 CPD ¶ 77, at 5 ("An agency's past performance evaluation is unreasonable where the agency fails to give meaningful consideration to all the relevant past performance information it possesses."); SCIENTECH, Inc., B-277805.2, Jan. 20, 1998, 98-1 CPD ¶ 33, at 7–8 (sustaining protest where protester's proposal cited its successful incumbent performance but the agency inexplicably failed to evaluate that performance).

365. B-404153, Jan. 13, 2011, 2011 CPD ¶ 2.

366. B-401871.5, May 24, 2010, 2010 CPD ¶ 126.

367. B-407111, Nov. 13, 2012, 2012 CPD ¶ 340.

example, the protester argued that the agency unreasonably failed to consider adverse past performance information about the awardee contained in three inspector general reports. GAO rejected the argument because the past performance evaluators neither knew nor should have known of the existence of two of the reports (even though they were issued by the same agency), and the third report was not finalized and issued until after contract award.

GAO has similarly declined to impute to evaluators knowledge of news reports, legal disputes, and other potential indicators of an offeror's adverse past performance without a showing of actual knowledge by the evaluators.[368]

GAO also has refused to apply the "too close at hand" rule to evaluation factors other than past performance.[369] For these other factors, the general rule is that agency evaluators *may* look outside the four corners of a proposal but are not *required* to do so.[370]

GAO also has consistently declined to require an agency to consider past performance information that the protester could have but did not include in its proposal.[371] In these circumstances, it is the "well-written proposal" rule that applies instead:

> Where an offeror is in control of the past performance information contained in its proposal—and not reliant on third parties to submit that information—it exercises its own judgment as to the information that the agency should consider. Under those circumstances, there is "no inequity" in an agency's decision to base its evaluation on an offeror's proposal as written, instead of supplementing the proposal with the agency's understanding of the offeror's performance under other contracts not cited by the offeror.[372]

368. *See, e.g.*, Thoma-Sea Marine Constructors, LLC, B-416240, July 16, 2018, 2018 CPD ¶ 245 (evaluators were not required to consider "publicly available information" concerning alleged performance problems involving the awardee's subcontractor where the evaluators had no knowledge of the dispute and the dispute did not involve the procuring agency); BillSmart Sols., LLC, B-413272.4, Oct. 23, 2017, 2017 CPD ¶ 325 (agency not required to consider outside sources of information, such as news reports that were not known to the evaluators, where there was no requirement for the agency to conduct an "independent review" or run Internet searches).

369. *See, e.g.*, Aero Simulation, Inc., B-411373, July 2, 2015, 2015 CPD ¶ 233 (declining to extend "too close at hand" rule to technical evaluations); SNAP, Inc., B-409609, June 20, 2014, 2014 CPD ¶ 187, at 8 (declining to extend "too close at hand rule" to corporate experience evaluations).

370. *See* Interfor US, Inc., B-410622, Dec. 30, 2014, 2015 CPD ¶ 19, at 7 ("We have held that an agency is not bound by the 'four corners' of an offeror's proposal, and *may* properly use information known by its own evaluators, as with any other references, to aid in the evaluation of proposals.") (emphasis added).

371. *See, e.g.*, FN Mfg. LLC, B-407936, Apr. 19, 2013, 2013 CPD ¶ 105 (denying protest where protester failed to include in its proposal the favorable past performance references it alleged the agency evaluators should have considered).

372. *Id.* at 3.

13. Responsibility Determinations

Before an agency awards a contract, it must determine that the prospective contractor is "responsible." "Responsibility" essentially means that a firm has the technical, financial, ethical, and other capabilities necessary to perform the contract.[373] Ordinarily, if the contracting officer determines that a firm is responsible, that determination is entitled to great deference and GAO will not review protests challenging the reasonableness of that determination. To this end, GAO's Bid Protest Regulations provide the following:

> *Affirmative determination of responsibility by the contracting officer.* Because the determination that a bidder or offeror is capable of performing a contract is largely committed to the contracting officer's discretion, GAO will generally not consider a protest challenging such a determination. The exceptions are protests that allege that definitive responsibility criteria in the solicitation were not met and those that identify evidence raising serious concerns that, in reaching a particular responsibility determination, the contracting officer unreasonably failed to consider available relevant information or otherwise violated statute or regulation.[374]

As noted in the regulation above, there are two narrow exceptions to this rule. First, GAO will consider a protest if the solicitation established "definitive responsibility criteria" that the awardee objectively did not meet or cannot meet by the time set in the solicitation.[375] For example, if the solicitation required the awardee to hold a certain security clearance or possess specific experience, GAO will review a protest alleging the awardee lacks that clearance or specified experience.[376]

In addition, GAO will consider a protest in which "the contracting officer unreasonably failed to consider available relevant information or otherwise violated statute or regulation."[377] Although rare, this may occur where the awardee is demonstrably tottering on the edge of bankruptcy or under a federal fraud investigation, but the contracting officer failed to give appropriate attention to that fact.[378] In *FCi Federal, Inc.*,[379] GAO concluded that the contracting officer's affirmative determination of responsibility was unreasonable where the contracting officer did not review and consider "specific allegations of fraud alleged by the DOJ, relying instead on general media reports," failed to consider the relationship of the awardee and its parent, and misunderstood the legal standards related to affirmative responsibility determinations.

---

373. *See generally* FAR Subpart 9.1.
374. 4 C.F.R. § 21.5(c).
375. *Id.*
376. J2A2 JV, LLC, B-401663.4, Apr. 19, 2010, 2010 CPD ¶ 102.
377. 4 C.F.R. § 21.5(c).
378. *See, e.g.*, FCi Fed., Inc., B-408558.4, Oct. 20, 2014, 2014 CPD ¶ 308.
379. B-408558.4.

Successful challenges to responsibility determinations are also rare at COFC. COFC will, however, consider protests of responsibility determinations alleging that "there has been a violation of a statute or regulation, or alternatively, if the agency determination lacked a rational basis."[380]

14. Impact of Corporate Transactions

In recent years, the government contracting community has seen a considerable amount of merger and acquisition activity, ranging from small company acquisitions to multibillion-dollar transactions. Offerors that submit proposals prior to being merged, acquired, divested, or reorganized, but win the award after the transaction has closed, may face protests arguing that the entity receiving the award was not the entity that submitted the proposal.[381]

In a particularly notable case, GAO sustained a protest challenging NASA's award of a $1.76 billion IDIQ contract to Science Applications International Corporation (SAIC) where the agency failed to reasonably consider the impact resulting from the company's expected reorganization of the company that submitted the proposal into two legally distinct corporate entities—"New" SAIC and Leidos.[382] GAO noted that the proposal submitted by SAIC "and the agency's evaluation thereof, was based on the technical approach, resources, and costs associated with 'old' SAIC," which was "a 40,000 employee, $11 billion per year organization."[383] In addition, GAO noted that the "'old' SAIC—the offeror and awardee—did not intend to perform as the prime contractor in this matter." Instead, a separate, "smaller entity with substantially fewer resources . . . would perform the contract as the prime contractor."[384] Although SAIC disclosed this plan to the agency during discussions, the agency never considered the impact of the divestiture on costs or technical approach, and GAO sustained the protest.

---

380. Impresa Construzioni Geom. Domenico Garufi v. United States, 238 F.3d 1324, 1333 (Fed. Cir. 2001).

381. Although this book focuses on potential grounds of protest, and does not address best practices that a contractor should employ when engaged in or considering such a transaction, it is worth noting that prudence warrants giving advance notice to the contracting officer (and specifically addressing in the proposal reasons the transaction will not impact the contractor's offer or performance). Doing so would deflect any post-transaction concerns that the change in performing entities came as a surprise (and could help ease the novation process, which can be difficult and lengthy, especially if the contracting officer believes he or she was caught off guard by the request). Advance notice would also arm the agency to respond to any protests by saying that the transaction was known about and considered when the proposal was evaluated.

382. Wyle Labs., Inc., B-408112.2, Dec. 27, 2013, 2014 CPD ¶ 16.

383. *Id.* at 5–6.

384. *Id.* at 7.

Less than a year after its decision in *Wyle*, GAO came to a different result in another protest involving the same transaction. In *VSE Corp.; the University of Hawaii-Costs*,[385] GAO denied a protest raising allegations that the agency failed to consider the impact of a proposed reorganization announced in a press release. GAO stated that the

> release was nothing more than an announcement of SAIC's board of directors stating its intentions to plan to examine the possibility of future action by SAIC, which did not trigger any obligation by SAIC to report or the agency to consider in the conduct of the procurement at issue.[386]

GAO contrasted the facts in *VSE* from those in *Wyle*:

> Here, in contrast, the protesters do not contend that SAIC's proposal specified how the company would be split or which company would ultimately perform the contract. In addition, unlike the situation here, in *Wyle*, SAIC expressly advised the agency during discussions of the pending split and identified which entities would be performing the contract. Further, SAIC offered to cap rates that might be affected by the approaching split and the agency declined their offer. On this record, where there was no discussion of the pending split, we see no basis to conclude that the agency was required to evaluate SAIC's past performance in the manner argued by the protesters.[387]

Three years later, GAO denied another protest asserting that the agency evaluated the old SAIC's past performance when it was the New SAIC's performance that mattered. In *DynCorp International LLC*,[388] GAO explained that "there was no question as to which entity's resources would be relied upon for purposes of contract performance," as the contracts novated to the new SAIC entity were used "for purposes of demonstrating New SAIC's experience and past performance."[389]

In *Wyle*, GAO sustained the protest because the agency failed to consider the impact of an *expected* restructuring—leading one to question: at what point does a contemplated corporate transaction require an agency to consider its impact in evaluating the proposal of an offeror involved in that transaction? GAO addressed this issue in *Lockheed Martin Integrated Systems, Inc.*[390] In *Lockheed*, GAO provided that "an agency should analyze the effect of a possible corporate restructuring on an

385. B-407164.11, June 23, 2014, 2014 CPD ¶ 202.

386. *Id.* at 6 (citing Metro Mach. Corp., B-402567, June 3, 2010, 2010 CPD ¶ 132).

387. *Id.*

388. B-411126.4, Dec. 20, 2016, 2017 CPD ¶ 333, at 15.

389. *Cf.* Target Media Mid Atl., Inc., B-412468.6, Dec. 6, 2016, 2016 CPD ¶ 358 (distinguishing the impact of a corporate transaction "resulting in the contract being performed by a materially different prime contractor").

390. B-410189.5, Sept. 27, 2016, 2016 CPD ¶ 273.

offeror's proposal when the transaction at issue is '*imminent and essentially certain*,'" adding that

> [i]ndices of whether a transaction is imminent and essentially certain include whether the timing and manner of the spin-off contemplated were within the control of the offeror, and whether the offeror had disclosed detailed plans to the SEC, including an anticipated time frame for closing the transaction.[391]

15. FSS Contract Issues

FSS orders may be protested on many of the same bases discussed earlier. There are two issues, however, that are unique to these contracts: alignment of labor categories and orders on expiring contracts, both of which GAO addressed in *AllWorld Language Consultants, Inc.*[392]

a. Labor Category Alignment

Unlike many procurements in which an offeror can propose labor categories to meet particular contract requirements, in an FSS contract, the labor categories have already been provided and described in the schedule contract. Thus, they cannot be altered to meet the specific government requirements at the order level. In *AllWorld Language Consultants*,[393] the GSA issued a solicitation to FSS contract holders to acquire linguistic support services. After award, the protester alleged that the awardee's quotation was technically unacceptable because it proposed a labor category that did not conform to the solicitation's specified labor category requirements.

GSA responded that contractors' FSS labor categories generally do not "align precisely" with solicitation requirements and that GSA accounted for this fact by considering the awardee's technical quotation to determine what duties its proposed linguists would actually perform.[394] GAO concluded that GSA's evaluation of the awardee's quotation was unreasonable because the awardee quoted a single FSS labor category to perform all linguist duties required by the solicitation, but that labor category did not address numerous solicitation requirements. GAO also found that although the awardee's quotation identified other labor categories of linguists that

---

391. *Id.* at 7 (quoting Nat'l Aeronautics and Space Admin.-Recon., B-408112.3, May 14, 2014, 2014 CPD ¶ 155, at 3).

392. B-411481.3, Jan. 6, 2016, 2016 CPD ¶ 12. The statutory bars that limit GAO's and COFC's jurisdiction over many task or delivery order protests do not apply to protests of FSS orders. *See* Coast Prof'l, Inc. v. United States, 828 F.3d 1349, 1354 (Fed. Cir. 2016); Panacea Consulting, Inc., B-299307.4, July 27, 2007, 2007 CPD ¶ 141, at 1 n.1.

393. B-411481.3.

394. *Id.* at 3.

could potentially satisfy solicitation requirements, these other labor categories were not included in the awardee's underlying FSS contract.

GAO rejected the GSA's position

> that [the awardee] could identify a labor category under its FSS contract that did not meet all of the requirements of the [Performance Work Statement], but could somehow enhance or alter the narrative description and qualifications of that labor category through the technical portion of its quotation.[395]

GAO stated that the

> labor categories identified and described in each firm's underlying FSS contract are fixed, discrete, specific labor category descriptions that are contractually binding and not subject to alteration, just as the technical specifications for products available under a firm's FSS contract are fixed, discrete, specific, contractually binding, and not subject to alteration.[396]

As such, GAO held that

> [t]o the extent a quoted labor category description under a firm's FSS contract does not, in the words of GSA, "align precisely" with the requirements of a given solicitation, the firm may not properly alter the underlying labor category description through the terms of its quotation. Rather, where a firm's quoted labor category description does not align with the requirements of the solicitation, it means that the quoted labor category does not meet the requirements of the solicitation, and therefore cannot serve as the basis for issuing a task order to the firm.[397]

As a result, GAO sustained the protest. Given this decision, agencies now must establish sufficiently specific solicitation requirements without being so specific as to prevent contractors from quoting labor categories that "align precisely."

b. Schedule Contract Expiration

In addition to the labor category alignment issue, the *AllWorld* protest decision also addressed an agency's ability to make awards and exercise options on an expiring FSS contract.[398] GSA issued the order to the awardee three days before its underlying FSS contract was set to expire. For years, federal agencies had issued orders under FSS and IDIQ contracts that included years of options extending well beyond the underlying contracts' ordering periods. And for years, agencies had exercised those options

395. *Id.* at 5.
396. *Id.*
397. *Id.*
398. *AllWorld Language Consultants*, B-411481.3.

without regard to whether the time for placing new orders under the underlying contracts had expired.

Notwithstanding long-standing agency practice, GAO concluded that an agency cannot exercise options included in an FSS order after the underlying FSS contract's ordering period had expired, even if the FSS order containing the option was issued during the FSS contract's ordering period (as was the case in *AllWorld*). Although recognizing that the schedule order's full *base* period could be performed despite expiration of the underlying FSS contract's ordering period, and that inclusion of the options did not render the order award itself objectionable, GAO opined that "GSA cannot legally exercise the options included in the task order without a valid underlying FSS contract."[399] GAO's rationale was that "orders under FSS contracts are not themselves stand-alone contracts" because "the rights and liabilities of the parties under every FSS task order are governed by, and subject to, the terms and conditions of the underlying FSS contract."[400] In addition, according to GAO, the exercise of an option creates "new contractual responsibilities."[401] Thus, the creation of these "new contractual responsibilities" requires "a valid underlying FSS contract."[402]

16. Flawed Best Value Tradeoff/Decision

One ground found in almost all protests is the allegation that the ultimate award decision was flawed. In many cases, this comes as an argument that the best value or price/technical tradeoff decision was unreasonable, or that the agency failed to conduct the required technical/price tradeoff either to justify paying a price premium for the higher rated technical proposal, or to award to the lower rated technical proposal because of its lower price. Protesters should be careful not to craft this ground so that it reads as nothing more than a rehash of previously asserted grounds, as GAO has been known to dismiss such arguments as derivative.[403] That said, there are several reasons why a protester might assert this argument.

399. *Id.* at 7.

400. *Id.*

401. *Id.*

402. *Id.*

403. *See, e.g.*, GCC Techs., LLC, B-416459.2, Nov. 19, 2018, 2018 CPD ¶ 394 (protest ground asserting flawed best value tradeoff dismissed as derivative of challenges to agency's evaluation of protester's and awardee's proposals); Emta Insaat Taahut Ve Ticaret, A.S., B-416391, Aug. 13, 2018, 2018 CPD ¶ 280 (same); Advanced Alliant Sols. Team, LLC, B-417334 ("derivative allegations do not establish independent bases of protest").

a. Unreasonable Underlying Evaluations

Agencies are required to evaluate offerors' proposals in accordance with the solicitation's evaluation criteria. In a best-value tradeoff procurement, the agency undertakes a meaningful analysis of the merits in each offeror's price and nonprice submissions, and based upon the solicitation's evaluation criteria, engages in a tradeoff analysis that explains why the awardee's proposal was selected. If the awardee's proposal was both rated higher technically and priced lower than the competitors' proposals, the analysis is fairly straightforward. If the proposal was technically stronger but more expensive, the agency must explain why the superior technical offering justified the price premium associated with it. If the proposal was technically inferior but less expensive, the agency must explain why the superior technical proposal was not worth the added price.

GAO does not second-guess an agency's documented determination that one offeror's superiority under nonprice evaluation factors is (or is not) worth a particular price premium in a best-value tradeoff. This means an agency might reasonably exercise its discretion to determine that some perceived technical superiority is worth paying a relatively large price premium, or that higher technical ratings are not worth a relatively modest price premium. GAO's review of a best value decision does not turn on the mere magnitude of the technical difference between the offerors or the size of the price delta, and it does not require agencies to quantify the dollar value of various technical merits. In the end, GAO's analysis focuses on whether the documented tradeoff decision is consistent with the terms of the solicitation and reasonably reflects the underlying merits of the competing proposals, and whether the articulated award rationale is *reasonable.*

When a protester has demonstrated that the underlying evaluations are prejudicially unreasonable, the tradeoff decision will also be considered unreasonable: "A source selection decision based on inconsistent or inaccurate information concerning the technical evaluation or the relative merits and contents of the offerors' technical proposals is not reasonable."[404]

b. Insufficient Documentation

Another often-raised challenge to an agency's best value decision is that the agency inadequately documented its tradeoff rationale. Just as the agency must document its

---

404. Ashland Sales and Serv. Co., B-291206, Dec. 5, 2002, 2003 CPD ¶ 36, at 6; *see also* Verdi Consulting, Inc., B-414103.2, Apr. 26, 2017, 2017 CPD ¶ 136, at 11 ("[B]ecause we find that the agency's price evaluation and the evaluation of [the protester's] past performance were unreasonable and fundamentally flawed, as discussed above, the agency's reliance (if any) on those evaluation judgments as part of its best-value tradeoff, is also flawed."). Evaluation errors that would not alter the final award decision are not prejudicial and are an insufficient basis for sustaining a protest.

underlying evaluation sufficiently to allow GAO an opportunity to understand the evaluation, so must the source selection authority document his or her rationale for why a particular offeror is being awarded the contract. The FAR specifically requires the documentation of the rationale underlying a source selection decision:

> The source selection authority's (SSA) decision shall be based on a comparative assessment of proposals against all source selection criteria in the solicitation. While the SSA may use reports and analyses prepared by others, the source selection decision shall represent the SSA's independent judgment. *The source selection decision shall be documented, and the documentation shall include the rationale for any business judgments and tradeoffs made or relied on by the SSA, including benefits associated with additional costs.* Although the rationale for the selection decision must be documented, that documentation need not quantify the tradeoffs that led to the decision.[405]

Failure to adequately document the tradeoff rationale may result in a sustained protest.[406]

Although the SSA must document any tradeoff, the pertinent explanation can be given in the award decision or evidenced by the documents on which the source selection decision is based.[407] Thus, the length of the source selection decision alone is not dispositive, especially where the SSA may have adopted by reference the findings of the evaluators or the recommendation for award provided in a lengthier, more detailed document.

c. Looking Behind the Ratings

A close cousin to the lack of documentation argument is the argument that the SSA failed to look behind the ratings of the offerors when conducting a best value tradeoff. GAO has long held that ratings, whether they are numerical, adjectival, or color, "are merely guides for intelligent decision making in the procurement process."[408] The

---

405. FAR 15.308 (emphasis added).

406. *See, e.g.*, Harmonia Holdings Grp., LLC, B-417475.3, Sept. 23, 2019, 2019 CPD ¶ 333, at 19 (sustaining protest where "the record contains no evidence that the selection official meaningfully looked behind the numerical ratings, and beyond the numbers of strengths and weaknesses, to determine that [the awardee's] higher-rated, higher-priced quotation was the best value"); ManTech Advanced Sys. Int'l, Inc., B-415497, Jan. 18, 2018, 2018 CPD ¶ 60, at 4 ("[A] tradeoff analysis that fails to furnish any explanation as to why a higher-rated proposal does not in fact offer technical advantages or why those technical advantages are not worth a price premium does not satisfy the requirement for a documented tradeoff rationale, particularly where, as here, price is secondary to technical considerations under the RFP's evaluation scheme."); Midland Supply, Inc., B-298720, Nov. 29, 2006, 2007 CPD ¶ 2 (sustaining protest where agency did not properly document its decision to award to the technically lower-rated, lower-cost offeror).

407. TRW, Inc., B-260788.2, Aug. 2, 1995, 96-1 CPD ¶ 11, at 2.

408. Systems Eng'g Partners, LLC, B-412329, Jan. 20, 2016, 2016 CPD ¶ 31, at 5.

SSA must look behind the ratings: "A source selection official is obligated to consider the underlying bases for ratings, including the advantages and disadvantages associated with the specific content of proposals, in a manner that is fair and equitable and consistent with the terms of the RFP."[409] In other words, ratings and adjectival labels cannot replace reasoned judgment and the need to consider the underlying qualitative merits of each offer.

Agencies may run afoul of this rule in a number of ways. One common procurement error is finding two proposals to be "technically equal" based solely upon a comparison of adjectival ratings.[410] Even if an agency properly rates two technical proposals as "Very Good," that does not mean they are technically equivalent. In *Arctic Slope Technical Services, Inc.*,[411] for example, the agency made award to an offeror based on its lower price after determining there were "no significant technical differences" between the offerors' proposals. The SSA concluded that the proposals were technically equal based solely on a comparison of the identical adjectival ratings, disregarding numerous differences between the proposals, including different strengths. GAO sustained the protest because the source selection decision was not based on any meaningful comparison of the underlying proposals' qualitative merits.

Another example of a failure to consider underlying merits is the mechanical counting of strengths and weaknesses. Because one strength may be of more value than a different strength, it is unreasonable to determine equivalence or superiority based upon a simple tally of strengths and weaknesses.[412]

d. Award Decision Inconsistent with Evaluation Scheme

Another argument often raised in the context of best value tradeoffs is that the SSA failed to make an award in accordance with the evaluation scheme. For example, if the solicitation stated that the technical evaluation factor would be significantly more important than price, yet the SSA plainly applied equal or more weight to the price factor than the technical factor, GAO may sustain the protest.[413] The most extreme version of this occurs when an agency essentially converts a best-value tradeoff

---

409. Arctic Slope Tech. Servs., Inc., B-411776, Oct. 20, 2015, 2017 CPD ¶ 6, at 7.

410. *See, e.g.*, Apogee Eng'g, LLC, B-414829.2, Feb. 21, 2019, 2019 CPD ¶ 85; Arctic Slope Tech. Servs., Inc., B-411776, Oct. 20, 2015, 2017 CPD ¶ 6.

411. B-411776.

412. *See, e.g.*, Nexant, Inc., B-407708, Jan. 30, 2013, 2013 CPD ¶ 59, at 8–9 (sustaining protest where SSA failed to identify any particular features that justified a price premium for the higher-priced proposal, and instead relied on "point scores or the generic number of strengths assigned to the proposals"); Apogee Eng'g, LLC, B-414829.2, Feb. 21, 2019, 2019 CPD ¶ 85, at 10 ("[T]he adjectival ratings (or the number of strengths) assigned to proposals are not dispositive metrics for an agency to express a proposal's merit.").

413. *See* DLI Eng'g Corp.–Recons., B-218335.2, Oct. 28, 1985, 85-2 CPD ¶ 468, at 4.

procurement into a lowest-price technically acceptable acquisition.[414] Likewise, if the solicitation provides that a technical subfactor will be given more weight than others, but the SSA does not apply these weights correctly, the protest may be sustained.[415] In *Blue Rock Structures, Inc.*,[416] GAO tied this issue to a failure to document as well, noting that a

> tradeoff analysis that fails to furnish any explanation as to why a higher-rated proposal does not in fact offer technical advantages or why those technical advantages are not worth a price premium does not satisfy the requirement for a documented tradeoff rationale, particularly where, as here, price is secondary to technical considerations under the RFP's evaluation scheme.

Another variation on this theme is when an agency's tradeoff analysis fails to give any meaningful consideration to cost or price and makes award based on technical merit alone. In *Technatomy Corp.*,[417] for example, GAO considered a tradeoff decision in a multiple-award procurement. The protester's price was substantially lower than some awardees' prices, but its technical ratings were generally no better than acceptable. The solicitation provided that the nonprice factors were more important than price. The agency selected for award the 14 proposals that demonstrated the highest technical merit based on the adjectival ratings assigned (which was a problem in itself), and excluded the proposals that fell below a "clear break" in technical merit, including proposals that were lower priced than the selected proposals. GAO sustained the protest, finding that the agency's source selection approach essentially eliminated the consideration of price, meaning that there was no price-technical tradeoff at all:

> Here, price was not considered in any meaningful way in the source selection decision. In this respect, the record shows that price had no material impact on an offeror's ability to be selected for award. Once the higher-rated proposals were identified, the agency did not perform a price/technical tradeoff; rather, award was based strictly on technical merit. In a tradeoff source selection process, however, an agency may not so minimize the impact of price to make it merely a nominal evaluation factor because the essence of the tradeoff process is an evaluation of price in relation to the perceived benefits of an offeror's proposal.[418]

---

414. *See* Patriot Sols., LLC, B-413779, Dec. 22, 2016, 2016 CPD ¶ 37, at 4–5 (sustaining protest where SSA disregarded any nonprice merit that exceeded mere acceptability and made award on the basis of price alone).

415. *See* ProTech Corp., B-294818, Dec. 30, 2004, 2005 CPD ¶ 73, at 8 (finding a source selection decision unreasonable when the SSA's best-value tradeoff accorded a factor less weight than specified in the solicitation).

416. B-293134, Feb. 6, 2004, 2004 CPD ¶ 63, at 3.

417. B-414672.5, Oct. 10, 2018, 2018 CPD ¶ 353.

418. *Id.* at 19.

e. Failure to Consider Weaknesses

Finally, GAO has sustained a number of protests where the agency's award decision has compared an awardee's strengths against the strengths of the protester but has not included a discussion of the purported awardee's weaknesses. For example, in *TRW, Inc.*,[419] the SSA was briefed on the strengths and weaknesses of each offeror and selected the low-price offeror for award. However, the awardee's weaknesses were not incorporated into the best value tradeoff analysis:

> Here, the source selection statement only listed the various [Awardee] strengths identified by the evaluation team in technical factors 1, 2, 3, and 8, but did not mention the more numerous corresponding identified weaknesses, nor any strengths or weaknesses for factors 4, 5, 6, and 7, despite the fact of [Awardee's] substandard "marginal" (yellow) ratings for factors 4, 5, and 6.[420]

In sustaining TRW's protest, GAO explained that consideration of an offeror's weaknesses in the best value decision is critical:

> [T]he source selection decision does not explain how [awardee's] low cost offsets its relatively low technical and high risk ratings. Consequently, in the absence of any comments in the source selection statement concerning relative technical merit, it appears that the source selection decision was based on the lowest proposed cost.[421]

17. Corrective Action Protest Issues (Scope/Solicitation Cancellation)

A protest that succeeds (either through a merits-based decision or voluntary corrective action by the agency before any decision issues) does not necessarily mark the end of the dispute process. Either the protester or the intervenor may be unsatisfied with the extent of the agency's corrective action and may seek to protest the agency's decision in that regard. From a timeliness perspective, it is important to remember that a challenge of the agency's corrective action must be filed before submission of revised proposals (if revised proposals are to be submitted) or, if filing at GAO, within ten days of the announcement of the extent of the corrective action if no new proposals will be submitted.

Broadly, challenges to corrective action tend to fall into two categories: arguments that the corrective action is too broad or too narrow. Challenges directed against corrective action that adopts a GAO recommendation (issued in connection

---

419. B-234558, June 21, 1989, 89-1 CPD ¶ 584.

420. *Id.* at 3.

421. *Id.* at 4; *see also* Keeton Corrections, Inc., B-293348, Mar. 4, 2005, 2005 CPD ¶ 44 (sustaining a protest where the SSA was provided with a recommendation that did not note the awardee's weaknesses).

with a sustain decision) should be brought at COFC. Although such protests are sometimes colloquially (and incorrectly) referred to as "appeals" from GAO decisions, COFC has no ability to reverse or vacate a GAO recommendation, which is not an enforceable judgment in any event. COFC does, however, have the power to enjoin an agency from adopting a GAO recommendation. Thus, although such COFC corrective action protests are technically directed against the reasonableness of the agency's decision, they necessarily involve COFC's assessment of the reasonableness of the underlying GAO recommendation. Finally, agencies may decide to cancel a procurement as part of their corrective action. Protesters can challenge cancellations, but such actions are subject to broad discretion by the agency.

a. Challenges to Overly Broad Corrective Action

Although some COFC judges previously held that agencies must "narrowly tailor" corrective action to fit the procurement errors the action is intended to resolve, a recent Federal Circuit decision may have put to rest any future challenges that an agency's corrective action is too broad. In *Dell Federal Systems, L.P. v. United States*,[422] the Federal Circuit reversed a COFC decision finding that the agency's proposed corrective action was unreasonable because it was not "narrowly tailored" to the particular errors of the procurement. COFC concluded that the proposed corrective action was overly broad because it involved reopening discussions, when more "narrowly tailored" clarifications would have addressed the "minor" errors at issue. Although recognizing that a number of COFC decisions had employed the "narrowly tailored" test to determine the reasonableness of proposed corrective action, the Federal Circuit rejected that approach as inconsistent with binding precedents imposed by the circuit itself: "[T]he Court of Federal Claims must follow relevant decisions of the Supreme Court and the Federal Circuit, not the other way around."[423] The Federal Circuit held that, under its own long-standing precedents, the highly deferential APA standard applies to protests of agency procurement decisions, including corrective action, and asks merely whether the agency's action had a rational basis and was in accordance with law:

> Instead, we have consistently reviewed agencies' corrective actions under the APA's "highly deferential" "rational basis" standard. The rational basis test asks "whether the contracting agency provided a coherent and reasonable explanation of its exercise of discretion."[424]

---

422. 906 F.3d 982, 998 (Fed. Cir. 2018).
423. *Id.* at 992.
424. *Id.* (internal citations omitted).

Although COFC recited this standard in its decision, the Federal Circuit held that the lower court failed to apply it when it analyzed the agency's corrective action using the "narrowly tailored" standard.

The Federal Circuit considered the facts of the protest under the highly deferential "rational basis" standard and found that the agency's plan to open discussions and receive proposal revisions from the offerors was "rationally related" to the errors at issue. On this basis, the court held that the agency's announced corrective action was unobjectionable. As a result, the standard of review of corrective action at COFC now is roughly equivalent to the standard already in use by GAO, that is, corrective action must be rationally related to the perceived errors but need not be narrowly tailored to those errors.

b. Challenges to Overly Restrictive Corrective Action

Protesters may have better luck in challenging agency corrective action when it is overly restrictive. This argument occurs most often when an agency seeks the revision or resubmission of certain aspects of offerors' proposals but will not allow revision to other areas of the proposals. Although agencies have a great deal of discretion in crafting corrective action to address the particular procurement impropriety that led to the need for corrective action, that discretion is not unbridled.

GAO has long held that "in conducting discussions to implement a recommendation of our Office for corrective action, [an agency] may reasonably decide to limit the revisions offerors may make to their proposals" and that, "[a]s a general matter, the details of implementing a recommendation for corrective action are within the sound discretion and judgment of the contracting agency."[425] Further, in the case of corrective action taken in response to outcome prediction or a GAO written decision, GAO has held that it "will not question an agency's ultimate manner of compliance, so long as it remedies the procurement impropriety that was the basis for the decision's recommendation."[426]

---

425. Consolidated Eng'r Servs., Inc., B-293864, Oct. 25, 2004, 2004 CPD ¶ 214, at 2 (denying protest challenging corrective action as unduly narrow in response to outcome prediction ADR where GAO identified narrow, specific issues it would sustain initial protest on).

426. *Id.*; *see also* NCS Techs., Inc., B-413500.2, Feb. 14, 2017, 2017 CPD ¶ 123 (denying protest and stating, "Where the corrective action does not also include amending the solicitation, we will not question an agency's decision to restrict proposal revisions when taking corrective action so long as it is reasonable in nature and remedies the established or suspected procurement impropriety."); Alliant Techsystems, Inc., B-405129.3, Jan. 23, 2012, 2012 CPD ¶ 50 (denying protest challenging scope of corrective action taken in response to GAO outcome prediction, noting that "an agency's discretion when taking corrective action extends to a decision on the scope of proposal revisions, and there are circumstances where an agency may reasonably decide to limit the revisions offerors may make to their proposals" and finding unobjectionable post-corrective action additional round of discussions that did not raise weaknesses identified during the protester's post-award debriefing because "[h]aving sufficiently led an

GAO has found the agency's corrective action to be unreasonable, however, where the agency allows revisions to certain aspects of offerors' proposals but does not allow revision of *other necessarily related areas* of the proposal:

> [W]here an agency amends a solicitation and permits offerors to revise their proposals, our Office has held that offerors should be permitted to revise any aspect of their proposals—including those that were not the subject of the amendment—unless the agency demonstrates that the amendment could not reasonably have an effect on other aspects of the proposals, or that allowing such revisions would have a detrimental impact on the competitive process.[427]

The rationale for this rule is sound. Changes to one aspect of a proposal may directly impact other areas of the proposal. For example, a change to key personnel or technical approach may also require a change to management approach or costs.

Another variation on this protest ground is when an agency's corrective action materially alters the solicitation's evaluation scheme. GAO may sustain a challenge to the corrective action if the agency does not allow offerors to revise those aspects of their proposals impacted by the alteration. In *Computer World Services Corp.*,[428] GAO sustained a protest where the agency's corrective action included the elimination of price realism from the evaluation criteria but did not allow for revised proposals:

> It is axiomatic that, where an agency makes a material change to the terms of a solicitation, it is required to issue an amendment to the solicitation and afford competing firms an opportunity to revise their proposals or quotations in order to provide all firms an opportunity to compete on a common basis. *Global Computer Enterprises, Inc.; Savantage Financial Services, Inc.*, B-404597, et al., Mar. 9, 2011, 2011 CPD ¶ 69 at 10. Among other things, a change to a solicitation's evaluation criteria constitutes a material change that requires permitting firms an opportunity to submit revised proposals or quotations. *See Power Connector, Inc.*, B-404916.2, Aug. 15, 2011, 2011 CPD ¶ 186 at 3-5.[429]

---

offeror to the area of concern in earlier rounds of discussions, an agency is not required to raise a matter again in any subsequent round of discussions, even where the matter continued to be considered a concern by the agency").

427. Power Connector, Inc., B-404916.2, Aug. 15, 2011, 2011 CPD ¶ 186; *see also* Deloitte Consulting, LLP, B-412125.6, Nov. 28, 2016, 2016 CPD ¶ 355 (sustaining protest where agency corrective action imposed unreasonably restrictive limitations on scope of proposal revisions, which prohibited revision of proposal information materially impacted by corrective action).

428. B-418287.3, June 29, 2020, 2020 WL 3545352.

429. *See also* Lockheed Martin Sys. Integration-Owego; Sikorsky Aircraft Co., B-299145.5, Aug. 30, 2007, 2007 CPD ¶ 155 (sustaining protest where corrective action materially altered the evaluation scheme but failed to provide offerors the opportunity to revise their proposals in response to those changes).

The common-sense rationale for this rule is that "the statutory requirement to notify offerors of the criteria upon which their offers will be evaluated is meaningless" if an agency changes the criteria but refuses offerors the opportunity to revise their proposals to respond to the new criteria.[430]

c. Challenges to Solicitation Cancellation

Finally, an agency may determine that its best action in the event of a successful protest is to cancel the solicitation and start over. This may happen where the agency decides that it must reconsider its needs, where the solicitation no longer reflects its current needs, where the solicitation does not provide sufficiently detailed information about the agency's needs, or where none of the offerors was technically compliant. GAO and COFC will generally review any challenges to an agency's decision to cancel a solicitation on the basis of rationality. If the agency has a rational reason for cancelling the procurement, the protest will be denied.

Protests have been successful, however, where the agency is unable to provide a rational justification for the cancelation or where the agency's cancelation is merely a pretext to make a sole-source award.[431] In *Superlative Technologies*,[432] GAO explained that, although agencies are given broad discretion to cancel a procurement,

> where a protester has alleged that an agency's rationale for cancellation is but a pretext, that is, the agency's actual motivation is to avoid awarding a contract on a competitive basis or to avoid resolving a protest, [GAO] will closely examine the reasonableness of the agency's actions in canceling the acquisition.

GAO then concluded that "the agency did not have a reasonable basis for canceling the RFQ" because its decision was based upon the fact that the contracting officer's technical representative had disclosed information to a contractor that may have given that contractor a competitive advantage, but then awarded a sole-source contract for the canceled requirements to a team that included that same contractor.[433] This was unreasonable and tended to support the protester's allegation that the cancelation was mere pretext to avoid competition.

---

430. *Id.* at 5.

431. *See, e.g.*, Walker Dev. & Trading Grp., Inc., B-413924, Jan. 12, 2017, 2017 CPD ¶ 21 (sustaining protest where agency canceled solicitation and extended incumbent's contract, while providing conflicting and unpersuasive explanations to GAO for the basis of the cancelation); Superlative Techs., Inc., B-310489, Jan. 4, 2008, 2008 CPD ¶ 12.

432. B-310489 at 3.

433. *Id.* at 4.

Chapter 7
What Lies Ahead

A. Statutory and Regulatory Changes

There have been several recent statutory and regulatory developments intended to streamline the bid protest process and reduce the perceived burden of protests on agencies.

First, the 2018 NDAA called for a pilot program designed to reduce the number of frivolous protests. The act provided that beginning on October 1, 2019, large contractors—defined as those with yearly revenues over $250 million—filing GAO protests against the DoD must reimburse DoD for the costs incurred defending a protest if the protest is denied.[1] As of April 2020, however, DoD has yet to seek reimbursement in those circumstances. After the pilot program ends on September 30, 2022, DoD must report to the Committees on Armed Services of the House of Representatives and the Senate on the viability of the program and whether it should be made permanent.[2]

The 2019 NDAA similarly aims to reduce the burden of bid protests on the DoD. It calls for a study "of the frequency and effects of bid protests involving the same contract award or proposed award that have been filed" at both GAO and COFC.[3] This study is expected to examine the following items:

1. The number of protests that have been filed with both tribunals and the results of each case;
2. The number of such protests where the tribunals differed in denying or sustaining the action;
3. The length of time, in average time and median time:
   a. From initial filing at GAO to decision in COFC;
   b. From filing with each tribunal to decision by such tribunal;

---

1. For the pilot program, contractors' revenues are measured in 2017 constant dollars. National Defense Authorization Act for Fiscal Year 2018, Pub. L. No. 115-91, 131 Stat. 1283, § 827.

2. *Id.* It is currently unclear, however, whether the reimbursement requirement would apply to protests that are dismissed by GAO, as opposed to those that are denied.

3. John S. McCain National Defense Authorization Act for Fiscal Year 2019, Pub. L. No. 115-232, § 822.

   c. From the time at which the basis of the protest is known to the time of filing in each tribunal; and
   d. In the case of an appeal from a decision of COFC, from the date of the initial filing of the appeal to decision in the appeal;
4. The number of protests where performance was stayed or enjoined and for how long;
5. If performance was stayed or enjoined, whether the requirement was obtained in the interim through another vehicle or in-house, or whether during the period of the stay or enjoining the requirement went unfulfilled;
6. Separately for each tribunal, the number of protests where performance was stayed or enjoined and monetary damages were awarded, which shall include for how long performance was stayed or enjoined and the amount of monetary damages;
7. Whether the protestor was a large or small business; and
8. Whether the protestor was the incumbent in a prior contract for the same or similar product or service.[4]

Under the 2019 NDAA, DoD is required to consult with the Attorney General of the United States, the Comptroller General of the United States, and COFC.[5] In addition, DoD is required to "establish and continuously maintain a data repository to collect on an ongoing basis the information" listed earlier, as well as any additional relevant bid protest data the secretary determines necessary and appropriate.[6] This will allow the DoD, GAO, and COFC to assess and review bid protests over time.[7]

The 2019 NDAA also calls for a new, expedited process for bid protests related to small-value contracts, defined as those worth less than $100,000. The statute does not provide additional detail on the program, but the RAND Corporation's 2018 report on DoD bid protests sheds some light into possible actions DoD could take, including (1) implementing a court akin to a small-claims court or traffic court designed specifically for protests related to small-value contracts, (2) requiring alternative dispute resolution, and (3) restricting low-value procurement protests to the agency level.[8]

In 2019, DoD issued a final rule (which took effect on October 1, 2019) amending the DFARS (and implementing certain sections of the 2017 and 2018 NDAAs) to limit the use of Lowest Priced Technically Acceptable (LPTA) procurements. Under

---

4. *Id.* § 822(a).
5. *Id.* § 822(b).
6. *Id.* § 822(c).
7. *Id.*
8. Mark V. Arena, et al., *Assessing Bid Protests of U.S. Department of Defense Procurements*, RAND Corp. xvii (2018), https://www.rand.org/content/dam/rand/pubs/research_reports/RR2300/RR2356/RAND_RR2356.pdf.

this rule, contracting officers may elect to use an LPTA evaluation approach only if eight factors are met: (1) minimum requirements can be described clearly and comprehensively, and expressed in terms of performance, objectives, measures, and standards that will be used to determine the acceptability of offers; (2) no (or only minimal) value will be realized from a proposal that exceeds minimum requirements; (3) the proposed technical approaches will require no (or minimal) subjective judgment when compared against competing proposals; (4) reviewing technical proposals will not result in identifying beneficial characteristics; (5) no (or minimal) additional innovation or future technological advantage will be realized by using a different source selection process; (6) goods to be procured are predominantly expendable in nature, nontechnical, or have a short life expectancy; (7) the contract file contains a determination that the lowest price reflects full life-cycle costs; and (8) the contracting officer documents the contract file describing the circumstances justifying the use of an LPTA approach.[9]

The FAR Council proposed a similar rule for LPTAs as DoD's final rule, except that it does not include the requirement that minimal innovation or technological advantage would be achieved, or that the goods being procured are predominantly expendable, nontechnical, or have a short shelf life.[10]

The 2020 NDAA directs that by June 17, 2020, the FAR is to be revised to provide unsuccessful offerors competing for an IDIQ task order or delivery order greater than the simplified acquisition threshold (currently $250,000) and less than or equal to $5.5 million, upon request, "a brief explanation as to why such offeror was unsuccessful."[11] The explanation is to include a summary of the award rationale and an evaluation of the significant weak or deficient factors in the offeror's offer. The fact that an offeror is entitled to such an explanation does not, however, change the dollar jurisdictional threshold for bringing task or delivery order protests.

B. Section 809 Panel

Section 809 of the 2016 NDAA established a panel to address the purchasing practices of the DoD. Before concluding its mission in July 2019, the Section 809 Panel issued 98 recommendations through an Interim and Final Report aimed at changing the overall structure and operations of defense acquisition both strategically and tactically. The goals of the panel included streamlining and improving the efficiency and

9. Defense Federal Acquisition Regulation Supplement: Restrictions on Use of Lowest Price Technically Acceptable Source Selection Process (DFARS Case 2018-D010), 84 Fed. Reg. 50,785 (Sept. 26, 2019) (to be codified at 48 C.F.R. pts. 208, 212, 213, 215, 216, 217, 234, and 237).

10. Federal Acquisition Regulation: Lowest Price Technically Acceptable Source Selection Process, 84 Fed. Reg. 52,425 (Oct. 2, 2019) (to be codified at 48 C.F.R. pts. 12, 13, 15, 16, and 37).

11. National Defense Authorization Act for Fiscal Year 2020, Pub. L. No. 116-92, § 874.

effectiveness of the defense acquisition process and maintaining a defense technology advantage, ensuring the financial and ethical integrity of the defense procurement programs, eliminating any unnecessary regulations, and establishing and administering appropriate buyer and seller relationships in the procurement system.

The Section 809 Panel released Volume Three of the Final Report on January 15, 2019, which contained 58 new recommendations intending to streamline DoD's acquisition process—including a number of recommended bid protest reforms. According to the report, the recommendations, which seek to "allow DoD to make purchases in a manner similar to the way private-sector businesses do," would, if implemented, "reduce barriers that deny DoD timely access to innovative technology and creative solutions from nontraditional companies and bridge the technical superiority gap that is beginning to develop today between the United States and near-peer competitors and nonstate actors."[12]

The recommended reforms to the bid protest system advanced by the Section 809 Panel were published under Section 6 of the report released in January 2019, entitled "Streamlining and Improving Compliance Section." These recommendations include enacting a bid protest purpose statement, eliminating the opportunities to file "second-bite" post-GAO protests at COFC, imposing GAO timelines on COFC protests, eliminating GAO and COFC protest jurisdictions for procurements under $75,000, and providing enhanced access to source selection decision and technical evaluation information to offerors during the debriefing process.[13]

Recommendation 66 suggests establishing a "purpose statement for bid protests in the procurement system to help guide adjudicative bodies in resolving protests consistent with said purpose and establish a standard by which the effectiveness of protests may be measured."[14] The panel fashioned this recommendation based on the rationale that the current lack of an established purpose statement "makes it difficult to evaluate the effectiveness of the current protest process and produces reform efforts intent on resolving discreet perceived problems rather than ensuring the process achieves the desired outcome."[15]

Recommendation 67 seeks to reduce bid protest processing time by eliminating the opportunity to file a protest with COFC after filing with GAO and requiring COFC (like GAO) to issue a decision within 100 days of ordering that a procurement be delayed.[16] The panel made this recommendation based on what it perceived

---

12. David A. Drabkin, et al., *Report of the Advisory Panel on Streamlining and Codifying Acquisition Regulations*, Vol. 3, Pt. 2 at 3 (Jan. 2019), https://discover.dtic.mil/wp-content/uploads/809-Panel-2019/Volume3/Sec809Panel_Vol3-Report_Jan2019_part-2_0307.pdf.

13. *Id.* at 341.

14. *Id.*

15. *Id.*

16. *Id.* at 345.

to be a problem of "two-bite" protests wherein an unsuccessful GAO protester has the opportunity to challenge the same procurement decision at COFC—creating the possibility that a single protest could be heard at the agency level, GAO, and COFC.

Under Recommendation 68, the panel endorses limiting the jurisdiction of GAO and COFC to only protests of procurements with values exceeding, or expected to exceed, $75,000.[17] The panel cited the RAND Corporation's study that, in an analysis of DoD protests filed at GAO and COFC, found that protests of procurements valued below $100,000 made up approximately 10 percent of GAO protests and four percent of those at COFC.[18]

In issuing Recommendation 69 for enhanced debriefings, the panel sought, in part, to "minimize the likelihood contractors will file protests because of a lack of information."[19] If adopted, this proposal would require that redacted Source Selection Decision Documents and technical evaluation materials be provided as part of required debriefings. The panel suggested this would lead to more fulsome debriefings as well as fewer protests filed only for informational purposes.

Each of the preceding recommendations would require legislation to implement and the report contains suggestions on implementation methods for the legislative and executive branches. Given the expansive nature of the recommendations, it would likely be difficult for Congress to adopt them in full, if at all.

---

17. *Id.* at 355.
18. *Id.* at 355–56.
19. *Id.* at 360.

Glossary of Acronyms

Acronym	Definition
A&AS	Advisory and Assistance Services
ADRA	Administrative Dispute Resolution Act
APA	Administrative Procedure Act
BI	BI Incorporated
CDA	Contract Disputes Act
CICA	Competition in Contracting Act
CLINs	Contract Line Item Numbers
COC	SBA's Certificate of Competency
COFC	Court of Federal Claims
COFC Rules or RCFC	Rules of the U.S. Court of Federal Claims
CPARS	Contractor Performance Assessment Reporting System
D&F	Determination & Finding
DFARS	Defense Federal Acquisition Regulation Supplement
DLA	Defense Logistics Agency
DoD	Department of Defense
DOJ	Department of Justice
EAJA	Equal Access to Justice Act
ENs	Evaluation Notices
EPDS	GAO's Electronic Protest Docketing System
FAA	Federal Aviation Administration
FAR	Federal Acquisition Regulation
FASA	Federal Acquisition Streamlining Act of 1994
FBO	Federal Business Opportunity website
FCIA	Federal Courts Improvement Act of 1982
FGCAA	Federal Grants and Cooperative Agreements Act

Acronym	**Definition**
FSS	Federal Supply Schedule
GAO	Government Accountability Office
GSA	General Service Administration
HCA	Head of the Contracting Activity
HUBZone	Historically Underutilized Business Zone
IDIQ	Indefinite Delivery/Indefinite Quantity
IFB	Invitation for Bids
J&A	Justification & Approval
LPTA	Lowest Price Technically Acceptable
MJAR	Motion for Judgment on the Administrative Record
NDAA	National Defense Authorization Act
NOI	Notice of Intent
OCI	Organizational Conflict of Interest
ODRA	Office of Dispute Resolution for Acquisition, Federal Aviation Administration
OTs	Other Transactions
OTAs	Other Transaction Agreements
PI	Preliminary Injunction
PIA	Procurement Integrity Act
RFI	Request for Information
SAIC	Science Applications International Corporation
SAR	Supplemental Agency Report
SBA	Small Business Administration
SDVOSB	Service-Disabled Veteran Owned Small Business
SSA	Source Selection Authority
STOP	Satellite Tracking
TRO	Temporary Restraining Order
VA	Department of Veterans Affairs
VBA	Veterans Benefits, Health Care, and Information Technology Act of 2006
WOSB	Women-Owned Small Business

Index

D

E

F

G